Style and Orchestration

Style and Orchestration

Gardner Read

Professor Emeritus
Boston University

Foreword by Nicolas Slonimsky

SCHIRMER BOOKS
A Division of Macmillan Publishing Co., Inc.
NEW YORK

c1979

Schirmer Books
A Division of Macmillan Publishing Co., Inc.
866 Third Avenue, New York, N.Y. 10022

Collier Macmillan Canada, Ltd.

Library of Congress Catalog Card Number: 77-15884

Printed in the United States of America

printing number

1 2 3 4 5 6 7 8 9 10

Library of Congress Cataloging in Publication Data

Read, Gardner
  Style and orchestration.

  Bibliography: p.
  Includes index.
  1. Instrumentation and orchestration—History.
2. Style, Musical. I. Title.
ML455.R4   781.6'4   77-15884
ISBN 0-02-872110-1

This book pays homage to no single individual; rather, it is dedicated to all *cognoscenti* of the symphony orchestra —past, present, and future.

Contents

List of Musical Examples

LIST OF MUSIC EXAMPLES

LIST OF MUSIC EXAMPLES

Foreword

"Le style est l'homme même," said Buffon in his speech of acceptance at the *Académie*. The great French naturalist was not so much indicating that the author's *character* is revealed by his style as he was stating a more profound philosophical truth: namely, that laws of nature and facts of science are common to all, while the manner of expressing these laws and formulating their interdependence remains a peculiarly personal act. It is the individual genius who assembles the similarities of disparate phenomena into a generalized hypothesis which we describe as a law of nature, until and unless refuted by new observations.

In this book Gardner Read follows Buffon's method of classification by observing similarities in the orchestral styles of selected composers and drawing up workable theories regarding the interdependence of these styles. He traces influences, but he also establishes what may be called spontaneous simultaneities: that is, accidents of identical usages occurring close together in time and reflecting the musical Zeitgeist. The history of science is full of such spontaneous simultaneities—the invention of calculus by Newton and Leibnitz, or the mathematical discovery of the existence of the planet Neptune by Adams in England and Leverrier in France. In music, the twelve-tone system was formulated almost simultaneously by Schoenberg and Hauer, and the latter claimed to the end of his days that he was the true progenitor of this technique, contesting Schoenberg's claim of priority.

In orchestration, too, there are such intriguing simultaneities, even if not so spectacular as the emergence of calculus or the twelve-tone method of composition. After all, orchestration is a highly practical science, which depends on the availability of musical instruments suitable for ensemble playing. The insertion of a saxophone in Bizet's *L'Arlésienne Suite,* or of the celesta in Tchaikovsky's *Nutcracker Suite,* represents not a stylistic change but a mere coloring device. But when saxophones, via jazz, massively invaded the symphonic scores of many modern composers, the orchestral style of the twentieth century was definitely affected. The tinkling celesta was a harbinger of such big-sounding keyed instruments as the marimba and the vibraphone, clangorous enough to have concertos written for them. Consistent employment of such instruments marks a stylistic change in orchestration.

Particularly remarkable is the rise of the role of percussion in the modern orchestra. The variety of drums in some contemporary scores is such as to place the percussion group as an orchestra within an orchestra. Here, undoubtedly, is a significant change of orchestral style.

Influences in orchestral styles are not as patent as in melodic or harmonic aspects of composition. Perhaps only the Wagnerian orchestral revolution was powerful enough to swing the direction of symphonic writing so that the post-Wagnerian orchestra differs quantitatively and qualitatively from the pre-Wagnerian orchestra in an immediately recognizable way. This was the first great revolution in the history of orchestral writing. But even in the Wagnerian orchestra the acoustical principles still apply; the overtone series, securing the mutual enhancement of harmonic ingredients, still stands.

The second revolution in orchestral writing was wrought by the Impressionists. It was even more far-reaching than the Wagnerian expansion of orchestral sonorities, for in its quest for exotic sonorities it finally upset the acoustical laws of euphony by disrupting and dislocating the natural overtone series. The conventional couplings all but disappear in the Impressionist scores; extreme low and extreme high registers are exploited for special effects; dynamic values become subtilized; the orchestra itself shrinks from Wagnerian proportions, approaching chamber music in the delicacy and precision of individual instrumental parts.

It is remarkable that such great innovators as Stravinsky and Schoenberg, who have changed the face of harmony, have not materially altered the basic concepts of orchestral writing. The third, and ultimate, revolution of orchestral style may come only with the abolition of the orchestral instruments themselves. Joseph Schillinger bemoaned the durability of the "heterogeneous aggregation of antiquated tools, wooden boxes and bars, wooden pipes, dried sheep's guts, horse hair and the like" that goes under the name of a symphony orchestra, and dreamed of an electronic future with instruments of unlimited capabilities and ultra-mathematical precision of rhythm and intonation. Schillinger's electronic future is now at hand, though as yet there are no signs that the old instruments made of pipes, gut, and hair will irrevocably vanish from the musical scene. The chances are that electronic conveyors of sound will do no more than supplement and enrich the existing methods of sound production.

Gardner Read, without attempting to write a general history of music, presents the evolution of orchestral style as an integral part of that history. Obliquely, he also illuminates the musical personality of each composer. Berlioz, Liszt, Mahler, and Scriabin were flamboyant personalities whose mystical visions of music as a universal art found expression in the grandiose dimensions of their orchestral works. In his symphonic poems Richard Strauss expressed a more pragmatic philosophy of music in a tremendously effective manner. The primitivistic colors of Stravinsky's early ballet-music reflect his ancestral Russianism, whereas the Neoclassical orchestra of his later works reflects his cosmopolitanism, even in the physical sense of his half-century absence from Russia. The fine clockwork of Ravel's symphonic writing somehow fits the image of Ravel the man. "Le style, c'est l'homme même. . . . "

Sometimes, a reluctance to employ certain sonorous resources becomes a distinct stylistic trait. The somber colors prevailing in the symphonic works of Sibelius are the result of his avoidance of ostentatiously brilliant sonorities, and of his concomitant predilection for low instrumental registers. And it is because of these very limitations that Sibelius formed an unmistakably personal style of orchestration. Some of his favorite devices, such as progressions of repeated, symmetrical sections of dynamic expansion and contraction in lengthy string passages, would be onerous in the works of another composer; but as applied by Sibelius, in the ambience of his subdued colors, these episodes sustain a mood of dramatic contemplation in a peculiarly effective manner.

The extreme expansion of orchestral sonorities was reached in the early decades of the twentieth century, in the works of Edgard Varèse and others. Paradoxically, in the same period the opposite aesthetic usage—tending toward extreme rarefaction of instrumental sonorities—manifested itself in the works of Expressionist composers. Particularly is this true in the miniature pieces of Anton Webern; some are subtilized to the vanishing point, and are marked by utmost brevity—one of them lasts but nineteen seconds.

Gardner Read is himself a composer who possesses a natural gift for orchestral color; he can judge the efficacy of symphonic scoring in the light of his own experience. In his Neoclassical works, such as the brilliant *Toccata Giocosa,* novel sonorities are achieved by an ingenious use of traditional orchestral combinations. On the other hand, in his dance symphony *The Temptation of St. Anthony* instrumental groupings are individualized in a series of virtuoso passages, after which the sonorous expansion reaches grandiose proportions in an orchestral tutti. In still another vein, his tone-poem *Night Flight* is conceived in Impressionistic colors, as an evocation rather than a descriptive musical essay. The composer's problem of creating a personal synthesis of such multifarious influences is, he feels, universal.

As an analyst and classifier, Gardner Read presents here the evolution of orchestral styles in a historical perspective, carefully noting the overlapping tendencies—for no art has evolved without transition periods that participate in both departing trends and new developments. In his *Thesaurus of Orchestral Devices* Read has classified, with enormous attention to detail, the technical applications of instrumental writing. In the present book he takes a larger view of the symphonic universe, integrating orchestral devices in a general concept of musical aesthetics as reflected throughout history in the changing orchestral styles.

Nicolas Slonimsky

Preamble

Style is something that evolves only slowly, and then never as an end in itself. It is not an outer manner, to be adopted at will, but an intrinsic part of a way of thinking.

Peter Heyworth

There is little doubt that one of the most significant phenomena in the history of Western music has been the conceptual evolution and artistic maturation of the symphony orchestra. Few aspects of any communicative art can compare in scope and importance with the creation and prolonged culmination of this great body of instrumentalists, organized into a diverse yet unified whole to delineate tonally the most complex expressions of creative man. For well over three hundred years the orchestra has been the mainstay of Western musical culture, and few composers in the entire period have failed to succumb to its eternal fascination and challenge.

The factual history of this cultural phenomenon is available to readers on many levels, from the rudimentary music-appreciation survey to the erudite musicological treatise. The techniques of instrumentation are thoroughly covered by authorities from Berlioz (the *Treatise on Instrumentation* of 1844) to Walter Piston (*Orchestration,* 1955).

1

PREAMBLE

There is, however, an unconscionable dearth of analysis of the creative orchestrational styles that distinguish one period from another and one composer from another. In the 488 pages of a recent biography of Serge Prokofiev by Israel Nestyev, for instance, exactly one page dealt with his highly personalized orchestral style. Other composers' biographies, standard and new, have done little better in the allotment of space to discussion and analysis of their subjects' orchestrational techniques. It is high time, then, to give attention to the creative alchemy by which a musical concept is born directly as a work for orchestra—the indissoluble link between a germinal idea and this specific form of external expression.

"The true art of orchestration," as Piston says in his admirable text, "is inseparable from the creative act of composing music. The sounds made by the orchestra are the ultimate manifestation of musical ideas germinated in the mind of the composer." The inspired unity of this single-minded process has little relation to the common commercial practice of assigning musical material to a ready-made agglomeration of twenty, sixty, or a hundred different instruments. This process, routine in film and television scoring, has little relation to the art of orchestration in the hands of its masters.[1] We may dramatize this fundamental truth by arbitrarily divorcing musical content from inherent orchestral style in excerpts from two well-known symphonic and operatic works: Wolfgang Amadeus Mozart's "Haffner" Symphony and Richard Strauss's *Salome*.

Typical of the period (late eighteenth century) and of the symphonic form as it existed for the Classical composers, the quoted passage from Mozart's "Haffner" Symphony is most assuredly typical of the composer himself. In this music all is melodic purity, harmonic simplicity, rhythmic regularity, and textural transparency. The scoring fits the expression like the proverbial glove—refined, polished, elegant, with not a superfluous note or instrument (Example 1).

What would result from the divorce of these complementary elements, a remarriage of Mozart's materials to, say, the late–nineteenth-century style of Richard Strauss? First of all, one must assemble a huge instrumental array, including a woodwind choir in fours, a brass section comprising six horns, four each of trumpets and trombones, and a bass tuba, plus harp, celesta, several percussion instruments in addition to timpani, and a vastly expanded string section.

In our Straussian "arrangement" (to put it euphemistically) melodic doublings at both the unison and the octave are consistently used. Furthermore, the basic harmony is thickened by the employment of

2

EXAMPLE 1
Wolfgang Amadeus Mozart: from Symphony No. 35, 3rd movement

"filler" parts and by rhythmic figuration. In spite of the modest dynamic levels indicated, a tremendous weight of sound will result. The commendable lightness and transparency of Mozart's music will be muddied and made opaque, the result not only of the sheer tonal weight of the instruments used but of the general busyness of all the component parts of the orchestral fabric. We may contend that the composer's intrinsic idea is still present in that no alterations of the original melodic lines or chord progressions have been permitted. But can one seriously maintain that the new orchestral guise any longer represents Mozart's original conception? (Example 2.)

To reverse our stylistic metamorphosis—it should be equally impossible to conceive of Mozart composing and orchestrating that apocalyptic passage in Strauss's opera *Salome* (1905) when the executioner rises from the depths of the cistern bearing the severed head of John the Baptist. This shattering orchestral outburst is expressed in terms of some ninety-six instruments playing at double *forte*, its overall density achieved by extensive doubling of melodic and harmonic voices (Example 3).

How can one shrink this Straussian eruption in terms of an orchestral body of forty-five: woodwinds, horns, and trumpets in pairs, two timpani, and a maximum of thirty strings? Acoustically, even at quadruple *forte*, forty-five instruments cannot match the sheer volume-impact of ninety-six instruments at double *forte*. To express this powerful musical idea in terms of the refined instrumental ensemble characteristic of the Classicists would necessitate a drastic reduction not only of the quantity of orchestral forces but also of the textural elements inherent to Strauss's dramatic conception. The harmonies must be thinned, and unison and octave doublings curtailed. But carefully as we calculate the requisite elements, the experiment must fail. The tumescent outpourings of the late Romantic cannot arbitrarily be forced into the mold of early Classical simplicity (Example 4).

Style in orchestration, then, is inextricably bound up with conception, content, and purpose. Indeed, we may truly say that the one cannot exist without the other. What a composer does with his orchestra is as significant as the melodies he fashions, the harmonies he chooses, the rhythms he feels, or the forms that stimulate and challenge him. A composer's orchestration is far more than just a personal stamp; it is, quite literally, the quintessence of his musical thought, expression, and artistic personality.

"Style is the particular way a composer organizes his conceptions and speaks the language of his craft," Igor Stravinsky once stated (*An Autobiography*); and Aaron Copland has written: "It is axiomatic that no

EXAMPLE 2

Excerpt from Mozart's Symphony No. 35 orchestrated in the style of Richard Strauss

EXAMPLE 2 *(Continued)*

6

EXAMPLE 3
Richard Strauss: from *Salome*

EXAMPLE 4
Excerpt from Strauss's *Salome* orchestrated in the style of Mozart

one can satisfactorily orchestrate music which was not conceived in orchestral terms in the first place" (*On Music*). Divested of their unique orchestral concepts, the *Symphonie Fantastique, Till Eulenspiegel, Daphnis et Chloé,* or *Le Sacre du Printemps* are each in their own way untenable, if not unimaginable. And not to recognize the stylistic earmarks that differentiate Haydn's and Mozart's orchestral writing from that of Strauss or Mahler, for example, is as unlikely as being unable to distinguish between the musical styles of Palestrina and George Gershwin.

In this book we propose to give long overdue attention to the specific elements—technical and artistic—that constitute orchestral style. Ranging from the embryonic Baroque ensembles of Bach and Handel and the newly formed symphonic and operatic orchestras of the Classicists to the Expressionistic chamber orchestras of Berg and Webern and the exotic groups of the twentieth-century avant-garde, we will cite typical compositions by many acknowledged masters of instrumentational thought. We shall attempt to isolate and to comment on their individual orchestral arcanum—a profile of each composer in question and of the historic period. For to recognize personal traits of orchestration is to understand the musical language of the composer. And, inversely, to comprehend the creator's musical personality is to know his unique way with the orchestra.

While writing this book I have been greatly—and constantly—encouraged by words written by the eminent Swiss playwright Friedrich Dürrenmatt: "Perhaps a writer should never talk about his art, but once he starts, then it is not altogether a waste of time to listen to him."

Notes

1. In an article on orchestration in the *International Cyclopedia of Music and Musicians* Philip James states: "The term Orchestration should be used in contradistinction to the term Instrumentation, the literalism of which would make the latter more concerned with the study of technical manipulation, compass, tone quality, limitations, and adaptability of instruments treated singly rather than in combination. Accordingly, Instrumentation is a Science; Orchestration is an Art."

1

The Preclassical Orchestra

The orchestra has always existed; it merely had to be discovered.
It represents, therefore, not so much an invention as a human
conquest, made under the impulse of musical intuition and
overcoming all the purely material obstacles.

Gian Francesco Malipiero,
The Orchestra

To discuss orchestrational style in a period when orchestral material was
largely the raw stuff of the military parade, ecclesiastical spectacle, and
castle hall is rather like discussing the style of a garment when the fabric
is still on four feet leaping from crag to crag in the South American
Andes. The orchestrational style of a Maurice Ravel or a Richard
Strauss springs from a unique manipulation of long-established components: perfected instruments with specialized techniques, complete
orchestral choirs with homogeneous voices for mixture, balance, or
opposition—and an accessible score to record one's intentions in careful
detail. But until the eighteenth century these precise elements existed
only in a formative state; hence the history of Preclassical instrumentation is only a hazard of the possible. Yet each tenuous advance is part of
the record as a rudimentary step toward a definitive orchestra, an in-

10

dividualized style. Briefly refreshing our memories of instrumental history, we can hear the potential of *Daphnis et Chloé* in the shepherd's flute or of *Till Eulenspiegel* in the hunter's horn.

Much early instrumental music was, strictly speaking, not primarily instrumental in concept; rather, it was vocal. A viola da gamba, for instance, might frequently double with a tenor voice—or substitute for the singer at will. The "orchestras" of the fifteenth and sixteenth centuries—random collections of lutes and viols, wind and keyboard instruments—played from vocal parts. Music designed to fit the human voice was considered equally suitable for instruments, and the effect of both together on a single part no less desirable than either alone.

Even the late sixteenth-century antiphons of Giovanni Gabrieli (1557–1612) give little evidence of advancing beyond an essentially vocal concept. Although the massive St. Mark's Cathedral in Venice, designed to accommodate two organs, offered the organist-composer of the *Sacrae Symphoniae* an unparalleled opportunity to exploit the exciting effects of choir echoing choir and of organ answering organ, the heterogeneous groups of wind-brass and stringed instruments which he requisitioned to support his choral material appear to have been aggregated without specific regard for contrasting instrumental timbres, and largely followed or imitated the vocal lines or organ accompaniment (Example 5). In none of Gabrieli's polychoral music is there evidence of clearly defined instrumental techniques, or of particularized instrumental color.

Yet in the "utility music" of this same era lay the essence of the well-defined choirs of the modern symphony orchestra. The cultivated music of the court employed the viols in mixed consort; recorders of various sizes were used in ensembles of household music, alone or blending their discreet tones with those of the gentle viols and lutes. The more vulgar-sounding shawms and bombards were grouped in open-air bands. Trumpets and drums, invariably used together, made the music of military life or royal pageantry, while the powerful sackbuts and cornetts were the mainstay of ecclesiastical music. The essential orchestral ingredients, then, were at hand: the primary colors, the dramatic and disparate timbres. Yet it seems not to have occurred to the Renaissance and pre-Baroque composers to join these individual elements into a new and satisfying artistic entity.

If this vision of a highly organized synthesis of wind-brass, string, and percussion was slow in appearing, the reason may lie in the inevitably prolonged evolution of the individual instruments. This was an intricate, overlapping process, involving interplay between instrument-maker, composer, and performer. From Gasparo da Salò and Jean Hotteterre to the modern inventor of the *ondes* Martenot, no instrument-designer has been

EXAMPLE 5
Giovanni Gabrieli: from *Surrexit Christus*

Cornetti

Violini

Tromboni

Voci

Bassi Organo

al - le - lu - ja, al - le - lu - ja:

am, al - le - lu - ja, al - le - lu - ja, al - le - lu - ja:

al - le - lu - ja, al - le - lu - ja, al - le - lu - ja: in

able to go it completely alone. Adolph Sax, for instance, invented the saxophone in 1846, but his instrument was seldom a member of the symphony orchestra until a few twentieth-century composers introduced jazz elements into their compositions. And even today the saxophone is not a basic orchestra member, only an "extra." The heckelphone, William Heckel's 1904 invention, appears sporadically in a few Strauss opera scores, but has intrigued few other composers. Only, in fact, when the designer's innovation solves a technical problem that has previously frustrated performers, and when, above all, it allows composers to express what they could not express before, is it likely to be perpetuated widely on the score page.

In the Preclassical and Baroque eras the most important instrument makers to fill these needs were the virtuoso stringed-instrument designers. For several decades—even before the early opera orchestras of Jacopo Peri (1561–1633) and Claudio Monteverdi (1567–1643)—the pale, characterless tone-quality of the viol family had coexisted with the newer potential of the violin members.[1] Then came da Salò, the Amati brothers, Antonio Stradivari, the Guarneris, and Jacob Stainer, giving composers a revitalized and highly responsive violin family with just the intense, brilliant color they demanded. It was thus inevitable that the greater expressive range of the violin, viola, and cello should be written into the instrumental foreground and the viols retired to an historic function. Systematized by Alessandro Scarlatti (1660–1725), the basic string choir—soprano (treble violin), alto (treble violin), tenor (tenor violin or viola), and bass (violoncello and double bass)—ultimately evolved during the Classical period into the core of the new symphony orchestra.

In the centuries since, these versatile instruments have incurred only minor refinements: a longer neck to give greater support to the strings; a more highly arched bridge; and François Tourte's longer, in-curved bow-stick (1780), which proved better suited to the technical demands of the early orchestral composers. But from the late Renaissance period to our own time, the basic design and construction of the string instruments have remained virtually unchanged.

All the woodwinds of our modern orchestra—with the sole exception of the clarinet, a late seventeenth-century invention—had their prototypes in the Middle Ages. Flute and piccolo evolved from the hollow-sounding flageolets and transverse pipes; oboe and English horn [2] from the coarse shawms and *oboi da caccia;* and bassoon from the crude bombards, which were the basses of the double-reed family. The ungainly wooden serpent of the military bands often lent its dubious tone to reinforce the bass register of the wind-brass group, being more generally available than the contrabassoon George Frederick Handel introduced in his 1727 *Coronation Anthem.*[3] By the closing years of the seventeenth century all of the woodwinds had assumed their modern form. Like the string instruments, they have since been affected only by mechanical and technical improvements.

The first brass voice to join regularly with the strings and woodwinds of the Baroque orchestra was the military trumpet; hunting horns were the next to assume an orchestral role. Trombones did not enter the regular complement of the orchestra, however, until the early nineteenth century. In the percussion area, kettledrums (timpani), though first associated with military life, attracted early attention to their dramatic potential by inclusion in such works as the amazing *Festmesse* of Orazio Benevoli (1605–1672). Composed for the 1628 consecration of the Salzburg Cathedral, this huge work calls for soloists with two eight-part choruses, each accompanied by three differently constituted ensembles. The printed score, comprising some fifty staves, is more formidable to the eye than many a late-Romantic score by Strauss or Gustav Mahler (Example 6).

By the last quarter of the seventeenth century the use of timpani was fairly common among orchestral composers. And in the forward-looking opera scores of Christoph Willibald Gluck, dating between 1741 and 1779, we find a number of other percussion instruments, including bass drum, cymbals, and triangle.

As the physical form and the technique of the instruments approached crystallization, novel instrumental effects and prophetic coloristic devices came into existence. Typical is the first-known instance of notated string harmonics in a now forgotten *opéra comique, Tom Jones* (1765), by François André Philidor (1726–1795), a prolific and strikingly original composer (and a noted chess expert as well). Many other notable devices and technical effects will be mentioned in our survey of individual Preclassical composers in the following pages.

Now at last the pattern of the embryonic orchestra began to take shape; stable instrumental components began to evidence their individualized potential. It must be repeated, however, that orchestral "style" in this, its evolutionary stage, was decidedly a nebulous matter. As the definitive form of the orchestra was still considerably in the future, so was instrumentational style a tenuous, indefinite element in the work of the composers of the Preclassical era. But no serious history of instrumental style can neglect the significant contributions of the pioneer composers of the Renaissance and the Baroque.

EXAMPLE 6

Orazio Benevoli: from *Festmesse* (Kyrie)

KYRIE.

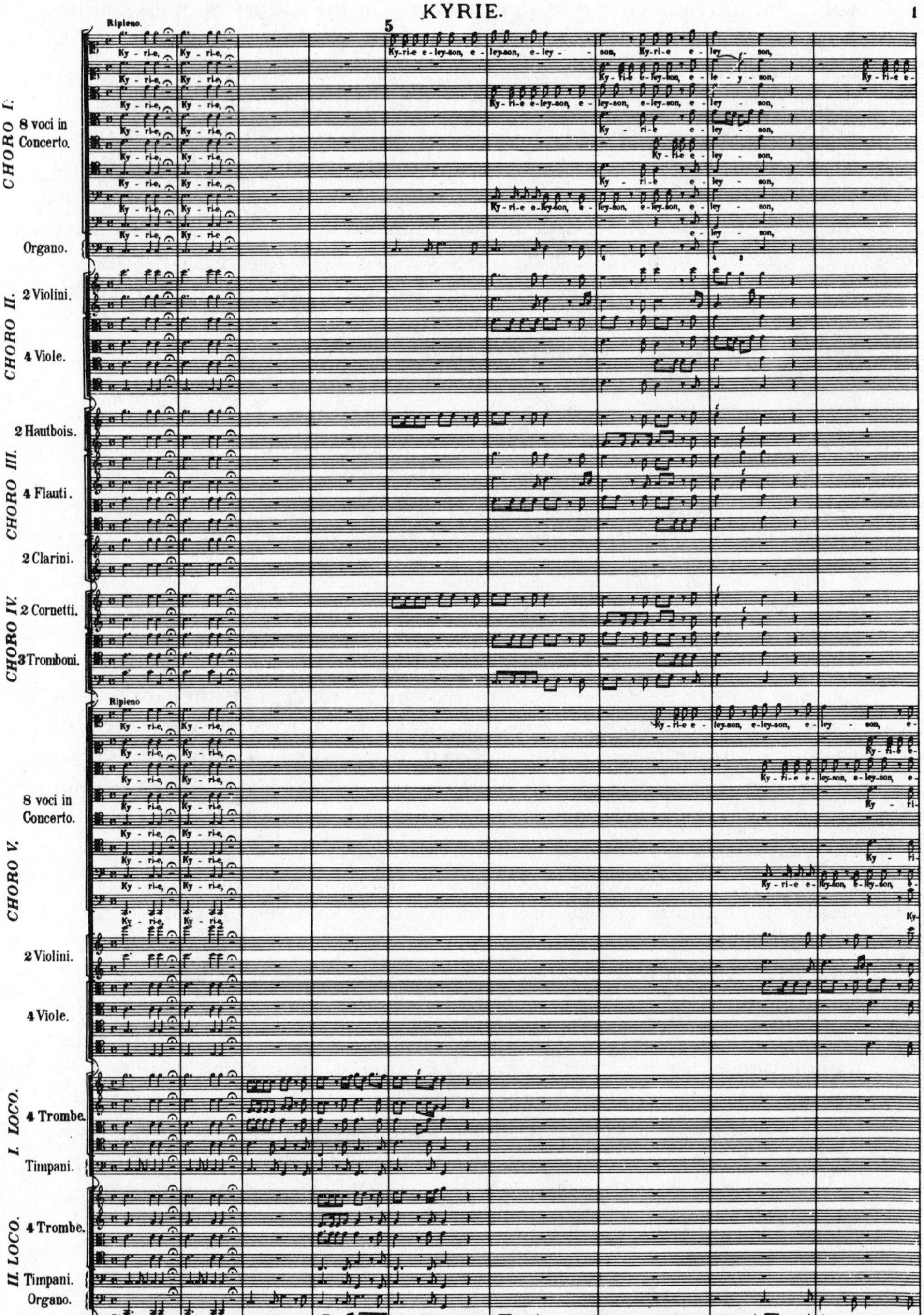

STYLE AND ORCHESTRATION

The first conscious attempts of composers to distinguish between vocal and instrumental style occurred early in the history of opera, dating from Jacopo Peri's *Euridice* (1600). Musicologists and historians usually refer, however, to the 1607 *Orfeo* of Claudio Monteverdi as the first instance of a "modern" orchestra. It is true that this opera represents the first conscious attempt of a composer to distinguish clearly between vocal and instrumental style; its fourteen interludes ("symphonies") and other purely instrumental passages give considerable independence to the orchestral ensemble. But the instruments called for in *Orfeo* were heterogeneous to an extreme, and many were to become virtually obsolete within the next decade or two. Can one rightly say, then, that this unfocused aggregation of portable organs, spinets, giant lutes, viols, harp, flute, trombones, and trumpets constitutes a "modern" orchestra?

Monteverdi's later *Il Combattimento di Tancredi e Clorinda* (1624), with its very selective resources, is far closer to the orchestral ideal of our modern era. This dramatic recitation was scored for a nucleus of the newly designed string instruments (the violin and the early forms of viola and violoncello), together with the older bass gamba and the keyboard clavecin. In the music for this ensemble (Example 7) the composer became the first to call for the pizzicato and tremolando effects that ever since have been the stock-in-trade of composers writing for the strings.[4]

"Quite as significant as the invention of these effects," says Adam Carse in his admirable history of orchestration (1925), "is the fact that in using them the composer necessarily broke away from the vocal style of writing for instruments. He produced music which is only possible on string instruments played with a bow, music in which the interest is that of harmony, texture, and tone color, and is completely independent of any polyphonic or imitative movement of parts."

Unfortunately, we cannot follow the detailed course of Monteverdi's innovations, as few of his scores have survived in printed form. The extant score of his last opera, *L'Incoronazione di Poppea* (1642), produced barely a year before his death, demonstrates no notable advance beyond his early works. In all the available scores, however, even his invention of specialized technical devices is not so important as is his exploration of the inherent dramatic potential of instrumental color. To musicians of our day this may hardly seem a daring exploit, but it represented a major advance in the musical thought and practice of the early seventeenth century. Regrettably, Monteverdi's compatriots (Giulio Caccini, Stefano Landi, and Luigi Rossi, for instance) failed to capitalize on his significant innovations.

EXAMPLE 7
Claudio Monteverdi: from *Il Combattimento di Tancredi e Clorinda*

STYLE AND ORCHESTRATION

In the ensuing period, however, a half-dozen composers did put something of a personal stamp on their orchestral writing: Lully, Corelli, Scarlatti *père,* Vivaldi, and Rameau. Jean-Baptiste Lully (1632–1687), court composer to Louis XIV, is considered the first authentic orchestral conductor, and his scores—all printed during his lifetime—demonstrate that in response to his monarch's constant demands for extravagant display he developed the first virtuoso orchestra. But, like Giacomo Meyerbeer some 200 years later, Lully tended more toward the sensational than the significant, as illustrated by the incidental music he supplied over a period of ten years for the stage works of the great Molière. Lully was not, moreover, an outstanding innovator, except for his introduction of mechanical mutes for the string instruments in his opera *Armide et Renaud* (1686). (Their first appearance occurs in the Prelude to scene three of Act Two.) His very conventionality, however, served as a model of stability for the lesser composers of the period inclined to imitate the "Music-Master to the Royal Family." Some measure of that conventionality may be gleaned from Example 8, a portion of the Passacaglia from Act Five, scene one of *Armide et Renaud.*

Arcangelo Corelli (1653–1713) gave the newly perfected violin the prima-donna status it retained in orchestration until the early Romantic era. The excerpt from one of his twelve *Concerti Grossi* (Example 9) demonstrates his typical handling of this starring role with two imitative violin solo lines and a supporting bass part (cello or gamba) comprising the *concertino,* together with a four-part layout in the accompanying string body (the *ripieno*). Corelli, like his confreres Giuseppi Torelli, Giovanni Baptiste Vitali, and Heinrich Johann Frank von Biber, was simultaneously the principal violin and the conductor of his orchestra. A solo performer as well as composer, he doubtless originated much of the florid figuration and virtuoso passagework new to this period. This highly specialized string technique, difficult if not impossible to match in other instrumental families, doubtless turned composers' attention to individualizing their woodwind and brass parts as well.

Alessandro Scarlatti (1659–1725), going a step further toward instrumental independence, was one of the first composers to write for the violoncello as a distinctive string voice, a unique string-color not to be squandered in invariable duplication of the bass part. Then, matching the new division of the strings into a four-part choir, he grouped his wind and brass instruments in complementary pairs. This procedure inevitably led to more independent parts for the wind instruments, which heretofore had almost obsessively duplicated the writing for the strings. As a result, Scarlatti was able—like his English contemporary Henry Purcell (1659–1695)—to exploit the natural contrast afforded by alter-

EXAMPLE 8
Jean-Baptiste Lully: from *Armide et Renaud* (Act 5, Scene 1)

EXAMPLE 9
Arcangelo Corelli: from Concerto Grosso No. 1, 2nd movement

nating wind-brass and string instruments, a refreshing change from the ingrained fugal habit common to most instrumental composers of the period.

Like Handel (whose contributions are discussed in detail below), the elder Scarlatti pioneered in regularly adding horns to the familiar components of the Baroque ensemble—strings, woodwinds (double reeds), trumpets, and timpani. This format, suggesting the firm outline of the later Classical orchestra, was stabilized by the "Mannheim School" (principally Johann Stamitz and Christian Cannabich) and by the founding of professional orchestras in Dresden, Leipzig, and elsewhere on the Continent.[5] Once established, the four-category pattern remained virtually unchanged until the twentieth century. Older members might be modified, or new instruments added, but there continued an association with one of the basic instrumental families.

Antonio Vivaldi (1680–1743) in his many concertos transferred to the realm of instruments alone the operatic concept of a solo voice against accompanying orchestra. Using considered economy of means in his treatment of the main body of instruments, he highlighted the florid figurations that characterize, for example, the solo violin part of his popular four-part concerto, *The Seasons* (1725). This solo-tutti contrast, a hallmark of the eighteenth century, remains even today a valid orchestrational technique (Example 10).

Jean-Philippe Rameau (1683–1764), author of one of the first significant treatises on harmony, *Demonstration du principe de l'harmonie* (1750), also developed several string techniques that long ago became staple orchestral effects. One of the first composers to use pizzicato chords in all the string instruments, he also called for the device of arpeggiation in which the bow undulates across the strings to produce broken chords (Example 11). It is thought that Rameau was also the first composer to use the newly designed clarinet. This instrument did appear in the works of somewhat later composers for the Paris Opera orchestra, but the designation *clarini* in Rameau's *Zoroastre* (1749) and *Acante et Céphise* (1751) could conceivably refer to trumpets rather than to clarinets.

Rameau's great contributions to the emerging art of orchestration were the elements of clarity, elegance, and general economy of means—aspects of instrumentation inherent in the French musical temperament. He is thus the first of a distinguished line of French masters of orchestration extending all the way to Pierre Boulez of our own time.

Yet despite the indubitable flair of the composers we have discussed (to say nothing of the efforts of C.P.E. Bach, Dietrich Buxtehude, Giovanni Carissimi, Johann Adolf Hasse, Heinrich Schütz, Gasparo Spon-

EXAMPLE 10
Antonio Vivaldi: from *The Seasons* (*Summer*)

EXAMPLE 11

Jean-Philippe Rameau: from *Castor et Pollux* (Act 3, Scene 5)

Fin du 3ᵉ Acte.
(On reprend le 1ᵉʳ Air des Démons page 196 pour Entr'acte.)

tini, and Georg Philipp Telemann, among others), it is evident that few Preclassical ensembles were orchestras in the same sense as our modern symphonic groups. More often than not they were collections of instruments aggregated largely in terms of availability.

This practice continued well into the Baroque period, as illustrated by the unsystematized orchestras of the six *Brandenburg Concertos* of Johann Sebastian Bach (1685–1750). All six, composed in 1721, call for string instruments, but no two were otherwise designed for the same basic instrumental forces. No. 1 in F Major calls for three oboes, bassoon, two horns, string choir, and *continuo* (harpsichord). No. 2, also in F major, is for solo oboe, flute, trumpet, and violin as a concerted group, accompanied by a main body of strings. No. 3 in G Major is scored for string orchestra alone, divided into three groups. No. 4, likewise in G major, calls for two flutes, solo violin, and string choir. No. 5 in D Major is for flute, violin, and clavier (harpsichord) as a solo group, and accompanying strings. Finally, No. 6 in B-flat Major employs cellos and double basses plus the older *viola da braccio* and *viola da gamba* in place of violins and violas.

Curiously, the bassoon required in the first concerto appears elsewhere in the Bach oeuvre only in the Overture (Suite) in C Major and in the Suite No. 4 in D Major (1736?). In the latter work, clearly intended for performance out-of-doors, the composer gives his non-string instru-

23

ments considerable independence, breaking away from the rather impartial distribution of interchangeable parts typical of the period. (With many of Bach's contemporaries, oboes and bassoons still doubled the strings, even playing from string parts, as they had done from the time of their first incursion into the evolving orchestra.)

Considered in the light of the modern orchestral ideal, the first two *Brandenburg Concertos* offer the greatest variety of tone color and instrumental contrast. No. 1, pitting the four woodwinds and two brasses against the string and keyboard instruments, comes closest to a clearly defined orchestral approach (Example 12). Even in this case, however, there is no marked contrast; instead of supplying individual color to the thematic material or to the implied harmony of the continuo, there is a wholesale duplication of polyphonic lines. This typical Baroque technique of instrumentation merely reinforces the contrapuntal strands, as various stops might be added to organ registration for the same purpose.

Similar reasoning also dictated the Baroque practice of "terraced" dynamics, as opposed to the later Romantic concept of expressive dynamics. In Bach's orchestral music, as well as in that of Handel and the other contemporaneous masters, dynamic contrasts were planned sectionally rather than between instrument and instrument or from measure to measure. Where there are major timbral contrasts it is between large structural elements. One instrumental scheme usually carries through an entire section or movement (as in the solo arias of the 1729 *St. Matthew Passion* or the *B minor Mass* of 1738). This is in contrast, of course, with the more modern practice of constantly shifting the instrumental tone-colors. Hence Bach's orchestrational style is compositional and contrapuntal rather than coloristic.

Like his distinguished forebears from Gabrieli to Buxtehude, Bach marshalled his material in terms of the instruments at his disposal, not in order to fit into a standardized ensemble of varied instruments, the later Classical practice. This former method of orchestration was soon to be outmoded, but the fresh sound of the *Brandenburg Concertos* and of the four orchestral suites is still permeated with the genius that created the *Art of the Fugue*—a masterpiece when performed by any combination of instruments whatsoever.

Bach's cosmopolitan contemporary, George Frederick Handel (1685–1759) was far more inclined than he to design his instrumentation for audience effect. His method with the strings, however, was even less enterprising than Bach's customary four-part treatment. Handel's violas had no separate and independent part, but followed the bass voices at

EXAMPLE 12

J. S. Bach: from *Brandenburg Concerto No. 1,* 1st movement

the upper octave or else filled in harmony notes—an unfortunate waste of color potential. His bass parts, like those of the other Baroque composers, served for cellos, double basses, bassoons, and the *continuo* (organ or cembalo).

Woodwinds, on the other hand, made a major contribution to the generally massive sound of Handel's orchestra. They frequently included as many as ten double-reed instruments against a string body rarely exceeding twenty-five. Any imbalance of tone, however, was probably not a problem, for eighteenth-century oboes and bassoons did not possess the power and intensity of their modern counterparts.

In his oratorio *Saul* (1739) **(1)** * Handel became the first composer to make the bassoon a solo instrument. Previously used only as a doubling agent, the bassoon was accustomed to follow the *basso continuo* and seldom had its own part written in Baroque scores. This time-saving practice on the part of composers led some later editors and publishers to assume that no bassoons were required in many works of the period. This misunderstanding applied even to certain of the Haydn and Mozart symphonies of a later era. Modern editions, of course, rightly supply these missing parts in the printed scores.

Handel's obvious fondness for horns and trumpets also gave great solidity and brilliance to his orchestration. He is now generally credited with being the first to use four horns in the orchestra (in the opera *Giulio Cesare* [1724]). Later, Mozart also called for four horns in his *Idomeneo* of 1780, but these instances are both the exception rather than the rule in the instrumentation of the Baroque and Classical periods.

Another "first" that can be credited to Handel is a solo role for timpani, notably in the two oratorios *Ode for St. Cecilia's Day* (1739) **(2)** and *Semele* (1743) **(3)**. Like the bassoons, the kettledrums had heretofore only supported and doubled existing parts, nearly always in conjunction with the trumpets. In several passages in the two oratorios, however, they are used quite independently.

Uniformly apt and always powerful, Handel's orchestration employed two broad methods of procedure. In his early period he duplicated all the component parts—oboes with violins, bassoons with cellos and double basses—as Bach did. Even his brasses would simply reinforce or imitate the string-wind voices, as in the excerpt from the *Water Music* of 1715–17 (Example 13).

Closer to the modern orchestral manner is the practice of Handel's later years, when he deliberately contrasted the three tone-colors of

* These bold-face numbers in parentheses refer to the List of Score References in the book, pp. 285–290.

EXAMPLE 13

George Frederick Handel: from *Water Music,* 3rd movement

strings, double-reeds, and combined brasses and timpani. By overlapping these groups, alternating them, and also combining them in the fashion of earlier duplicating procedures, Handel exemplifies what the later Romantic composers took for granted—an orchestrational technique rooted in the principle of contrast by choirs.

Even as the Baroque masters at mid-century were perfecting a method of instrumentation still largely contrapuntal, forces of change were already at work. Typical of the transition from Bach and Handel to the early harmonic, formal Classicism of Haydn and Mozart (and even beyond) was the expert orchestrational art of Christoph Willibald Gluck (1714–1787). Here for the first time the wind-brass instruments were treated as a sustaining and binding element; they and the strings, with their motion and ornamentation, functioned in independent yet inter-related roles. In applying this approach, Gluck pioneered in the use of horns, trumpets, and timpani for soft effects instead of the massive or brilliant sounds invariable with previous composers. Thus was born the new idea in music of harmony versus melody–of sustained sonorities against active thematic strands—in the treatment of the orchestral choirs.

Gluck's operas and oratorios, in their instinctive use of this new application of instrumental color, go far beyond the works of such con-temporaries as Johann Christian Bach, Domenico Cimarosa, François Joseph Gossec, Niccola Piccinni, or Giovanni Sammartini. On occasion Gluck made an effective dramatic device of the entire string body playing in unison or in octaves (Example 14). In his *Alceste* (1767) (4) he cleverly imitated Charon's conch horn by having two horns, placing the bells of their instruments together, play in unison, thus creating a mutual muffling effect. (It was a contrivance ingenious enough to command the respect of Hector Berlioz some eighty years later.) And though this dramatic flair for unusual orchestral effects had little systematic applica-tion beyond stage works, intensified tone-color generally began to develop in its application to sections and whole movements of compositions, as well as in terms of individual instruments. Here, indeed, are the germinal elements of Romanticism and Expressionism that lay dormant for much of the following century.

In his very selection of instruments, Gluck's orchestra also came to foreshadow the orchestra of the nineteenth century, rather than clinging to that of the eighteenth. From time to time he requisitioned piccolo and contrabassoon, clarinet and trombone—none of them regular com-ponents of the orchestra until the Beethoven era. His operas also call for the early form of the English horn (termed a "tenor hoboy" by Henry Purcell) and for the harp, which like the English horn did not become a

EXAMPLE 14
Gluck: from *Alceste* (Act 1, Scene 4)

full-fledged member of the symphonic ensemble until the Berlioz and Liszt period a half-century later. In Gluck's *Iphigenie en Tauride* (1779) the orchestra was comprised of piccolo, two each of flutes, oboes, clarinets, bassoons, horns, and trumpets, three trombones, and strings. These were the exact forces Beethoven employed, with the addition of contrabassoon and timpani, in the Fifth Symphony of 1805.

It is evident, however, that despite such creative anachronisms as Gluck's, conscious orchestrational style was not an aspect of the Preclassical period. Far more characteristic are the products of groping and experimentation in the fields of orchestral writing and of instrument design. The constructive elements of Preclassicism, as far as orchestration is concerned, must certainly include the discarding of some instruments, the improvement of others, and their grouping into families where a fundamental and generic timbre is common to all within each separate choir. It was a period in which a growing, sometimes extravagant, preference for extreme contrasts branded indelibly the evolving instruments and the malleable techniques of instrumental writing. Instinctive empathy for the original instrument, the human voice, eventually resulted in the dominance of those orchestral instruments capable of highest melodic expressivity. This concept of "instrumental song," common to all composers of the time, was to influence the whole art of music until well into the present century.

Notes

1. The viol was a sixteenth-century metamorphosis of the earlier *vielle,* or *fiedel.* Because the viol was held by the performer between the legs, it was commonly referred to as the *viola da gamba.* By the end of the sixteenth century an entire family of viols had developed, ranging from the sub-bass instrument (over seven feet high) to the tiny descant viol, some twenty-eight inches in length. Not all viols, of course, were capable of being held between the player's knees, but the generic term persisted. The *viola da braccio (braccio:* "arm") also descended from the ancient *vielle,* was played at the shoulder. It was the direct forerunner of the violin and the viola proper. Although because of its size the violoncello is played like the *viola da gamba,* its design stemmed from the newer violin family rather than the earlier viol.

2. This nomenclature is a corruption of the French *anglé,* meaning an "angled" or bent horn—not *anglais* ("English").

3. The serpent was superseded during the mid–nineteenth century by the ophicleide, and this in turn by the bass tuba.

4. The devices of col legno (playing with the back of the bow) and sul ponticello (close to the bridge) were apparently first specified in compositions of the violin virtuoso, Carlo Farina, printed in 1627.

5. At its maximum size the Mannheim Orchestra consisted of a pair each of flutes, oboes, and bassoons, four horns, one trumpet, two kettledrums, twenty violins (in two sections), and four each of violas, cellos, and double basses.

2

The Classical Orchestra

The orchestra is such a beautiful instrument in itself that, provided one has common sense and observes certain rules, it requires positive genius to make it sound ugly.

> Gerald Abraham,
> *A Hundred Years of Music*

In the formal beauty of the Classical period, with its dedication to symmetry, finish, and repose, we reach a welcome point of consolidation in the development of the orchestrational art. Composers of this era, devoted like their contemporaries in the other arts to established and elegant patterns, came to gladly abandon the sprawling suites of galliards and gavottes characteristic of Preclassical composition in favor of the calculated designs of the sonata and the symphony. These ordered forms, perfectly realized in the orchestral works of Franz Joseph Haydn (1732–1809) and Wolfgang Amadeus Mozart (1756–1791), became the epitome of Classical expression.

Both the sonata and the symphony grew out of the new concepts of harmonic writing; both are an admirable blend of formalism and subjectivity, an ideal balance of structural logic and musical content. If the orchestral symphony has surpassed the instrumental sonata in mass ap-

31

peal, it is owing to the colorful and sensuous impact of massed instrumental sound. And, conversely, we owe the subsequent maturing of this orchestral sound, with its textural consistency and subtle gradations of nuance and dynamics, to the firming up of the symphonic format during the Classical era.

The first characteristic of the definitive Classical orchestra was its selectivity of resources, in contrast to such ill-assorted agglomerations as Monteverdi's flutes, viols, theorbos, and harpsichords. Over the years, as we have previously indicated, composers had been serving as the agents of natural selection when they stopped writing for instruments that functioned imperfectly or were limited in their expressive capacity. By the middle of the eighteenth century composers were also assessing instruments on the basis of their collective timbres, placing them in one or another of the four basic orchestral groups.

Above all, the essence of the Classical spirit favored economy rather than extravagance, clarity and precision rather than lavish display. The orchestra of Haydn and Mozart, the end-result of these critical standards, was therefore frequently smaller than the Baroque ensembles of Handel and Bach. The normal complement of the Classical orchestra included: flute, oboe, and bassoon—sometimes in pairs, sometimes not; two horns; often, but not invariably, two trumpets; two kettledrums hand-tuned to the tonic and dominant pitches of each movement; and, finally, from fifteen to twenty-five string players (first and second violins, violas, violoncellos, and double basses).

These components, it will be noted, do not include the clarinet, which was not a regular member of the orchestra of the Classical period. Haydn used the instrument only sparsely, and only in his later symphonies; Mozart used it in only five of his symphonies, including the revised version of Symphony No. 40 in G minor (1788). Even when it appeared in eighteenth-century scores, the emerging clarinet often lacked a well-defined mission. For example, in Mozart's Symphony No. 39 in E-flat Major (1788), the clarinets substituted for oboes. When both instruments were included, as in the "Haffner" Symphony (No. 35 in D Major [1782]), the single-reed instrument often merely reinforced the double-reed one; where independent parts were written, oboes invariably had the more active role. One should point out that Mozart called for the *corno di bassetto*, a form of tenor clarinet, in several of the operas and in the great *Requiem Mass* (left incomplete at the time of his death).

Trombones, though widely used in church music of the seventeenth and eighteenth centuries, were also exceptional rather than standard in Classical scores. Haydn, of course, made exemplary use of these instruments in *The Creation* (1798), but never requisitioned them in any of his 104 symphonies. Likewise, no trombones appeared in any of Mozart's forty-one symphonies, although they functioned with dramatic power in *Don Giovanni* (1787), *The Magic Flute* (1791), and in the *Requiem Mass*. The tuba, as previously pointed out, did not take its place in the orchestra until well into the nineteenth century.

Neither Haydn nor Mozart used the harp (the single-action instrument) in any operatic or symphonic works, with the exception of Mozart's rather routine concerto for flute and harp (1778). Even Beethoven employed the harp in only one work, his ballet *The Creatures of Prometheus* (1800). As for the percussion instruments, with the exception of the timpani, they were likewise only an occasional element in the Classical milieu. Mozart's exquisite utilization of the keyed glockenspiel in *The Magic Flute* (5), and Haydn's apt cymbals, bass drum, and triangle in the "Military" Symphony (No. 100 in G Major [1794]) (6) are both rarities in Classical scoring.

Nor were there notable structural changes in the individual members of the late eighteenth-century ensemble; significant improvements in the instruments themselves occurred only in time for the development of nineteenth-century Romantic orchestration. Classical composers, then, were able to concentrate on expanding the musical potential and improving the performing techniques of their refined instrumental gamut. In the technical area the greatest single advance concerned the register domain of the various strings; the extension of the left-hand finger technique that increased the upper range of violin, viola, and cello was of paramount importance in the development of modern instrumentation.

With almost universal agreement on orchestral constituents which were limited in number and of firmly established technical range, composers of the Classical period achieved a unanimity of instrumentational style present in no other era of musical history. The exemplars—Haydn, Mozart, and Beethoven in his early period—faced identical possibilities and identical limitations; they therefore of necessity subscribed to the same instrumental procedures. To the informed musician, then, it is not so much a variance in orchestrational style that distinguishes Haydn from Mozart as it is certain melodic and harmonic individualities, not to mention obvious differences of temperament and musical personality.

But if the orchestral style of Mozart, Haydn, and the young Beethoven was circumscribed by Classical patterns and a restricted number of instruments, it was by no means a matter of "black and white", as some misguided musical historians have described it. Until the era of the mature Beethoven, it is true, the subjective use of instrumental color—meaning the exploitation of individual and characteristic instrumental timbre—was not of major importance in composing for the orchestra. Prophetic experiments of Monteverdi, Gluck, and others notwithstanding, the concept of orchestral color for its own sake simply did not exist for the Classical composers. Their treatment of the newly stabilized orchestra, however, was in no way pallid or monochromatic.

Both Haydn and Mozart frequently scored in such a way as to emphasize distinctive instrumental sounds, regardless of the technical limitations of those instruments. "I have only just learned in my old age how to use the wind instruments," Haydn ruefully remarked, "and now that I understand them I must leave the world." In the slow movement of the "London" Symphony (No. 104 in D Major [1795]) he artfully contrasted the limpid colors of the woodwinds alone with the previous quiet string passage (Example 15). And in the first movement of the "Military" Symphony (7) the principal subject is given to flute and oboes, with no other instruments in support. "So revolutionary a treatment of the high woodwind instruments, which in the earlier symphonies are almost never used independently," Karl Geiringer observes in his life of Haydn, "shows us that the aged Haydn did not cease experimenting and trying out new effects."

We should remember, too, that Haydn was the composer responsible for discarding the then widely prevalent notion that once the woodwinds commenced a passage in a certain pattern, this plan should continue until a change of texture occurred. For instrumentation, as well as for Haydn himself, it was a salutary decision.

As fresh and piquant in effect as the Haydn excerpt from the "London" Symphony is the Trio of the minuet (third movement) of Mozart's Symphony No. 39 in E-flat Major (1788). Here two clarinets simultaneously outline both melody and harmony, the one in a brilliant, clear-cut tessitura, the other in a low and warmly suave register (Example 16). This particular color relationship must have especially intrigued the composer, for he used it also in two of his operas, *Don Giovanni* and *Così fan tutte* (1789).[1] By modern standards this is a carefully muted palette, it is true; but in the opinion of the celebrated modern photographer Ivan Dmitri: "A great picture need not scream with color."

Within the overall pattern of the Classical orchestra there are subtle permutations especially characteristic of one composer or another. In the case of Haydn, we have already noted the care with which he gave the woodwinds a new flexibility, independence, and commendable pliancy of expression. It is a sad commentary on the twentieth-century passion for exaggeration of amplitude that his delicately calculated balances between winds and strings are so frequently contravened in modern performance. Many an eminent maestro, insensitively employing an enlarged string section with Haydn's specified complement of

34

EXAMPLE 15
Franz Joseph Haydn: from Symphony No. 104, 2nd movement

woodwinds, quite destroys the originally intended relationship between the two choirs.

It is all too easy to overlook the contrasting definitions of wind-string balance in the Classical orchestra and in today's major ensembles. In Haydn's day, some twenty-five strings would usually be arrayed against three to six each of oboes and bassoons, and about four each of flutes and horns. The parts, of course, were written in pairs, but were quite frequently played by more than two instruments of each kind. For tutti passages, the paired wind parts were always doubled, indicating that extra players were esssential for a full and satisfying balance. But even granting the increased dynamic strength of the modern winds, they cannot achieve a true Classical balance when pitted against a string choir of over sixty players in our major orchestras of today. The in-

35

EXAMPLE 16

Wolfgang Amadeus Mozart: from Symphony No. 39, 3rd movement

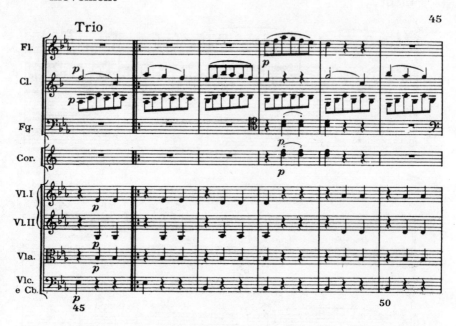

formed conductor, we may be sure, will wish to perform the Haydn and Mozart symphonies with the instrumental complement that is imperative for Classical balance and contrast: eight woodwinds, four brasses, two timpani, and not more than thirty strings.

Haydn's brasses, in contrast with his creative attention to the woodwinds, usually received conventional treatment. He wrote for his trumpets generally in a routine—almost primitive—fashion; and nowhere in Haydn's oeuvre do we find more than two separate horn parts, not even in *The Seasons* (1801), where four instruments are specified.

A representative example of Haydn's customary approach to his horns and trumpets is the quoted passage from Symphony No. 99 in E-flat Major (1793). Here the brasses, in alliance with the woodwinds, merely outline the harmony, moving in parallel motion and utilizing the most conventional rhythmic pattern (Example 17). Haydn was restricted, of course, by the inherent limitations of the brass instruments available at the time. Neither the horns nor the trumpets could easily play pitches outside the natural series of notes derived from the fundamental key-note of the individual instrument. Stopped notes, an invention of the virtuoso horn player Anton Joseph Hampel (1700–1771) for

EXAMPLE 17
Haydn: from Symphony No. 99, 4th movement

lowering the natural tones of the horn a half- or whole-step, seldom appeared in the scores of Haydn or Mozart, no doubt due to the fact that the stopped notes resulted in faulty intonation and inferior tone quality.

Occasionally Haydn's cautious approach to the brasses gave way to something as fresh as the canonic play of horns and trumpets in the minuet movement of Symphony No. 99 (Example 18). Here the composer was not handicapped by technical limitations, since the melodic strands merely outlined the natural series of notes available to the E-flat instruments.

Seemingly unusual for the period were the muted trumpets and horns in the *adagio* movement of Haydn's Symphony No. 102 in B-flat Major (1795). The Eulenburg edition of Haydn's score includes the direction *con sordini* over both parts, but according to Karl Geiringer (*Haydn—A Creative Life in Music*) the direction ought to be placed

EXAMPLE 18
Haydn: from Symphony No. 99, 3rd movement

over the timpani part instead, thus indicating muffled kettledrı
The color resource of muted brass was extremely rare in Classical orchestration; even Beethoven utilized muted horn in only one of his
symphonies—at the very end of the Pastoral (No. 6 in F Major [1808])
(8)—and at the conclusion of the slow movement of the Violin Concerto
(1806) (9).

Haydn's percussion resources were seldom as imaginatively employed as in the "Military" Symphony, previously mentioned. For the
most part, his timpani simply reinforce the bass voice in tutti passages as,
for instance, in the slow movement of Symphony No. 101 in D Major
("Clock" [1794]) (10). Notably less conventional is the effective one-
measure roll, solo, that opens the aptly named "Drumroll" Symphony
(No. 103 in E-flat Major [1795]) (11), and the soft tapping rhythm in the
Menuetto of Symphony No. 88 in G Major (1787) (12).

In the domain of the strings Haydn relied—as did the younger
Mozart—mainly on a four-part texture; only occasionally did the double
basses assume an independent part. When they did go their own way,
the bassoon or low horn was usually present to lend necessary support. A
rare instance of a relatively unsupported double-bass part occurs in the
opening measures of the slow movement of Symphony No. 88 (13). Here
the thin harmonic texture quite justifies the notable lack of bass reinforcement. Also worthy of note in this passage is the intense color produced by the oboe with the solo violoncellos an octave lower, backed up
by the dark timbres of bassoon, low horn, and violas—hardly monochrome orchestration.

In one aspect, however, Haydn's instrumentation needlessly adhered to Baroque practice: in his first forty-odd symphonies the composer indicates a *continuo* part to double the bass line; thus a harpsichord or cembalo is indispensable to correct realization. Since the linear
concepts of the Baroque were already being supplanted by the new
harmonic style, it is singular that Haydn should not have been emancipated from this prominent feature of early instrumental composition. As
all the harmonic voices in Classical orchestral writing were now assigned
to specific instruments, the need for a figured-bass part was obviated.
Perhaps it was only from force of habit that Haydn and certain other
composers continued to include a *basso continuo* part long after it had
become inessential.

Even so, Haydn is universally recognized as one of the great masters
of the art of orchestration. His unique contribution lies not so much in
distinctive and highly personal use of the individual instruments as in his
treatment of the orchestra as a whole—as a perfectly balanced ensemble,
an entity supremely capable of elegant Classical expression.

STYLE AND ORCHESTRATION

If Haydn made only understated use of the color of characteristic instrumental tone, the symphonies, concertos, and operas of Mozart display the most advanced conception of orchestral timbre prior to the Romantic period. Beethoven, Weber, and Berlioz owed this supreme Classicist a substantial debt; even Johannes Brahms, a century later, readily acknowledged the Mozartian inspiration.

A large portion of Mozart's felicitous color palette lies in the area of the woodwinds, treated either as solo voices or as a sectional timbre artfully contrasted with that of the strings. Hallmarks of his approach are melodic ideas uniquely suited to the individual technical facility and tonal character of the separate woodwind instruments. This grateful scoring is superbly illustrated in the excerpt from his Symphony No. 39 previously referred to (see Example 16, p. 36), and throughout Symphony No. 41 in C Major ("Jupiter" [1788]) (14). It is noteworthy that in one particular passage the composer flexibly placed the oboe above, rather than below, the flute in a scale passage in thirds. Incidentally, it is singular that Mozart's Symphony No. 38 in D Major ("Prague" [1786]) was the last to require two flutes in the complement of paired woodwinds. In his final three symphonies Mozart used but one flute—perhaps because he shared the opinionated verdict of Cherubini, "The only thing worse than a flute is two flutes."

Be that as it may, a single flute appears in one of Mozart's favorite melodic combinations—the three colors of flute, clarinet, and bassoon separated by octaves—as demonstrated in the final movement of Symphony No. 39 (15) and in the first movement of the Piano Concerto in A Major (1786) (16), for instance. Also frequent (in other Classical composers as well as Mozart) were parallel thirds or sixths given to three different winds: flutes on top, oboes or clarinets in the middle, and bassoons at the bottom. Owing to the different levels on which each pair of instruments moves, the separate timbres sound clearly and do not mix to create a neutral blend. The passage illustrated (Example 19) also exhibits another of Mozart's apt woodwind melodic combinations: flute and bassoon not one, but two, octaves apart. A coloristic extension of this device is Mozart's predilection for an interchoir melodic coupling of violins doubled at the octave above by flute and at the octave below by bassoon. This combination may be seen on page after page in Mozart's works for orchestra.

In his treatment of the brasses Mozart, like Haydn, seemed philosophically resigned to the limitations of the extant instruments. He invariably used them in orchestral tutti for sonority and brilliance but seems to have been untempted to exploit them, with their faulty intonation and regrettable technical restrictions. Mozart called for four horns

EXAMPLE 19
Mozart: from Overture to *The Magic Flute*

in several of the early symphonies (Nos. 18, 19, 25, and 32), although there they played only two parts, but in the later sequence of symphonies fell back on the more conventional pair. Whether he became impatient with the bad intonation of inferior players or was merely striving for better dynamic balance, is uncertain.

As for the timpani, Mozart's scoring is practically indistinguishable from Haydn's; if anything, Haydn was the more venturesome of the two. The concept of percussion as a solo voice in the orchestra did not appear until Beethoven wrote the dramatic Scherzo of his Ninth Symphony (see Example 23, p. 53).

On the other hand, Mozart's strings enjoyed considerably more freedom and independence than did Haydn's, within an orchestra equally conservative in size and variety of instruments. Haydn had usually entrusted melodic lines only to the first violins, with the seconds and violas providing harmonic parts and the cellos and double basses creating the underpinning. Mozart, to the contrary, habitually used both first and second violins—in unison or in octaves—on a principal thematic voice, letting violas and woodwinds supply the inner harmonies. What is more, he was apparently the one to discover the rich color alchemy of violin and viola in octaves on a melodic strand, a device found in many of his string quintets as well as in the orchestral compositions. His mature works also strikingly illustrate the expanded palette offered by violas subdivided on inner harmonic voices.[3]

A remarkable distillation of Mozart's approach to the strings appears in the final movement of the "Jupiter" Symphony with a notable passage for five independent string voices (one line of polyphony for each instrument of the section [Example 20]). Five-part string writing now seems hardly noteworthy, but in the available literature of the eighteenth century this passage is unique. Here Mozart's instrumentation enhances the contrasts essential to the Baroque-style counterpoint (the five subjects are each invertible), yet it demonstrates at the same time an instinctive insight into the new harmonic idiom.

For all this deft amalgamation of seemingly opposed styles, Mozart's approach to the orchestra remained essentially that of all the Classical composers (including, in addition to Haydn: Stamitz, von Dittersdorf, Cimarosa). Though Mozart saw the newly formulated orchestra as a collection of individual instruments, each capable of a special contribution within the formal design of the symphonic form or the dramatic demands of the opera libretto, he never allowed individualism to dominate the overall scheme. Thus, in orchestration that is architectonic rather than subjective, Mozart's music is the quintessence of Classicism,

EXAMPLE 20
Mozart: from Symphony No. 41, 4th movement

and is the ideal realization of eighteenth-century thought in the realm of musical composition.

In the actual presentation of their printed scores, Haydn and Mozart lacked the settled standards that characterized other aspects of their instrumentation. Only since the time of Beethoven have composers come to place their woodwinds at the top of the score-page, with brasses next, percussion below them, and strings at the bottom. The Baroque composers had to choose between two contrasting plans, neither of which was standardized in the sectional order of the instrumental parts. The Italian-French method placed violins and violas at the top of the score-page, followed in order by flutes, oboes, horns, trumpets, and kettledrums; at the bottom of the page was the *continuo* line, comprised of bassoons, the lower strings, and a keyboard instrument (usually the cembalo). On the other hand, the German-English system put timpani and brass instruments at the top of the page, woodwinds below them, strings beneath the winds, and in the lowest position the thorough-bass line (incorporating the same instruments functioning in the *continuo* mentioned above).

The two basic plans, moreover, were varied on occasion. Certain French operatic composers—one being Daniel François Esprit Auber (1782–1871)—arranged all the wind instruments, wood and brass, together in order of pitch, with the higher instruments at the top and the lower at the bottom. In all these systems, basic or variant, any solo or choral vocal parts were always inserted just above the *basso continuo* line.

Even within each choir, regardless of sectional organization on the score-page, the printed scores of the period show no standard order for the individual instruments. Most Baroque and Classical composers grouped the violas with the violins, regardless of the position of the higher strings on the page. Gasparo Spontini (1774–1851), however, in his opera *La Vestale* (1805), put the violas just above the *continuo* staff. This would seem to indicate that they were used to double the bass line at the upper octave, instead of supporting the violins or providing inner harmonies.

In one of Haydn's holograph scores the flute part is situated below the oboe and clarinet lines, above the bassoon. Perhaps this represents a momentary lapse on Haydn's part, for such an odd arrangement does not show up in any of his other scores. But Mozart in his "Coronation" Concerto for Piano (1788) put the timpani below the double-bass line, as did also Étienne Méhul (1763–1817) in his opera *Joseph* (1807) and Cherubini in his *Eliza* (1794). And in Domenico Cimarosa's *Indica Marina* (1792) the timpani are separated from their traditional brass allies and placed just below the violin and violas, immediately above the choral parts and the inevitable *basso continuo* line.

Yet even with the visual presentation in such a state of flux, Classical principles of composition—as pointed out earlier in this chapter—created an orchestrational style that was fairly universal, orderly, and subtly colored within a limited instrumental gamut. This instrumentation was characterized first of all by the four basic groupings that even today remain the foundation of symphonic ensembles: woodwinds, brasses, percussion, and strings. Of these four sections, the strings were sovereign, and largely upheld the dual responsibilities of melody and harmony. The violins, having extended their upward compass through the sixth position (up to g'''), were the uncontested prima donnas of the orchestra and carried most of the principal thematic lines. Sometimes they were doubled at the unison or the octave by the higher woodwinds, generally in tutti passages, but just as frequently they played alone.

Violas customarily provided inner harmonic figuration or supported the lower strings and other instruments of the harmonic underpinning. Cellos and double basses nearly always carried the bass line in conventional octave doubling, only infrequently being entrusted with independent parts. For the first time in the history of orchestration, however, we find the composers of the Classical period writing for pizzicato cellos and basses against the sustained effect of arco violins and violas—a simple yet efficacious device now common coinage with orchestrators the world over. Further extension of string technique included the common use of mutes to soften string tone when appropriate, tremolando effects, and frequent uses of chordal stopping in all but the double basses.

As a choir, the woodwinds were next in importance to the strings. The flute was almost invariably melodic in its role as the high soprano woodwind, joining the violins either in unison or at the upper octave if the range were not extreme. Clarinets (when present) and oboes were treated in an interchangeable manner, with the oboes achieving as a rule the greater importance. Frequently they moved with the bassoons in parallel, mellifluous thirds or sixths, serving either as melody or harmony. Bassoons most often reinforced the bass lines of the lower strings, unless providing a tenor duplication of thematic outlines in the upper woodwinds or strings.

Brass instruments (crooked horns and trumpets) and associated drums (timpani) were the least in evidence in Classical instrumentation. And generally speaking, they were the least effective of the orchestral instruments of this period. Both the horns and the trumpets—invariably written as harmonic support—served to add power and brilliance to tutti passages. Only occasionally were the two horns entrusted with relatively uncomplicated thematic elements, usually of a "hunting call" nature, or given the responsibility for sustaining an inner pedal-note if the bassoons and lower strings were otherwise occupied. The timpani provided rhythmic emphasis (usually in reinforcement of the trumpets) on tonic and dominant pitches in passages for full orchestra, or pulsated unobtrusively on a pedal-point in support of the low strings, with or without the bassoons.[4]

STYLE AND ORCHESTRATION

This, then, was the instrumentational approach of the Classical composer to the newly established symphonic and operatic orchestra. At all times he aimed for transparent texture and for complete clarity of melodic, harmonic, and rhythmic elements. For him the individual tone-color of the various instruments at his disposal was still a matter of secondary musical consideration.

Ahead lay the nineteenth century, with its steadily impinging conception of tone-color as a means to an end—a dominating artistic tenet of the Romanticists and the later Impressionists. Ahead lay an era of incredibly rich resources of massive orchestral sonority, of the diversified and trenchant voices of new instruments. But above all else, ahead lay the intense individualization of personal styles that was to raise the art of orchestration to its highest peak of attainment.

Notes

1. See also the final movement of Beethoven's Fourth Symphony, measures 215–218.

2. Admittedly unusual for the Classical period, muted timpani show up also in Luigi Cherubini's *C minor Requiem,* and in the first act of Mozart's *The Magic Flute.*

3. The slow movement of the Symphony No. 34 in C Major offers a prime example of divisi violas, used both harmonically and melodically.

4. The solo flute and timpani "duet" in the final act of *The Magic Flute* is an exceptional rather than standard treatment of the timpani in the Classical orchestra.

3

The Early Romantic Orchestra

Not only can it [music] agitate the sea, animate the flames of a
fire, make the brooks flow, the rains fall, and swell the torrents;
it can paint the horror of a desert, darken the walls of a
subterranean prison, calm the tempest, render the air tranquil
and serene and, through the orchestra, diffuse a new freshness
through the woods.

Jean Jacques Rousseau,
Dictionary of Music

We have viewed the Classical period as a point of comparative repose in
the leisurely evolution of the science and art of orchestration. The works
of Haydn and Mozart give the impression of creative impulse operating
in the restricted tonal palette and formal patterns of the eighteenth century. Inevitably, however, there appeared other creative minds for whom
these same elements came to represent confinement. These new Romanticists, feeling with the poet Keats that "the excellence of every art
is its intensity", came to reach beyond the cultivated Classical designs for
freedom and fantasy, size and strangeness. It was this Romantic impulse
that liberated and transformed earlier concepts of orchestral sound, for
tone-color as an indispensable element of orchestration—only faintly

47

foreshadowed in the symphonies, oratorios, and operas of Haydn and Mozart—was to become the enlarging prepossession of orchestral thought and practice in the early nineteenth century.

Any study of Romantic orchestration properly begins with Ludwig van Beethoven (1770–1827). His Classical inheritance notwithstanding, it was Beethoven who, in Robert Haven Schauffler's often quoted aphorism, truly "freed" music. His instrumentation sought new expressive qualities that led to a conscious exploitation of instrumental timbre—an approach completely realized in the later scores of Carl Maria von Weber, Giacomo Meyerbeer, and Hector Berlioz. Beethoven placed at the service of this expression an expanding orchestra transformed into a true virtuoso body of instrumentalists, devoid of shallow exhibitionism, and dedicated entirely to musical ends.

The aura of virtuosity that marks the Beethoven orchestra begins with his string instruments, which the composer approached from the standpoint of personal mastery of the violin. Evidently a pioneer in writing for violin above seventh position, he took these instruments to heights of pitch extreme for his time in the *Egmont Overture* (1810) **(17)**. His violas generally assumed astonishing independence in comparison with their Classical use, and in the final movements of the Ninth Symphony (1823) were extensively divided as inner string voices.

Beethoven also quite literally freed orchestral cellos and double basses from the strict confines of incessant octave duplication. So invariable had been the previous practice that in many a Classsical symphony and opera score these two strings shared a common staff. But in Beethoven's Fifth Symphony (1805) **(18)** the violoncellos in their upper, tenor register (here doubled with violas) carry a long expressive melody, an assignment rarely matched before this time. In the Scherzo of the same symphony **(19)** both cellos and double basses are required to toss off extraordinarily tricky passagework. No less difficult are the thunderous rumbles that accompany the "storm" in the Pastoral Symphony (1808) **(20)**, an obvious yet telling moment of tone-painting.

In all these passages, and in such others as the entire second movement of the *Eroica* Symphony (1804), it is evident that in Beethoven's hands the string section became truly a five-voice choir. His frequent and judicious use of divisi further increased the voice parts available within the string family, although it remained for Weber and the later Romantics to exploit this device in their descriptive music.

Beethoven's woodwinds also demonstrate his inclination to explore new expressive means. The piccolo, a comparative newcomer to the symphonic and operatic ensemble, appears in a number of his scores: the Fifth, Sixth, and Ninth Symphonies; the *Egmont* music; the incidental music for *The Ruins of Athens* (1811), and the *Wellington's Victory* Symphony (1813). In their frequent solo assignments Beethoven's flutes are limpid and his oboes pastoral. And while he did not originate the description, he would have relished the rough wit that anonymously characterized the clarinet as being "particularly happy in smooth, sustained, very legato melodies, in which the almost imperceptible joints between note and note remind you of breaking off pieces of a very ripe banana." By the date of the First Symphony (1800) this instrument had become a standard member of the woodwind choir, and from the *Eroica* on it was given numerous solos written with complete understanding and unfailing effectiveness—as, for instance, numerous passages in the Fourth Symphony (1806) (21), and in the Trio of the Eighth Symphony's Minuet (1812) (22). This type of scoring firmly established the characteristic rapport between the Romantic orchestrator and the individual expressive capacity of each instrument at his disposal.

The tenor range of the bassoon seemed to Beethoven particularly suitable for solo work; with quite evident partiality, he wrote a number of highly effective melodic passages for the instrument, notably in the Fourth Symphony (23), the *Coriolanus* Overture (1807) (24), and the Violin Concerto in D Major (1806) (25). And surely bassoonists of the time must have savoured the furious scampering allowed them, quite unsupported by other instruments, in *The Consecration of the House* Overture (1822) (26).

The contrabassoon, previously neglected by symphonic composers, was given specific assignments in Beethoven's Fifth and Ninth Symphonies, in his one opera, *Fidelio* (1805), and in the *King Stephen* Overture (1811). We cannot be sure, however, that the part was always performed by this instrument. More often than not, contrabassoon parts were probably played by the serpent or the ophicleide; the somewhat unrealistic writing for contrabassoon in the Ninth Symphony (27) may well indicate that Beethoven wrote what could not be easily performed except by instruments considerably more flexible than those available today. The remaining woodwind instruments—English horn and bass clarinet—do not appear in any of Beethoven's compositions.

Frequently Beethoven's brass writing was cruelly hampered by the limitations of the instruments he inherited from the Classical orchestra. A case in point occurs in the recapitulation section of the initial movement of the Fifth Symphony: the main theme, originally given to the powerful horns (Example 21a), returns in the dynamically weaker bassoons (Example 21b.) Beethoven's horns could not, of course, negotiate it in the new tonality, restricted as they were to the harmonic series of the former key of E-flat. What should be a powerful and dramatic restate-

EXAMPLE 21
Ludwig van Beethoven: from Symphony No. 5, 1st movement

a.

b.

ment of the "fate" motive is thereby watered down by this enforced shift of instruments—unless the conductor takes the liberty of doubling the returning theme with modern chromatic horns. It would seem that this constitutes one of the rare instances where judicious tampering with a composer's original instrumentation is fully justified.

In other works, however, Beethoven made audacious demands for purely musical reasons, with the expectation that both instruments and players would progress to meet them. As early as his opera *Fidelio,* Beethoven wrote three independent horn parts, all elaborately conceived and no doubt causing the players of his day considerable anguish. And the trio sections of the *Eroica*'s Scherzo contains a fanfare-like passage for three horns that can still be the undoing of tired or careless players (Example 22). No passage in a Classical work—symphony or opera— can compare in technical difficulty or in compositional brilliance with this moment of typical Beethovian jubilation.

The finale of Beethoven's Seventh Symphony (1812) **(28)** demonstrates vividly the wide leap in technical proficiency and orchestral concept in the twenty-four years separating this work from Mozart's last symphony, the "Jupiter" (1788). The horns in this movement are in A, which means that in several instances the first horn ascends to e'', a dangerous note for even the modern instrument.

In the Ninth Symphony Beethoven wrote four horn parts, a symphonic "first," though Handel had earlier required four horns in the orchestra of his opera *Giulio Cesare.* The florid solo assigned the fourth horn in the slow movement of the Ninth has puzzled many students of instrumentational history; why the fourth horn instead of the first, or even the third? This demanding solo, it appears, was written for a *corno basso,* normally either the second or the fourth player of the horn quartet. Beethoven's choice of the fourth rather than the second horn was determined by key (E-flat), the first and second horns being in B-flat, and therefore unable to encompass all the required notes of the solo line.[1]

Brilliant as were Beethoven's horns, his trumpets received less imaginative treatment, although the offstage trumpet call in *Fidelio* is entirely suited to its dramatic purpose. Trombones, on the other hand, achieved full symphonic status for the first time in his Fifth Symphony; they were, nonetheless, held in reserve until the final movement. Of special interest is Beethoven's specifying three varieties of trombones: alto, tenor, and bass. The alto instrument is now obsolete, and the part is always taken by the modern tenor trombone. Last, the tuba does not appear in Beethoven's orchestral works, since it had not yet been invented.

Timpani in Beethoven's scoring were at long last emancipated from their routine use in *forte* passages, and assumed such highly soloistic

EXAMPLE 22
Beethoven: from Symphony No. 3, 3rd movement

activities as we find in the Scherzo of the Ninth Symphony. The instruments, moreover, were not restricted solely to tonic and dominant pitches; in both the Eighth and Ninth Symphonies they were tuned (in one movement in each symphony) to tonic octaves, a procedure unheard-of before this time. The octave tuning in the Scherzo of the Ninth, of course, enabled the principal motive to be played antiphonally by the timpanist

52

EXAMPLE 23

Beethoven: from Symphony No. 9, 2nd movement

(Example 23). The soft timpani double-notes at the close of the moving Adagio of the symphony—in all probability the first appearance of this effect—may also be considered a purely compositional expedient.[2]

Beethoven's orchestral style, seen as a whole, illustrates both the culmination of Classical practices and the early Romantic treatment of the expanding orchestra. Even as his deafness increased, his imagination, in terms of orchestral sound, gained in variety and in subtlety. Like all great orchestrators, who hear in the mind what goes onto the score page, Beethoven rarely miscalculated balance, over-scored, or asked the technically impossible from the instruments he could no longer hear. His scores, ushering in a new and revolutionary era of orchestration, are the true beginnings of the nineteenth- and early twentieth-century modern orchestral concept.

When compared with the orchestrational approach of Carl Maria von Weber (1786–1826), however, even Beethoven appears a sober Classicist. The first of the great German Romantics of opera, Weber found in the glowing sonorities of the evolving orchestra the ideal vehicle for an innate theatricalism. To his contemporaries he appeared at times to over-emphasize effect—for example, the combination of shimmering string tremolandi, sepulchral tones of the low clarinet, and the ominous thud of timpani and pizzicato double basses depicting the forces of evil in *Der*

53

hütz (1820) (Example 24). Such obvious pictorial devices in r's orchestration did frequently take precedence over musical con- His basic aim was always to induce a certain emotional and psychological frame of mind in the listener by a calculated system of exaggerated technical device, and in this effort he was highly successful. But to compare Weber with Beethoven is obviously unfair; Weber's premise was not that of the great master of the symphony.

Weber's desire to achieve theatrical realism, to simulate nature's sounds, led to many innovations in his scoring for the orchestral instruments. And as the first virtuoso composer for the clarinet, Weber showed succeeding generations of composers the full potential of this newest arrival in the woodwind choir. His solo parts for the instrument take it gracefully from the bottom to the top of its compass, exploiting each register in a highly effective manner. (See, for instance, the *Der Freischütz* Overture (**30**), the *Ruler of the Spirits* Overture (**31**), and the two clarinet concertos—all dating from 1811.) If he were aware of the clarinet's limitations in the hands of inexperienced players—as described anonymously: "Few phenomena are more agonizing than the rat-squeaks and caterwauls, the duck-quacks and claxon-horn squawks of this instrument when inefficiently handled"—the knowledge did not temper his expectations.

Weber seems to have been the first composer to standardize the complement of four horns and three trombones in the brass section, in addition to the usual pair of trumpets. He also called regularly for three kettledrums (see the overtures *Peter Schmoll* and *Ruler of the Spirits,* for example), a previous isolated instance being in Handel's *Music for the Royal Fireworks.* Weber was among the first orchestrators to subdivide the violin sections into more than the customary two parts each, doing so for special harmonic effects. In the 1823 *Euryanthe* Overture (Example 25) he presaged similar string divisi in the later scores of Berlioz and Wagner and the multitudinous string voices in Richard Strauss and Gustav Mahler.

It is Weber's lot to be known to music history mainly as the composer of three hopelessly outdated operas, now rarely staged. In his concept of the orchestral entity, however, he must certainly be considered an indispensable precursor of full-bodied German Romanticism. As Alfred Einstein remarked: "Weber revolutionized classical instrumentation; Berlioz and Wagner are inconceivable without him" (*International Cyclopedia of Music and Musicians*).

If Weber appeared to his contemporaries to strive for obvious theatrical effect, what can one say regarding Giacomo Meyerbeer (1791–

EXAMPLE 24
Carl Maria von Weber: from Overture to *Der Freischütz*

EXAMPLE 25
Weber: from Overture to *Euryanthe*

1864)? No symphonist, but a prodigal composer of elaborate operas, the German-born Meyerbeer seemingly embraced every known trick of instrumentational sensationalism and ostentatious musical display. Even Richard Wagner, though he professed to have a very poor opinion of Meyerbeer, appropriated many of his orchestral effects, such as unison brass melodic material against heterophonous string figurations.[3]

Whatever our pejorative observations, we must admire Meyerbeer's extraordinary sense of instrumental color, applied both in new technical devices and in the introduction of unusual instruments. Even more than Weber, he subdivided his strings into numerous solo or harmonic voices, scoring, for example, for four solo cellos in the introduction to the second scene of Act 3 of *L'Étoile du Nord* (1854) (32). This effective application of tone color, also used by Gioacchino Rossini in the overture to *William Tell* (33), was appropriated by Wagner for a scene in the first

56

act of *Die Walküre* (1856) (34), barely two years after the first production of Meyerbeer's opera.

Meyerbeer was also one of the first composers to ensure two distinct qualities of basic string-tone by muting only part of the string section, leaving the others to play unmuted. A parallel innovation is illustrated in the finale of Act III of *Robert le Diable* (1831) (35): for a lengthy passage here the cellos play arco and the double basses pizzicato. Also quite exceptional was his lavish use of string lines played tremolo, sul ponticello, or at the point of the bow, or his employment of string glissando—almost in the manner of Béla Bartók—as in *L'Étoile du Nord*, Act 3 (Example 26).

We are apt to think of such colorful devices as the inventions of such late-Romantic instrumentational wizards as Strauss or Mahler. But they are found, with many other tonal ingenuities, in the operatic scores of Meyerbeer—stage works that exhibit a fascinating blend of Italianate lyricism, Germanic thoroughness, and French esprit. The first solo for the newly developed bass clarinet, to cite one instance, is found in *Les Huguenots* (1836) (36). Prophetic in its virtuosity, this passage takes the instrument through its entire compass, antedating by a century the brilliant toccata solo in William Schuman's Third Symphony (1941) (37).

The English horn (so rarely used in concert works that it created a critical scandal even when Cesar Franck used it in his 1888 D minor Symphony) appeared in the operatic scores of Meyerbeer and, as well, in orchestral writing by François Boïeldieu, Jacques Halévy, and Gasparo Spontini. And finally, though his treatment of the instrument was by modern standards quite conventional, Meyerbeer was evidently the first composer to consistently use Sebastien Érard's newly developed (1810) double-action harp. The original harp had been at first too imperfect in construction to attract orchestral composers to its potential; only after more than a century of mechanical improvement did it become a potent orchestral asset. Then the effective harp-writing of Meyerbeer and other early composers of Romantic opera helped give the instrument a regular and honored status in the symphonic ensembles of Berlioz and Liszt as well.

Meyerbeer's was truly an inquiring mind with a bold attitude toward the problem of colorful orchestral combinations, and there are few who have surpassed him as a dramatic painter in tone.[4] Whether in *Robert le Diable, Les Huguenots,* or in his final opera, *L'Africaine* (1864), his instinct for theatrical flamboyance never deserted him. "The obvious signs of a composer who took orchestration seriously—," Adam Carse observes, "the finish and careful attention to detail in his scores— all testify to Meyerbeer's keen interest and concern for orchestral effect

EXAMPLE 26
Giacomo Meyerbeer: from *L'Étoile du Nord* (Act 3)

and orchestration which is, indeed, too often worthy of better musical matter" (*The History of Orchestration*).

At the same time that the orchestration of the German Romantics was growing increasingly heavy-handed, the Italian Gioacchino Rossini (1792–1868) balanced with almost Classical stylistic clarity his Romantic explorations of orchestral sound. This facile opera composer is popularly remembered in terms of orchestration for ingenious innovations in two of his overtures: that to *William Tell* (1829) begins with five solo violoncellos, while that to *Il Signor Bruschino* (1813) commences with the violins tapping on their music stands. Rossini's specific direction in the latter, however, was simply "col legno"; thus the desk-tapping may be some early conductor's gratuitous interpretation rather than the composer's unique inspiration.[5]

But Rossini more nearly approached the status of a significant orchestrator in his exploitation of the long orchestral crescendo, contriving a general increase in dynamic strength by successive instrumental entrances adding up to a rousing orchestral tutti (Example 27). The aurally satiated sophisticate of the twentieth century may not be impressed by such modest theatrics, but to Rossini's audiences they must have seemed like an eruption of Vesuvius.

At its worst, Rossini's orchestration annoys the sensitive listener with its vulgar brass-band aura, a sound and fury that often signifies very little. But at its best his clear orchestral sound permitted a welcome breath of fresh air to permeate the current Romantic hothouse, anticipating in its brilliance and élan the writing of Berlioz.

Not all the composers contemporary with Meyerbeer and Rossini were absorbed in the development of new or experimental instrumentation. For reasons of temperament and training, many notable nineteenth-century composers worked outside the grand orchestral sweep from Beethoven to Berlioz—among them Schubert, Mendelssohn, Schumann, and Chopin. Franz Schubert (1797–1828), as the gentle lyric voice of German Romanticism, applied universally (even in his purely orchestral scores) a concept of melody and accompaniment particularly suited to the setting of poetry. Where his orchestration is especially effective it may be counted an instinctive reflection of natural skill rather than the product of an intellectual technique. Schubert was, at one and the same time, a superb melodist and an indifferent polyphonist. But the fact that he did not advance the science or the art of instrumentation is no reason to overlook the validity of his natural skill with the instruments.

Schubert's solo windwinds often engage in charming little dialogues, as in the second movement of the "Unfinished" Symphony (1827) (38). And his use of pianissimo trombones on a melodic passage, which illuminates the slow movement of the Seventh Symphony (1828), is as unusual for the period as it is effective (Example 28). On the whole, however, Schubert's orchestration is almost too modest and unassuming, and in this history of styles of instrumentation we may, as a consequence, seem to minimize his genius. Yet if one should consider genuine musical

EXAMPLE 27
Gioacchino Rossini: from Overture to *La Gazza Ladra*

qualities alone, Schubert might well outweigh the flamboyancies of a Meyerbeer or a Berlioz.

Felix Mendelssohn-Bartholdy (1809–1847), though a Romantic composer in point of time, partook more of the earlier Classical spirit and technique than of the liberalizing new musical philosophy. As his compositions constantly exhibited perfect order, inner logic, and neatness, so

EXAMPLE 28
Franz Schubert: from Symphony No. 7, 2nd movement

did his orchestration reflect his antipathy to anything turgid or diffuse. Delicacy and clarity—Mozartean ideals—are always present in Mendelssohn's scores, and their transparency and guileless charm owe more to the Rococo than to the musical freedoms of the Beethoven-Berlioz era.

Like Schubert, Mendelssohn orchestrated with instinctive effectiveness, without revealing anything basically new in device or instrumental exploitation. His woodwinds and strings, in keeping with his penchant for clarity of texture, were treated with exceptional felicity. The Scherzo from his incidental music to *A Midsummer Night's Dream* (1843) is possibly history's most engaging example of delicately articulated flute, oboe, clarinet, and bassoon passages. His brasses, however, seldom displayed the same poetic insight into brass color as the evocative horn solo in the Nocturne (39) of the same work. Yet there is no lack of richness in Mendelssohn's scoring when it is needed, such as in the warm, cushiony mixture of clarinets, bassoons, and cellos for the theme of the *Ruy Blas* Overture of 1834 (Example 29).

An aristocrat among the Romantics, Mendelssohn always exhibited patrician taste in his scoring. In instrumental clarity and mastery of form, Mendelssohn's scores still offer orchestrators a salutary example.

The instinctive instrumentational flair of Mendelssohn and Schubert was unfortunately lacking in the entire output of Robert Schu (1810–1856). Fresh and exuberant in their musical ideas, his fou phonies and the concertos for piano and for cello continue to be p

EXAMPLE 29
Felix Mendelssohn: from *Ruy Blas* Overture

despite their awkward, thick, and occasionally even inept orchestration. As Vincent d'Indy once commented: "The clumsiness in the instrumentation will never prevent the *Rhenish* Symphony [No. 3 in E-flat Major (1850)] from remaining one of the beautiful manifestations of the human spirit in music." Still, it is unfortunate that Schumann—strangely handicapped by his early pianistic training—never learned to think orchestrally.

A study of specific aspects of this ineptitude may illustrate how a composer of significant stature could still fail conspicuously in the very area where one might reasonably have expected the most dazzling success. How was it possible, for example, for a composer of Schumann's genius to write the 879 measures of his Fourth Symphony (1851) during which the strings play not one measure by themselves? Furthermore, like many student orchestrators with no real understanding of the orchestral instruments, Schumann doubled everything. It is truly distressing to hear the many instances of unnecessary duplication in his scores; it is astonishing to see a highly regarded composer overlook the most obvious opportunities for effective orchestrational contrast, clear spacings, and proper tonal balance.

A prime example of such faulty instrumentation may be drawn from the opening measures of the Romanze movement of the Fourth Symphony (Example 30). Here the oboe and violoncello theme is backed up by a disarmingly simple accompaniment in the pizzicato strings. The effect is maddeningly ruined, however, by a completely unnecessary duplication in the clarinets and bassoons. Even the most insensitive conductor will instinctively consider cutting out these wind parts in performance; in fact, many a conductor—notably, Gustav Mahler—has taken the law into his own hands and rescored large segments of the Schumann symphonies.

One further example of instrumentational miscalculation: in measures 79–86 of the *Rhenish* Symphony (40), the scherzo movement, the melodic line in the low woodwinds is marked *mezzo-forte,* the same level as the brass and violin accompanying chords. Obviously the sound of the latter, more weighty instruments will predominate; thus the scoring completely contravenes Schumann's evident compositional intention. Were the first violins to be omitted and the horns, trumpets, and timpani marked *mezzo-piano,* the passage might possibly come into proper focus.

Even with his flaws and miscalculations, however, an artist's expression represents his personal way of thinking and doing. Its very imperfections give it a special dimension, a unique value that may be unreasonably diluted by the extensive administrations of another hand. Therefore, in spite of the fact that what is orchestrally apt in Schu-

EXAMPLE 30
Robert Schumann: from Symphony No. 4, 2nd movement

mann's music is overshadowed by passages in which crudities are painfully manifest, we must either accept (and enjoy for what they are)
Schumann's orchestral works as imperfect as he left them, or else tolerate
the well-intentioned polishings of Mahler and other conductors.

Like Schumann, Frédéric Chopin (1810–1849) directed his best gifts
more to the solo keyboard than to the diversified timbres of the symphony

orchestra. Not that his orchestration—in the two piano concertos, the *Grande Fantaisie,* and a number of other scores for piano and orchestra— does not sound; it does, and very agreeably. But Chopin never made full use of the "many-splendored fabric" of sound that was the Romantic orchestra. Even the skillful use of col legno strings in the finale of the F minor Piano Concerto (1829) (41)—an unusual device for the times— must be considered an exceptional, rather than regular, Chopin instrumentational practice. This narrowed field of vision does not make him a lesser composer, but it does minimize his contributions to the evolution of the Romantic orchestra.

With the career of Hector Berlioz (1803–1869), however, we return to the grand tradition of Romantic instrumentation. If Weber should be rightfully considered the progenitor of the Romantic point of view on orchestration, Berlioz surely represents its epitome. His merits as a composer may be—and frequently are—hotly debated, but his brilliance as an orchestrator is unquestioned. A grudging compliment may be inferred even from such a caustic comment as that by the critic William J. Henderson: "Meyerbeer was a veritable trickster with instruments, and could produce a theatrical effect with a penny-ballad idea, while Berlioz could enchant an audience with no idea at all" (*The Orchestra*).

For the first time in the history of orchestral composition there emerged, in Berlioz, an artist for whom dramatic tone-color was both the means and the end of his expression. With the natural instinct of a great orchestrator he needed neither teacher nor textbook to point the way to his vivid tonal images. Although there were, of course, a few rather elementary tracts on instruments and instrumentation extant during Berlioz's lifetime, they could hardly have provided him with very many viable ideas for unusual instrumental effects. As a matter of fact, Berlioz himself wrote the first-known treatise on the modern orchestra, published in 1844. As a source work it still has considerable validity, notwithstanding its references to some obsolete instruments and outmoded techniques; especially informative and pertinent is the revised edition by Richard Strauss, with its terse and pungent commentary.

In such works as the *Symphonie Fantastique* (1831), *Roméo et Juliette* (1839), and *La Damnation de Faust* (1846), Berlioz made the brass choir—for the first time in the history of symphonic instrumentation—the peer of woodwinds and strings. This brilliant, full-voiced brass harmony would not have been possible, however, without many contemporary improvements in the instruments themselves. The development of the valve system in the period between 1818 and 1830, roughly, enabled the brasses to lengthen their tubing and so produce overtones from new fundamentals. No longer tonally limited, they achieved a new romanticism that literally revolutionized the music written for them. The trombone, retaining the slide mechanism that dated from the sixteenth-century, was unaffected by these changes.

This new flexibility in the brass choir was a great temptation to the theatrical Berlioz, and he made amazing use of it at both ends of the dynamic scale. In his *Requiem* (the *Grande Messe des Morts* [1837]) (42) he requires twelve horns and sixteen trombones, which might appear to be synonymous with power and overwhelming volume of sound. Yet Berlioz created an extraordinary effect in this work by putting eight unison trombones, played softly, on the low pedal-tones B-flat, A, and G-sharp, separated by three and a half octaves from three flutes with nothing in between. This is an aural inspiration that must be heard to be believed—"a magnificent experiment in sepulchral sonority," as Paul Henry Lang remarked.

Berlioz may, in fact, be credited with discovering and exploiting the pianissimo value of the brass instruments. No better example can be cited than a passage from the "Queen Mab" Scherzo, the fourth movement of the *Roméo et Juliette* symphony (Example 31). This entire movement is a tour de force of musical delicacy, of faint color-tints and wispy iridescence, for Berlioz's keen ear for unusual timbres led him unerringly to such mixtures as flute and English horn in octaves, or antique cymbals (*crotales*) doubling the high glitter of harp.

One of the last of the older brass instruments to leave the scene during Berlioz's time was the picturesque serpent, an instrument that now "leads a respectable secluded life among the mermaids and stuffed alligators of local museums," as Cecil Forsyth tells us. But even by the time of the Requiem, composers were writing for the ophicleide instead of the dubious-sounding serpent; Berlioz eventually substituted the newly invented bass tuba for both.

The luster of his brass writing, however, does not minimize Berlioz's inventiveness with the string choir as well. We are apt to think of the technique of subdividing the strings into numerous solo voices as the exclusive province of the late Romantics—Wagner (as in the "Forest Murmurs" from *Siegfried* [43]), or Richard Strauss (as in *Also Sprach Zarathustra* [44]). But Berlioz, even more than Weber and Meyerbeer, frequently resorted to this practice, sometimes dividing the violins alone into as many as eight independent parts. With his instinctive grasp of novel orchestral color, he similarly subdivided his double basses (as in the "March to the Gallows" from the *Symphonie Fantastique* [45]). One further bit of string alchemy must also be mentioned: the use of artificial violin harmonics to outline a high-placed chord, which cunningly illuminates several passages in the *Roméo et Juliette* (46).

EXAMPLE 31
Hector Berlioz: from *Roméo et Juliette*, 4th movement ("Queen Mab" Scherzo)

STYLE AND ORCHESTRATION

Even the orchestral percussion lost its Classical reticence in Berlioz's creative scoring. In the *Symphonie Fantastique* he called for two timpani players (Example 32), and for the monumental *Grande Messe des Morts* he requested no fewer than eight pairs of kettledrums. This specification appears never to have been exceeded subsequently by any composer. Notable, too, is the use of the timpani for three- and four-part chords in the *Symphonie Fantastique,* probably the first instance of this original concept (though Beethoven had used more modest two-note chords in the Adagio of the *Ninth* Symphony [47]).

Surpassing even his technical skill with the instruments themselves was Berlioz's instinct in employing them dramatically. To him the orchestra in full panoply became a theatrical medium, offering through the instruments alone the essential drama of his favorite literary characters. Without this form of theatre in terms of the symphonic medium— without, in other words, *Roméo et Juliette* and *La Damnation de Faust*—Wagner could hardly have conceived in their present form the operas of *Der Ring des Nibelungen* or *Tristan und Isolde,* for example.

For parallel dramatic content one might well compare the somber pastoral qualities of two famous solos for the English horn: One is from the third movement of the *Symphonie Fantastique* (Example 32), the other from the opening of the third act of *Tristan und Isolde* (48). The Berlioz passage depicts a young artist's fevered dreams of fields and meadows; the Wagner excerpt, a bleak Cornish seascape near Tristan's castle. Could any two passages in all music share a more common approach, a more skilled evocation of gentle melancholy? This is true painting in tone—hallmark of the Romantic and Impressionist alike— carried to satisfying culmination.

In the final analysis it is likely that Berlioz's most individual contribution to Romantic musical art resides in his transferral of theatrical concepts from the stage to the domain of the orchestra alone. We may, or may not, agree with Richard Strauss when he writes: "One might say . . . that he was not dramatic enough for the stage and not symphonic enough for the concert hall." But we cannot deny to Berlioz the position of supreme orchestrator in the pantheon of early nineteenth-century composers.

With the achievements of Beethoven, Weber, and Berlioz as the exemplars of early Romantic orchestration, many other names fade into historic oblivion. Bellini, Donizetti, Spohr, and Spontini, for example, or Auber, Boïeldieu, Halévy, Hérold, LeSueur, and Méhul—all were well-known in their day, yet each made only meager contributions to the art of orchestration. Others, such as Glinka in Russia, Raff in Germany, and Goldmark in Hungary, added their one or two bricks to the founda-

EXAMPLE 32
Berlioz: from *Symphonie Fantastique*, 3rd movement
(*Scene in the Country*)

69

tion of the symphonic and operatic orchestras. But we can no more eulogize each than we can single out for posthumous glory each anonymous artisan who helped fashion Chartres Cathedral.

An historic synthesis of early nineteenth-century orchestration is not as easy as a survey of the instrumentation of the entire eighteenth century, and from that era to the present the task has grown more difficult year by year. Individuality—that is to say, the personality of the composer—was by the early Romantic period impressing itself with ever greater force and conviction on the concept of orchestration. Personal style was more clearly visible in the orchestral scoring of the early Romantic era; analytical generalities no longer suffice in discussing it. Nonetheless, certain cardinal characteristics clearly distinguish this instrumentational period from the previous Classical era.

To begin with, the relationships of string instruments had changed. True, they still reigned supreme in early Romantic orchestration, despite increasingly insistent claims registered by the woodwind and brass sections; even a casual glance at representative scores will demonstrate that the strings still dominated the orchestra, whether as a melodic or harmonic element in the composer's expression. But the violins were no longer the uncontested prima donnas; both violas and violoncellos had expanded their performing techniques, ranges, and expressive usefulness to an equal status. Even the double bass had achieved a degree of independence that would have amazed the more conservative Classicists.

Divided and subdivided string parts became more and more common, and the upper range of all the strings was noticeably extended. The effective use of pizzicato, including multiple-stops, was standard; the authentic bow-tremolo (as opposed to the measured variety prevalent in Classical scores) was routine in dramatic situations. The use of artificial harmonics was still comparatively rare, but mechanical mutes were frequently called upon to veil or alter the string timbre in quiet passages.

As in the Classical orchestra, the woodwinds took second place in early Romantic instrumentation. Their individual functions, however, had been immeasurably increased and their overall expressiveness greatly refined. Frequently the wind choir operated as a self-contained unit within the orchestra, outlining both primary and secondary melodic material, as well as subsidiary harmony and figuration. As with the strings, their possible and effective ranges were widened, their playing techniques vastly facilitated (mainly by means of mechanical improvements in the instruments themselves), and their tonal qualities enhanced and refined.

Although the flute and oboe were still most often employed in their middle to upper register, both the clarinet and the bassoon had been made more flexible—and hence more useful—in their extremities, the low one for clarinet and the high for bassoon. The piccolo had become a fairly standard member of the woodwind group, while the English horn remained an infrequent component and the contrabassoon was still used only occasionally. The bass clarinet, last of the modern standard winds to join the orchestra, did not do so until about the middle of the century—and then made its bow principally in stage works.

In early Romantic orchestration the brass choir still ranked third in most composers' treatment of the orchestra. Horns and trumpets, however, were far more versatile than in Haydn's day and were no longer compelled to serve principally as essential components of tutti sections. This welcome expansion of brass technique and musical potential had been made possible by important mechanical improvements; the metamorphosis of the brass instruments from limited diatonic to full-scale chromatic voices is one of the most significant developments to have taken place in the symphony and opera orchestras.

Although a pair of trumpets still sufficed for most of the early Romantic orchestrators, the horns had been increased in number to three and then to four; three trombones had also become fairly standard. For a bass voice in the brass section, a few composers used the ophicleide or the newly developed tuba. This latter instrument, despite the importance assigned it by Berlioz, was not yet a standard member of the orchestra. Moreover, passages dominated by brass color were still comparatively rare, though the solo capabilities of all the instruments—particularly the horns—had been vastly strengthened.

Even more important than the increased numbers of brass instruments is the fact that all eventually became independent voices. At its minimum size the brass section provided the composer with eight separate parts; at its maximum strength, ten brass voices were available.

By the end of the early Romantic era the number of kettledrums included in the orchestra had increased to three; in exceptional instances (Berlioz scores, principally) more were required. Furthermore, the previous custom of tuning the drums only to tonic and dominant pitches had been outmoded by the stipulation of other harmonic tones. The use of supplementary percussion—bass drum, cymbals, and triangle, usually—was still largely conservative; only in rare instances were they called upon to provide coloristic embellishment rather than obvious rhythmic or dynamic support. The harp was just beginning to be used in the orchestra, symphonic and operatic, and very routinely at that. The keyboard instruments (harpsichord, piano, organ) in the role of orchestral voices, not soloists, were to be only a late nineteenth-century revival.

STYLE AND ORCHESTRATION

One final consideration: even in the early Romantic period there was no unanimity on the presentation of the printed orchestral score-page. In the operas of Meyerbeer, for instance, the high strings (violins and violas) were inserted on the page between the woodwinds and brasses, while the cellos and double basses were placed at the bottom, almost as if the parts constituted a *basso continuo*. And in his Third Symphony, Schumann reverted to the older Italian-Baroque layout, with violins and violas at the top of the page, cellos and double basses at the very bottom. Evidently the composers had still not decided whether to group the instruments according to their register or to separate them by orchestral choirs into their modern format. Even in a score as late in the century as Giuseppe Verdi's *Otello* (1887), this dilemma was still unresolved.

Early Romantic orchestration—from Beethoven to Weber, through Berlioz and on to Wagner—may be seen as the essential foundation for the subsequent rapid growth of the symphonic and operatic orchestra, a flowering that was to reach its apex by the end of the century. In writing for this enlarged instrumental gamut, composers were thus constantly widening their strands of orchestral color and increasing their realization of the orchestra's dramatic potential. By the final decade of the century composers were to create some of the most dynamic orchestral music of all time.

Notes

1. At the Vienna premiere of the Ninth Symphony the solo fourth horn was played by the virtuoso E. C. Lewy. He was not, however, a regular member of the orchestra.

2. The first instance of cross-handing for the timpani—the technique by which rapid repeated notes alternating between two or more drums are played by alternate hands—occurs in the Gloria of Beethoven's *Missa Solemnis* (1822).

3. The technique of heterophony—by means of which basic melodic and/or harmonic elements are figurated in various ways by different, but homogeneous, instruments—is one that assumes an important position in the orchestrational styles of Wagner, Strauss, and many other late Romantic composers.

4. Meyerbeer, incidentally, was the first composer to give melodic material to the timpani, in contradistinction to the rhythmic motive as used by Beethoven in the Ninth Symphony. The opera *Robert le Diable* contains several melodic passages for kettledrums.

5. Confusion still surrounds Rossini's intent; a modern score of the overture published by Carisch (Milan, 1937) indicates the bow-striking passages with x-shaped noteheads for the second violins only, marked "col legno." However, a French edition of the piano-vocal score (1858) contains the note: *"2ds Viols. frappez sur le pupitre"* at the first appearance of the effect. However, a note at the outset of the overture states: *"Dans le courant de cette ouverture il y a plusiers passages ou on a écrit frappez.*

Cet effet ne peut être comique que si le quatuor frappé avec le dos de l'archet sur une plaque de fer blanc adaptée à chacun des pupitres." ("During the course of this overture there are several passages where striking is indicated. This effect will not be humorous if the strings will strike with the back of the bow on the metal part of each music stand." Thus it is unclear whether the entire string section or only the second violins are to do the desk-tappings or, indeed, whether the directive itself originated with the composer or the publisher.

4

The Late Romantic Orchestra

> To orchestrate is to create, and this is something that cannot be
> taught. . . . A work is thought out in terms of the orchestra,
> certain colors being inseparable from it in the mind of its creator
> and native to it from the hour of its birth.
>
> Nikolay Rimsky-Korsakov,
> *Principles of Orchestration*

If a single word could characterize most late nineteenth-century orchestration, that one word would be *complex*. In the hands of the supertechnicians, Wagner and Strauss—and Mahler, Scriabin, and early Schoenberg, as well—the symphonic and operatic orchestra assumed the gigantic proportions and the incredible complexity that inevitably carried Romantic orchestration to a dead end. For all their unquestioned mastery of massive instrumental effect, many late Romantic composers were seemingly blind to the incalcuable value of restraint in handling huge orchestral forces. In their hands the orchestra, like Atlas shouldering the sky, was made to support a well-nigh impossible burden of sonority piled upon sonority.

In this complex of complexity, audiences eventually lost sight of the pristine colors inherent in the various orchestral instruments and of the transparent textures they can produce. Acoustically speaking, there is a point of aural saturation beyond which the ear cannot take in further duplication (unison or octave) of melodic strands and harmonic voices. To mass together many different-hued instruments playing identical parts creates, then, an inescapable neutrality of sound. Strings, woodwinds, and brasses in constant mixture can produce a thick overlay of instrumental sonority, like a painting built up by impasto in which successive heavy layers of paint disguise the original character of each layer.

Amplitude, too, by the close of the nineteenth century seemingly could go no further. Thirty-six violins playing *double-forte* are not four times as loud as eighteen violins playing *forte*. Two each of horns, trumpets, and trombones at *double-forte* can almost match the volume produced by four horns and three each of trumpets and trombones at the same dynamic level. In other words, the intensity ratio varies [1]—the degree of loudness is not in direct proportion to the actual number of instruments involved.

To test this thesis one might first listen to the opening measures of the finale of Beethoven's Fifth Symphony, with its fifty-sixty instruments at *double-forte*. Then listen to the two final pages of Mahler's Eighth Symphony (1907)—the "Symphony of a Thousand"—with its 140-odd instrumental performers at the levels of *double-* and *triple-forte*.[2] Does the Mahler actually sound twice as loud as the Beethoven? Even a scientific measuring of the decibels of each passage in turn would demonstrate that the law of diminishing returns is no less valid in orchestration than in other manifestations of human energy.

To survey the ramifications of the late Romantic orchestral style is largely to provide a resumé of the orchestrational technique and practice of four outstanding composers of the period: Wagner, Tchaikovsky, Mahler, and Richard Strauss. Certain of their contemporaries also enter the picture to the extent that they influenced orchestral evolution. Yet the individualism of the era, the keynote to Romantic expression, complicates any approach to an overall survey; most composers resist any effort to pigeonhole them neatly on grounds of style.

The late Romantic orchestral style, then, must be approached with the understanding that it has many precincts. To some, it is possible to apply a nationalistic label. Others are only loosely bound together by a common predilection for the overblown that marked the final years of the century. Still others, although contemporary historically, are by-paths scarcely touched by the powerful surge of giganticism.

It is in the music of Richard Wagner (1813–1883) that the true beginning of *fin de siècle* Romantic orchestration resides. If Wagner himself is inconceivable without the earlier models of Weber and Berlioz,

EXAMPLE 33
Richard Wagner: from Prelude to *Parsifal*

so his contemporaries and successors—Mahler and Strauss, in particular—
are indebted to him for the potential of their instrumentational styles.

It is inappropriate for a treatise on orchestral style to go into
Wagner's philosophy of the arts—his detailed conception of the "music-
drama" combining music, poetry, and staging in perfect and complementary balance. We must be concerned, instead, with his instrumental
concepts and techniques, concepts that are chapter, book, and verse of
Romantic orchestration. Quite apart from the historical significance of
Wagner's achievement is our amazement that his virtuosity did not evolve
gradually through trial and error, the process common to most other
composers. Wagner's orchestral concepts were born fully matured and
expressed with utter conviction and nearly always with complete
effectiveness.

The melodic leitmotif associated with the composer's dramatic
and operatic elements is basically a compositional device, and will not be
dealt with here. Wagner's orchestrational leitmotif, from *Der fliegende
Holländer* (1841) to *Parsifal* (1877–82), is a constant mixture of the
timbres of two, or even three, different instrumental choirs. All of his
woodwinds, for instance, acted as important melodists as well as harmonic components—the flute and clarinet throughout their total ranges,
the oboe and English horn in their lower registers, and the bassoon and
bass clarinet in both tenor and bass compass. Yet these melodic lines
were almost always duplicated by the horns or other brasses or, even
more often, by strings.

Wagner often joined the horns to his harmonic woodwinds as well,
thus continuing the tradition of treating the horns as a tonal link between
the woodwind and brass sections. The bassoon frequently joined the
horns as a bass voice, almost like an extension of horn timbre—as in the
introduction to Act 3 of *Die Meistersinger* (1862–67) **(49)**. Even on his
score-pages Wagner sometimes placed the horns within the woodwind
choir—in *Siegfried* (1856–71), for example—thus further emphasizing
the strong ties of horns with woodwind timbre.

A typical example of Wagner's extensive doubling practice is the
beginning of the Prelude to *Parsifal* **(50)**, in which the woodwind line
and the strings strongly reinforce each other. Later in this work we see
another instance of Wagner's habitual heavy-textured scoring: both
primary and secondary melodic lines (harmonic counterpoint, properly
speaking) are thoroughly doubled between the three orchestral sections
(Example 33).

These mixed timbres are basic to Wagner's modus operandi, despite
his practice of making chords complete in homogeneous fashion within

each of the three sections of the orchestra capable of outlining harmony. This method of complete vertical delineation is commonplace in scoring for strings, but for lack of complete instrumental families even the early Romantic composers were forced to mix woodwind and brass colors in full chords. Wagner, however, thanks to the recent technical and mechanical advances, could create sonorities of a uniform tone-color within twelve to sixteen woodwind voices, just twice the number available to the Classicists under optimum conditions. He could also outline a complete harmonic profile with three or four instruments of identical or closely related timbre, and in this way became the first composer to group each family within the woodwind choir in units of three: piccolo (or third flute) and two flutes; two oboes and English horn (or third oboe); two clarinets and bass clarinet (or third clarinet); and two bassoons and contrabassoon (or third bassoon).

As Wagner customarily wrote for either six or eight horns, he thus had at his disposal as many as twenty-four fairly analogous voices, exclusive of the strings, for vertical sonorous structures. From the lowest B-flat of the contrabassoon to the highest B-flat or C of the piccolo a seven-octave span was available. The combinations possible to woodwind and brass instruments, with their concomitant timbral variations, would require tabulation by a high-speed digital computer. Add the strings, with the subtle shadings possible in inner-choir divisions, and the total number of melodic and harmonic combinations available to Wagner and his contemporaries soars to astronomical heights.

Timbral mixtures, however, are only one facet of the Wagnerian style; he also made distinctive innovations with single instruments and with the orchestral choirs. He was the first composer, for instance, to exploit the sinister color of hand-stopped horns, as in "Siegfried's Funeral Music" from *Götterdämmerung* (1869–74) **(51)**. This device, indicated in Wagner's scores by a small cross (+) over the notes to be so played, is known to orchestrators as "gestopft," a German word admirably suited to the effect produced.

Wagner's brasses, when used thematically, assumed even more expressive voices than in Berlioz or Meyerbeer. Their power was often reinforced by unison passages: horns and trumpets, horns and trombones, or trumpets and trombones. (See, for instance, the Overture to *Tannhäuser* [1843–45] **(52)**; the Prelude to Act Three of *Lohengrin* [1846–48] **(53)**, and the "Magic Fire Music" from *Die Walküre* [1854–56] **(54)**. Yet Wagner understood fully as well as Berlioz the sonoric advantages of brass instruments played softly. The subdued warmth and soft-textured solidity created by quiet tenuto harmonies in horns or trombones appears on page after page of his scores; the first few measures of the "Liebestod" from *Tristan und Isolde* (1857–59) **(55)** are the very epitome of this telling resource. This is a far cry from the more blatant brass writing in his early *Rienzi* (1838–40), a work that, incidentally, included both the serpent and the ophicleide in its orchestral arsenal.

In Wagner's harmonic scheme the brass instruments, like the wood-winds, are invariably spaced so as to produce the full chord required, with like instruments grouped in close position. The ear thus assimilates the chord as an affinitive timbre, despite the presence of four separate brass instruments. This is orchestration with all the holes plugged up, providing a continuous and hypnotic tonal foundation. It is the very antithesis of the "ventilated" instrumentation of Igor Stravinsky in his Neoclassical period, for instance, or the attenuated Expressionistic fabric of Anton Webern. Orchestration of such continual thickness is apt to sound louder than its actual measurement in decibels. As Oscar Wilde cogently put it in *The Picture of Dorian Gray:* "I like Wagner's music better than anybody's. It is so loud that one can talk the whole time without people hearing what one says."

If Wagner accorded perfunctory treatment to any section of the orchestra, it was the percussion. Three or four timpani [3] were customarily required by the composer, but were utilized in a fairly routine manner—except for isolated instances such as the bell-like ostinati for two players in *Parsifal* **(56)** (during the entrance of the Knights of the Grail), or the "Funeral Music" from *Götterdämmerung* **(57)**.

The other percussion instruments, such as bass drum, cymbals, triangle, and tubular bells, are of course essential to many passages in the Wagner operas. One thinks, too, of the charming use of glockenspiel in the lively "Dance of the Apprentices" from the final act of *Die Meistersinger* **(58)**, and in the "Forest Murmurs" section from *Siegfried* **(59)**. The climax of the "Magic Fire Music" from *Die Walküre* **(60)** is immeasurably enhanced by crisp flashes from glockenspiel and triangle. But even the use of castanets in the *Venusburg Bacchanale* from *Tannhäuser* **(61)**, however brilliantly their unusual sound meshes with the music, cannot be considered exceptional. Wagner could apparently think of nothing better for them to do here than to engage in incessant trills, along with the triangle, bass drum, and cymbals—thus adding only sheer noise to the instrumental background. Generally speaking, then, Wagner's percussion writing does not notably contribute to the singularity of his instrumentation.

In his handling of string instruments, on the other hand, Wagner was at his most brilliant. Where in all orchestral literature is there a more imaginatively conceived example of string scoring than the opening of the Prelude to *Lohengrin* (Example 34)? The ethereal sounds of the four solo violins (three playing harmonics, the remainder of the section divided into four parts) accompanied by the overlapping entrances of soft flutes and oboes all blend to create an imperishable aural impression.

Wagner carried all of the string members, save the double basses, to extreme heights, markedly extending their effective ranges. And no composer was ever more adept than he at weaving an intricate web in which greatly subdivided strings engaged in related legato arpeggios or in heterophonous melodic figuration. Practically the entire second act of *Tristan und Isolde* demonstrates this sort of instrumental alchemy.

The hyper-critical listener errs when he thinks that Wagner cared a fig whether or not the audience's ears clearly heard all the component parts of such passages. Nor did he expect his listeners to hear every single one of those glittering note-sparks flung out by violins and violas in the "Ride of the Valkyries" (from the last act of *Die Walküre* [62]). At the tempo Wagner indicated for this music (*vivace*), a complete and accurate execution on the part of the strings is virtually impossible. But what one player misses his desk partner may catch; between them the passage will produce the scintillation the composer aimed for.

Wagner's notation for the string instruments, however, does not suggest emulation. He was in the habit of writing phrase-marks on the different string parts rather than the conventional (and more accurate) bowing slurs. A single phrase-sign, often covering a half-dozen or more measures over several pages of score, is of no help to string players, who must thereupon work out a practical bowing pattern. (See, for instance, the "Wotan's Farewell" scene from *Die Walküre* [63].)

Woodwind and brass players also have to make certain phrasing compromises when confronted with Wagner's superhuman expression marks. Since the wind player's breath cannot last indefinitely, added breathing commas are a physical necessity. One sometimes feels that in writing about gods and goddesses, dragons, giants, and Valkyries, Wagner was apt to forget that his music was to be performed by ordinary mortals.

Even the much-admired harp parts in certain of the Wagner operas are generously besprinkled with technical impracticabilities that are evident to any professional harpist. There are, for example, broken chords or arpeggios of five or more notes for each hand (the little finger is not used in harp playing), and excessively chromatic passages quite unsuited to the pedaling limitations of the instrument. As a consequence, harpists must extensively edit their parts in the Wagner scores to make them more idiomatic.

It is true that harp passages such as those that illuminate the "Magic Fire Music" in *Die Walküre* (64) are often praised extravagantly. But

EXAMPLE 34
Wagner: from Prelude to *Lohengrin*

despite the obvious effectiveness of the six harps in this particular opera, Wagner's harp scoring was frequently uninspired—or at best, routine. In the Prelude to *Die Meistersinger,* for example, the harp contributes only a few measures of duplicating chords. Certainly the instrument is not essential in Wagner's scheme, nor are the rather saccharine arpeggios in the later *Prize Song* more than ordinary.

Any implication that the Olympian Wagner was also a human does not lower his position in the musical hierarchy. To balance his flaws in the science of notation we have his mastery in deploying orchestral pedal-point, and his dexterous use of low, rich-hued sonorities above which his melodic lines were always clear. If he did not fully understand the anatomy of the harp, he knew the acoustical anatomy of a chord, and always spaced his chord members according to the physical law of over-tones—wide spacing at the bottom, close spacing at the top. Above all, we are fortunate that Wagner was not a pianist, for he never made the mistake of orchestrating like one. A too-heavy reliance on the keyboard frustrated many a potential orchestrator, with Brahms, Chopin, and Schumann as prime examples. Whatever his excesses, Wagner approached the orchestra for what it is: a multitudinous collection of musical timbres, capable of producing an astounding gamut of expressivity and dynamic power.

An unquestioned virtuoso of the Romantic era, Peter Ilyich Tchaikovsky (1840–1893) has only recently been restored to proper historical perspective. For many years it was fashionable for the musical elite to sneer—albeit politely—at his impassioned orchestral manner; his compositional approach was pronounced bombastic and embarrassingly obvious, as though the ability to score in a sure-handed manner were a despicable achievement. Yet many musicians—drawn to Tchaikovsky's music during their formative years, but afterward surfeited with his ro-manticized utterances—have now rediscovered his extraordinary flair for brilliant and effective orchestration.

The orchestra Tchaikovsky chose for his six symphonies [4] was of essentially the same size that had served Beethoven up to his Ninth; to this Tchaikovsky added only tuba and extra percussion. Strangely enough, for all the gloomy quality of much of his music, he did not call upon either bass clarinet or contrabassoon in any symphony score; he did, however, use the bass clarinet in the *Manfred* Symphony of 1885 (ac-tually a tone-poem rather than a symphony), the opera *Pique-Dame* (1890), and the ballet, the *Nutcracker* (1891–92).

In choosing this traditional, pliable ensemble Tchaikovsky was clearly apart conceptually from the instrumentational prepossessions of his German contemporaries. In the tone-poems and dramatic works, however, he came closer to German practice, adding English horn, cornets, harp, and a wider variety of percussion instruments to his orchestral palette. Even the organ is requisitioned for the finale of the *Manfred* Symphony (65), and large tubular bells and cannon contribute to the clangor of the *Festival Overture*, "1812" (1880) (66).

To deploy these forces Tchaikovsky subscribed, as did all the Rus-sian nationalists from Michael Glinka on, to Franco-Italian concepts: in a word, to the principle of instrumental opposition rather than unification, to the grouping of homogeneous timbres rather than the constant mixing of heterogeneous tone-colors. The manner in which this procedure became the hallmark of Tchaikovsky's orchestrational style is well illustrated in the finale of his Fifth Symphony (1888). Here each compositional idea is concentrated in one instrumental section: the principal theme in a two-octave spread in stringed instruments; the secondary theme in octaves in the brasses; and harmonic figuration in octaves in the woodwind choir—all this supported by an animated octave pedal-point in the lower brass and double basses (Example 35).

All Tchaikovsky's mature orchestration embraced the credo of this example; all his melodic lines, primary and secondary, stand out in sharp contrast to supporting harmony and figuration, and this contrast is achieved by employing a single concentration of blending colors for each element of the musical whole. This principle, persisting even through the diversities of twentieth-century instrumentation, may also be observed in scores of Paul Hindemith (see Example 70, p. 203) and William Schuman (Example 79, p. 230).

In temperament, Tchaikovsky resembled Robert Schumann in his paradoxical amalgam of intellectual Classicism (Mozart was one of Tchaikovsky's musical gods) and Romantic emotionalism. But unlike Schumann, he was a born orchestrator, and every note of his scores does exactly what he intended. To demonstrate his instrumentational cunning we might choose at random the entire Scherzo movement of the Fourth Symphony (1877), with its effortless group instrumentation: first, the pizzicato strings; second, the woodwinds, answered by brasses and timpani; and last, the skillful joining of the three sections, with each pursuing its own independent idea.

Equally adroit are the opening measures of the "Pathétique" Symphony (1893), with the murky, somber colors of low bassoon, violas, and divided double basses; also, the ingenious crossing of string voices that opens the final movement of that symphony, its melancholy mood enhanced by the low flutes and high bassoons (Example 36). The single reticent stroke of the tam-tam at the climax of this movement (67) is still further evidence of the composer's discriminating ear, as are the thin tonal slivers of the celesta answered by low bass clarinet in the first *Nutcracker* Ballet Suite (68).[5] And what listener can forget the pale, dry bassoon in its highest tessitura, linking the suave low clarinet with the faint rustle of the tambourine in the *Danse Arabe* (69) from the same ballet score?

If everything sounds in all these delicately adjusted moments, it is because Tchaikovsky heard each idea in its instrumental investiture be-

EXAMPLE 35

Peter Ilyich Tchaikovsky: from Symphony No. 5, 4th movement

EXAMPLE 36
Tchaikovsky: from Symphony No. 6, 4th movement

fore putting down a note in score. "I never compose in the abstract," he wrote his patroness, Madame von Meck; "that is to say, the musical thought never appears otherwise than in a suitable external form. In this way I invent the musical idea and the instrumentation simultaneously." It is in the singleness of this concept that Tchaikovsky rose above frequent banality and lapses of taste to become a Romantic orchestrator second to none.

Nikolay Rimsky-Korsakov (1844–1908), Tchaikovsky's brilliant compatriot, clothed exotic and fantastical musical ideas in a sophisticated, transparent orchestral style closely akin to that of late nineteenth-century French composers. But even more significantly, his insight into the science and art of orchestration became an intrinsic element in the instrumentational development of his contemporaries Anatol Liadov, Alexander Glazounov, and Reinhold Glière, of the youthful Serge Prokofiev and Igor Stravinsky (who studied with Rimsky-Korsakov), and even of such rising foreign luminaries as Claude Debussy, Maurice Ravel, and Ottorino Respighi. This he accomplished by his own example, by his penetrating teaching, and most especially by his text, *Principles of Orchestration,* a work that even today is widely consulted.

Of all the orchestral virtuosi of the period, Rimsky-Korsakov—along with Wagner—practiced most knowingly the precepts of instrumental balance as governed by the fundamental law of acoustics: that wide spacing of chord components in the lower instruments makes for greater clarity in the orchestral mass, regardless of close juxtaposition of harmonic and melodic voices in the upper reaches of the orchestra. But his keen ear for colorful sonorities and piquant effect was doubtless the first element to attract the attention of other orchestrators to the scores of this member of the "Mighty Five." In his most popular work, *Scheherazade* (1888) **(70)**, for instance, the combination of high bassoon, solo, with the support of only four double basses is as unorthodox as it is adroit. Instinctively—as in the deliberate mixing of the four basic woodwind timbres in unison on the plain-chant opening of the *Russian Easter* Overture (1888–89) **(71)**—he often chose precisely the right instrumental color for the moment. Somewhat less convincing, however, is a later passage in the same work in which another liturgical melody is entrusted to solo trombone over divided cellos and double basses **(72)**; the brass color here seems inappropriate to the effect desired.

It is even possible to corroborate Rimsky-Korsakov's extensive sphere of influence by comparing specific works. For instance, there is a striking parallel in the orchestral attitude of a passage from the Russian's *Capriccio Espagnol* of 1887 (Example 37) and a passage from Debussy's *Ibéria* of 1906 (see Example 52, p. 130), composed some nineteen years

EXAMPLE 37

Nikolay Rimsky-Korsakov: from *Capriccio Espagnol* (4th movement: Scene and Gypsy Song)

Nor should it be surprising that Rimsky-Korsakov anticipated the coloristic devices that were to loom important in the evolving al style of Prokofiev, for the two were teacher and pupil. The crisp flashes tossed out by celesta, glockenspiel, harps, and piano in Prokofiev's *Scythian Suite* of 1914 (see Example 71, p. 208) assuredly have their counterpart in the 1907 *Le Coq d'Or* Suite of Rimsky-Korsakov (Example 38). The bell-like scintillations of the first *Cinderella* Ballet Suite (1941–44) **(73)** of Prokofiev were also clearly foreshadowed fifty years earlier in Rimsky-Korsakov's jubilant *Russian Easter* Overture **(74)**.

Conscious tributes to a style greatly admired and well assimilated can be found in the orchestral works of Sergei Rachmaninov (1873–1943). Though the greater part of his life was spent in the twentieth rather than the nineteenth century, Rachmaninov's music is indisputably late Romantic in character. Of his former teacher, Rachmaninov once wrote, "In Rimsky-Korsakov's scores there is never the slightest doubt of the meteorological picture the music is meant to convey. When there is a snowstorm, the flakes seem to dance and drift from the wood instruments and the soundholes of the violins; when the sun is high, all instruments shine with an almost fiery glare; when there is water, the waves ripple and splash audibly through the orchestra. . . . He was a great master of orchestral sound-painting, and one can still learn from him" (*Composers on Music,* ed. by S. Morgenstern).

Rachmaninov's own works, however, look backward more to the Tchaikovsky style than to the pictorial qualities of his teacher's music. Even in a work as late as the admirable *Symphonic Dances* (1940) he treated the orchestra exactly as he had in the popular Second Symphony of 1907, the four piano concertos (dating from 1890 to 1938), the somber tone-poem *The Isle of the Dead* (1907), and the unjustly neglected choral symphony of 1913, *The Bells* (after the Edgar Allen Poe text).

Of the remaining Russian Romantics of the period, only Anatol Liadov (1855–1914) followed Rimsky-Korsakov's basic technique, but he rarely ventured into the domain of orchestrational invention. The others—Mily Balakirev (1837–1910), Alexander Borodin (1833–1887), Alexander Glazounov (1865–1936), Reinhold Glière (1875–1956), and Michael Ippolitov-Ivanov (1859–1935)—all continued the traditions established by Glinka, founder of Russian nationalism in music. Modest Mussorgsky (1839–1881), despite the roughness of his style, had a more wide-ranging understanding of orchestral potential, and his opera *Boris Godunov* (1868–72), in spite of many crude moments of instrumentation, is a remarkable achievement.

It can easily be proved that both of the reorchestrated versions of *Boris Godunov,* one by Rimsky-Korsakov and the other by Dmitri

Shostakovich, are superior in craftsmanship to that of the composer. But equally valid arguments can be advanced that in polishing the rough edges of Mussorgsky's score a good deal of the original power and emotional impact has been needlessly sacrificed. Indeed, Igor Stravinsky went even further in his denunciation of such "improvements": ". . .even to an influenced mind . . . Rimsky's Meyerbeerization of Mussorgsky's technically 'imperfect' music should no longer be tolerated" (*Conversations with Igor Stravinsky*).

The peculiar Russian felicity with instrumentation was not, unfortunately, the birthright of the German Romantic Johannes Brahms (1833–1897). One is constantly more impressed with Brahms's musical ideas than with their orchestral fulfillment; the loftiness and nobility of his musical conceptions touch one more convincingly than the dramatic coloration of his orchestra. We cannot, of course, compare Brahms with Robert Schumann, for if Brahms's instrumentation was in no way remarkable, neither was it ever downright inept. It was unremarkable only because it was basically conservative—a plain reflection of his philosophy of absolute music, stripped of all nonessentials. He aimed to avoid shallow rhetoric, and erred in the direction of being overscrupulous concerning virtuosity and orchestral effect.

Instinctive orchestrators write what they wish to hear, and expect instruments and instrumental technique to catch up with their "impossible" ideas. Brahms, on the other hand, succumbed too easily to technical problems such as occur at the very outset of his Second Symphony (1877). After the initial phrase in D major, given to the cellos and double basses in octaves, the germinal idea returns in E minor, given in the same instruments. But as the lowest note then available to most double basses was E, Brahms wrote a quarter-rest for them at the point where the cellos play D-sharp, rejoining the two groups on the following beat to continue as before. In modern performance, of course, the double basses are equipped to play down to low C—as indeed some of them were even before Brahms's time—and the missing note is rightly included.[6]

The general heaviness and thickly greyed patina of the Brahms scoring is often engendered by the prevalence of low chord-spacings, frequently with the third of the harmony present in the bass register, as in the excerpt from the Fourth Symphony of 1885 (Example 39). Clarity of voice-leading is thus sacrificed to a thick harmonic texture, a mannerism of his piano music as well as his orchestral scoring. Elsewhere, as Max Reger indicated somewhat testily, "Only too often did he [Brahms] orchestrate so that the most important passages lie in the 'weak' ranges of certain instruments so that it is impossible to bring them out. . .

EXAMPLE 38
Rimsky-Korsakov: from Suite from *Le Coq d'Or*, pp. 10–11

He gives passages to bassoons which can only be conceived in the horns. The bassoons blow for dear life and the result is a horrible squeak. Give the identical passages to the horns and they 'sound' immediately."

Above all, Brahms's string parts are frequently awkward and ungrateful to negotiate, as in a number of passages in the concerto (1887)

(75) for violin and violoncello. Though he seldom wrote anything actually unplayable, he did not seem to fully comprehend the special problems inherent to the stringed instruments: hand position, fingering, crossing strings, and the like.

Still, the Brahms oeuvre has many moments of felicitous scoring,

91

EXAMPLE 39
Johannes Brahms: from Symphony No. 4, 2nd movement

such as the graceful oboe solo in the third movement of the Second Symphony (76), with its quiet background of clarinets, bassoons, and pizzicato cellos. Also notable is the poignant horn melody toward the close of the slow movement of the Third Symphony (1883) (77), and the massive wind chords that launch the chaconne-like finale of the Fourth Symphony (78).

All in all, we would do well to accept Brahms—and gladly—for what he is, and not for what he might have been. The favorable balance has perhaps been best assessed in our own century, oddly enough, by Charles Ives: "Some accuse Brahms's orchestration of being muddy. This may be a good name for a first impression of it. But if it should seem less so, he might not be saying what he thought. The mud may be a form of sincerity which demands that the heart be translated, rather than handed around through the pit. A clearer scoring might have altered the thought" (*Essays Before a Sonata*).

Camille Saint-Saëns (1835–1921), Brahms's French contemporary, possessed the easy technical facility with the orchestra that the German master lacked. It has been said of Saint-Saëns that he knew everything in music, and used everything. Clearly, his technical aptitude produced many ingenious touches in his scores—for example, the *scordatura* solo violin and clattering xylophone in *Danse Macabre* (1874); the use of piano four-hands in the finale of the Third Symphony (1886) (79); the brief but telling appearance of a military bugle in *La Jeunesse d'Hercule* (1877) (80); and the three timpani players requisitioned in *Phaëton* (1873) for the moment of the young god's fiery descent from the heavens (Example 40).

Certainly the "off-beat" instrumentation of the highly popular *Le Carnaval des Animaux* (1886) is in intriguing contrast to the prevalent grandiosity of the late Romantic period. Calling only for flute (piccolo), clarinet, harmonica, xylophone, a string quintet, and two pianos, this "zoological fantasy" assumes a chamber-music texture, especially as only in the finale does the composer utilize his full resources. With its satirical thrusts at Jacques Offenbach and Leo Delibes, the work appeals to modern ears by its exemplary clarity and succinctness.

These two elements often redeemed Saint-Saëns's musical practice, for in all his vast output of tone-poems, symphonies, concertos, and operas he stressed clearly separated orchestral tone-colors. With an intimate knowledge of the orchestra and with enviable ease he solved the problems of proper balance, weight, and texture. But this very facility, coupled with a marked disdain for "inspiration," gave to Saint-Saëns's music a cold and contrived brilliance. Even while admiring the fluency of his expression one is seldom deeply moved by it.

EXAMPLE 40
Camille Saint-Saëns: from *Phaëton*, p. 40

THE LATE ROMANTIC ORCHESTRA

Of a sizable list of French composers contemporary wit
Saëns, we may eliminate from comment such lesser orchestration
as Gustave Charpentier, Leo Delibes, Gabriel Fauré, Charles (
Victor Lalo, Henri Pierné, and Ambroise Thomas—mainly becau
instrumentational achievements are minor in comparison to the work of
Franck, Bizet, Chabrier, and Chausson.

César Franck (1822–1890), the chief protagonist of symphonic music
in a country dominated by opera, was an expert orchestrator in a less
exuberant version of the German Romantic tradition. An organist of
exceptional repute, he exhibited in his ever-popular Symphony in D
minor (1886–88) the same organ-like conception of the orchestra that one
finds in Anton Bruckner's nine symphonies, and the same tendency to
manipulate orchestral "registration" as one would change the stops of an
organ. Both composers steadfastly pursued a Wagnerian style, while
adding their own brand of religious mysticism.

Unlike Bruckner, however, Franck embodied in his symphonic
poems a colorful and apt instrumentational technique. The use of four
bassoons in *Le Chasseur Maudit* (1882) stems directly from the Wagnerian orchestra (Example 41), as does the sudden infernal blast on four
muted horns in unison (81), an effect worthy of the grand tradition of the
dramatic tone-poem and opera. Typical, too, was Franck's customary
use of a pair each of trumpets and cornets, a brass requirement dear to
most of the late French Romantics.[7]

Georges Bizet (1838–1875) can claim orchestrational fame mainly by
virtue of the brilliant score for his opera *Carmen* (1875), along with the
incidental music for Daudet's *L'Arlésienne* (1872). One cannot maintain, however, that his orchestration—polished and economical though
it was—created any new viewpoint or added any notable substance to
the practice of the period. His youthful Symphony in C (1855) recalls,
in fact, the earlier style of Rossini, and of Mozart before him; even his
mature scoring was only a natural extension of the French style and
technique established by Meyerbeer and Berlioz.

Ernest Chausson (1855–1894), a pupil of Franck, was similarly
devoid of innovation in his orchestration. His two major works, the
Symphony in B-flat of 1890 and the *Poème* for violin and orchestra (1896)
are thoroughly imbued with the Franck methodology. Although Chausson wrote several other orchestral works, and a number of compositions
for voices and orchestra (including several operas), they are seldom if
ever performed now. It is safe to assume that their orchestral investiture
is of the same cut as the symphony and the *Poème*.

Emmanuel Chabrier (1841–1894), on the other hand, displayed in
his *España* Rhapsody (1883) a flair for piquant instrumentation that

EXAMPLE 41
César Franck: from *Le Chasseur Maudit,* p. 60

presaged the virtuosity of Maurice Ravel's early *Alborada del Gracioso* (1912) in its orchestral version. And indeed the wit and fastidious craftsmanship of Chabrier's comic opera, *Le Roi Malgré Lui* (1887), may be considered ancestral to Ravel's sophisticated *L'Heure Espagnole* (1907) and even to Francis Poulenc's racy *Les Mamelles de Tirésias* of 1944.

It is evident that for all the intense compositional activity of late nineteenth-century France, no composer for the orchestra achieved an eminence comparable to that of Berlioz in the early Romantic period. And until Impressionism produced that solitary phenomenon, Claude Debussy, few French musicians were aware of how decisively the foundations of their musical world were to be shaken.

In the Italy of the late Romantic period, orchestration was only one aspect of the total operatic concepts of both Verdi and Puccini. For Giuseppe Verdi (1813–1901) wrote little but operatic music, even when under the title of *Messa da Requiem* (1874), and he had very definite ideas about the center of importance in that form: "Opera is opera, symphony is symphony," he said. "I don't think it is a good idea to insert a symphonic piece into an opera just for the pleasure of letting the orchestra cut loose once in a while."

To Verdi opera was a drama performed by singers. The stage on which they appeared, the lighting, the costumes, and the orchestra—all were at the service of the vocalists and existed solely to support and amplify their performing roles. In Wagner's operas, to the contrary, the main protagonist is the orchestra. But Verdi's orchestra was in effect eternally the servant—constantly busy in a useful way, but without the distinctive physiognomy to dominate the stage picture. Clearly, Verdi heartily agreed with Erik Satie, who once wrote: "There is no need for the orchestra to grimace when a character comes on stage."

Because the cardinal tenet of Verdi's operas was their vocality, orchestral timbres and textures were selected largely as they amalgamated with the color of the human voice. As the strings, of all the instruments of the orchestra, blend most subtly with vocal timbre, it is inevitable that Verdi should have strongly favored the use of pure string tone. Page after page in the Verdi scores has an undeviating accompaniment by strings alone. Even in the storm music of *Rigoletto* (1851) (**82**) and *Otello* (1887) (**83**) the composer's principal attention was fixed on his singers. A purely orchestral composer would probably have thought in terms of more inventive instrumentation (Sibelius in his incidental music to *The Tempest,* for example), yet Verdi limited himself to Classical "storm" patterns: chromatic scales, trills, diminished-seventh chords, and tremolos that were instrumental innovations a century before his time. *Aida* (1871), with all its exotic trappings, might be thought to have offered the composer many unusual orchestral possibilities. But here, too, the devices are conventional and stylized, made wholly subservient to the dominant vocality of the music. Even in the ballet music Verdi by-passed the opportunity for novel orchestration, relying on stereotyped combinations and predictable sounds.

As a practical man of the theater, Verdi subordinated orchestrational inventiveness not only to the needs of his singers but also to the exigencies of stage action. And as that action became increasingly important in the late veristic operas, extended overtures or preludes disappeared. Instead, a few measures of arresting music usually sufficed to raise the curtain on the first act. Once it was raised, the theater was a place of action and Verdi's orchestral writing pulsed with a rhythmic vitality characteristic of the composer from the early *Nabucco* (1842) to the mature *Falstaff* (1893). (In Wagner's operas, on the other hand, rhythm was a factor of only minor importance.)

Yet throughout Verdi's long career there was a definite evolution in orchestrational style. The earliest operas were scored, as one might expect, in the Donizetti-Bellini-Rossini tradition. In Verdi's middle period there were certain dynamic exaggerations: blatant brass harmonies and undue crashing of bass drum and cymbals, *à la* Meyerbeer or Berlioz. And there are those who profess to see some Wagnerisms in the culminating *Otello* and *Falstaff*. If this be so, they are elusive, and merely prove that the octogenarian Italian had a questing and unbiased mind while remaining far removed from any Wagnerian conversion.

For all his emphasis on the vocal elements of opera, however, Verdi did produce some striking examples of instrumental tone-painting. In the first act of *Rigoletto* (**84**), for instance, there is a duet accompanied by clarinets, bassoons, and divided lower strings, pizzicato—their dark timbres reinforced by the soft thudding of a bass drum. But the most notable color in this passage comes from the combination of muted solo violoncello and double bass on the melodic line—an effect worthy of Weber.

In the score of *Otello* we have Verdi's most massive orchestra and two outstanding moments of orchestral theatrics. In one, sinister low woodwind trills introduce Iago's malevolent "Credo" (Example 42); in the other, at the conclusion of Desdemona's "Ave Maria" in Act 4 (**85**) there is a sudden dramatic shift of tessitura from the high A-flat major string chord to the ominous low E in the solo double basses as Otello stealthily enters his wife's dimly-lit chamber. It is interesting to hat Verdi marks this passage for double basses with *four* strings. n the late nineteenth century in Italy, three-stringed double basses were commonly used in operatic orchestras. But only a four-stringed instrument could play the first half-dozen measures of this passage, the remainder of the section joining in at the *tutti* designation. Today, of course, the passage is played generally by the entire section, with the players often disregarding Verdi's dynamic indication of *double-piano* and attacking the first note with an accent, diminuendo.

Falstaff, the quintessence of Verdi's art, contains no patent instrumentational theatrics—only miracles of felicitous melody and orchestral color accomplished with an ensemble of almost chamber-music character.

The *Messa da Requiem,* Verdi's one significant quasi-symphonic work, was still scored for an operatic orchestra, despite the composer's demand for four bassoons, four trumpets, and ophicleide as part of his total resources. Even without knowing who wrote the work, the listener would sense that its composer was steeped in the traditions of the theatre. In the passages of massive orchestral trills in the "Dies irae" **(86)** are echoes of the storms of *Rigoletto* and *Otello.* Diametrically opposite in mood and effect are the soft tremolos of the violins alone, divided into six equal parts, at the beginning of the "Lux aeterna" **(87).** Also noteworthy from the orchestration standpoint is a later passage in the same movement in which the soft, double-tonguing piccolo decorates the violin tremoli **(88).**

With complete justification, then, Verdi dominated the Italianate world of opera as Wagner ruled the Teutonic world. These two composers represent antipodal approaches to operatic instrumentation, just as Tchaikovsky and Bruckner may be said to embody polarities in symphonic orchestration. No succeeding composer of lyric opera has wholly escaped Verdi's influence; few have equalled his unique gifts.

The strongest contender as Verdi's logical successor was Giacomo Puccini (1858–1924), excepting that his tendency toward self-deprecation led him to assert, "I am not made for heroic gestures." Nor were the Puccini operas heroic in any way; with the possible exception of *Turandot* (left incomplete at the time of the composer's death), they were relatively unostentatious in effect, tasteful and elegant in essence, and a natural extension of his unique abilities as a melodist.

Puccini's orchestra, like that of Verdi, underlies and supports rather than dominates. Rarely is it independent of vocal lines or of meaningful stage action; seldom does it comment alone on dramatic situations or character involvements, seldom even paint a picture or establish a strong subjective mood. Quite exceptional, therefore, is the orchestral commentary in the closing moments of Act 2 of *Tosca* (1900) **(89),** when Tosca places a pair of candelabra beside the dead Scarpia and silently

EXAMPLE 42
Giuseppe Verdi: from *Otello* (Act 2, Scene 1)

101

glides from the room. *Madama Butterfly* (1904) **(90)** contains the only other instance of such potent mood-delineation: in spite of its old-fashioned sentiment, the quiet, poignantly simple music while Butterfly patiently waits through the night for the arrival of her American husband remains extremely moving. A similar nocturnal evocation highlights the opening of *Turandot*'s last act **(91)**, although here the offstage voices contribute more to the mood-painting than does the orchestra.

Like Verdi, Puccini usually opened his first-act curtain after only a brief orchestral passage. Thereafter, his orchestra assumed—as did Verdi's—a function definitely secondary to that of the singers. As for specific techniques of orchestration, Puccini's scoring relied heavily on unison and octave doubling, particularly in the strings. Rarely did the violins have completely independent parts, and the melodic combination of cellos with the higher strings was so frequent that it assumed the status of a mannerism.

It may be taken for granted that Puccini would favor the sentimental contributions of the harp, celesta, and tuned percussion. His use of the more clangorous resources of this orchestral department was, however, commendably restrained; seldom did Puccini indulge in the welter of percussive sound that characterized Verdi in his less reticent moments. His occasional use of unusual instruments—such as the bass xylophone, Chinese gongs, and tam-tam in *Turandot*—was obviously justified by a specific exotic background.

All the orchestral instruments were normally used by Puccini in their most effective ranges, and all functioned largely in the traditional manner. One significant exception is his substitution of the bass clarinet for the bassoon in the woodwind harmony of *La Bohème* (1896). And clearly dictated by the exotic milieu of *Turandot* is the sharp brilliance of a pentatonic theme in the piccolo, doubled two octaves lower by a muted trumpet, and backed up by triangle, celesta, and tremolando violins on a glittering pentachord (Example 43). Also admirable in conception and sonoric effect are the chilling sounds made in a later scene of this opera by low bassoon, contrabassoon, and pizzicato double basses, reinforced by bass-drum thuds and timpani chords **(92)**. In every case, however, the requirements of the vocal drama governed Puccini's orchestration, and, as these citations illustrate, called forth the stylistic amalgam peculiarly suitable to the situation at hand.

Puccini's contemporaries—Ruggiero Leoncavallo, Pietro Mascagni, Italo Montemezzi, and Amilcare Ponchielli—merely maintained the instrumentational practices solidly established by the long line of Italian operatic composers from Rossini to Verdi. None of them advanced the

EXAMPLE 43
Giacomo Puccini: from *Turandot* (Act 3, Scene 2)

103

science and art of orchestration to the same degree as did Verdi and Puccini, to say nothing of the Russian, French, and German masters of the late Romantic period.

Of the composers already discussed, only Richard Wagner was a conductor as well as a creator. In this respect he shared with Gustav Mahler (1860–1911) the advantages of a special insight into the potentiality of the orchestra, one that is denied the composer who knows the orchestra only at second hand. The instrumentation of both Wagner and Mahler, however, like that of Ravel, refutes the Hindemith thesis that orchestration can only be learned by playing as many instruments as possible. Some of the greatest examples of the orchestrational art have been produced by composers who played no instrument other than piano.

"What first strikes one about Mahler's instrumentation," wrote Arnold Schoenberg, "is the almost unexampled objectivity with which he writes down only what is necessary." Certainly few composers have ever been more fastidious and precise in score directives than Mahler. The nine completed symphonies, as well as *Das Lied von der Erde* (1908) and the several other song cycles with orchestra, are replete with footnotes regarding tempo alterations, the qualities of tone production desired, or unusual devices required. In Mahler's First Symphony (1885–88) **(93)**, for instance, below a col legno passage for the violins one finds this stern warning to the conductor: "Not a mistake! Played with the wood of the bow."

With the practiced security of a skilled conductor, Mahler was prolific with such special orchestral devices as flutter-tonguing in wind instruments, muting in all the brasses, and glissandi in nearly all the woodwind, brass, and string instruments. He frequently wrote "bells up" [8] to insure maximum strength in oboes and clarinets as well as in horns and trumpets—a device whose effect is visual as well as aural. Mahler also requested that the timpani be struck with two mallets simultaneously, and that a wide variety of sticks be used to strike the drums, cymbal, and gong. Furthermore, he constantly indicated all the unusual ways of producing string tone: sul ponticello and sul tasto, pizzicato, tremolo, col legno, and harmonics. To these he added a personal invention: *col arco battuto,* a method of sharply striking the string with the bow hair, used extensively in the Fourth Symphony (1900) **(94)**. All these devices were quickly to become the common property of twentieth-century orchestrators—Romantics, Impressionists, and Expressionists alike.

Mahler frequently called for offstage instruments for distant and dramatic effects: trumpets alone in the First **(95)** and Second (1894) **(96)** Symphonies; a solo posthorn in the Third Symphony (1896) **(97)**; trumpets and horn in the Second Symphony **(98)**; trumpets and trombones in the Eighth Symphony (1907) **(99)**; cowbells in both the Sixth (1904) **(100)** and Seventh (1905) **(101)** Symphonies, and a snare drum in the Third Symphony **(102)**. Commonplace enough in operatic literature, from Beethoven's offstage trumpet in *Fidelio* to Wagner's shepherd's horn in *Tristan und Isolde,* the device of using offstage instruments had been quite rare in works designed for the concert hall. Mahler's behind-the-scene trumpets in the first two symphonies antedate by a dozen years Richard Strauss's distant fanfare of three trumpets in *Ein Heldenleben* (1898) **(103)**.

Although not essentially an orchestral device, Mahler's use of voices, both solo and choral, was a basic part of his symphonic conception and thus must be regarded as an important facet of his compositional technique. *Das Lied von der Erde,* while not a symphony, ranks in every way as the very epitome of Mahler's art of orchestration and musical expression.

In this field of expressivity one Mahler innovation may be considered especially subtle. The composer consistently wrote into his scores a fluid "dynamic counterpoint"; that is, crescendos and diminuendos employed simultaneously rather than consecutively, with one group of instruments increasing in intensity while another diminishes or otherwise varies its tonal volume. The effect is clearly contrapuntal, not antiphonal, for several degrees of amplitude (and their concomitant shadings) are present at the same time. A technique of opposition, in other words, is applied both to the pitch components and to their intensities. The excerpt from Mahler's First Symphony (Example 44) well illustrates this characteristic technique of the composer.

So accomplished, in sum, was the instrumentational art of Mahler that it can hardly be characterized without verbiage as overblown as the musical subject. We might at this juncture turn to just such a summary, written by the musicologist Gabriel Engel:

> Each instrument was for him a living, breathing, feeling creation with an individual voice, inflection, and song. . . . Solo flutes, which the custom of the former masters had made the vehicles of sweet melodies are . . . heard sounding ethereally, totally bereft of pathos, as though issuing out of a boundless distance. The brilliant little E-flat clarinet, a queer foundling inherited from Berlioz, is revealed a full-blown symphonic soloist, bursting forth in occasional mockery, grotesque, often to the point of scurrility. The oboe, no longer the high-pitched voice of poignant melancholy, sings with unrestrained accents in its natural, middle register. The droll bassoon, suddenly become the voice of suppressed pain, cries out,

EXAMPLE 44
Gustav Mahler: from Symphony No. 1, 1st movement

most eloquent in its high tones. The contrabassoon makes coarse, bizarre remarks all alone. The horn . . . seems never to have played so important a role. To the noble level of expressiveness it attained in Bruckner's hands Mahler has added a new power, enabling it by means of dying echoes to carry smoothly an idea already exploited into a charged musical atmosphere. Sometimes a solo horn emerges with overwhelming effect from a whole choir of

106

horns among which it has been concealed or, singing in its deepest tones, lends a passage the air of tragic gloom.

Short, sharp fanfare-like trumpet motifs . . . attained apotheosis with Mahler; for either disappearing gently in a soft cadence or singing bravely on, they soar with ever increasing intensity and breadth to a powerful dynamic climax, to be finally crowned with the triumphant din of massed brass and percussion. . . . Above a sombre rhythm powerfully marked by a choir of trombones over percussion, he sets a solitary trombone to pour out grief in noble, poignant recitative (*International Cyclopedia of Music and Musicians*).

It is unfortunate that in a body of work freighted with such potential the craving for massive expression, symptomatic of the late Romantic style, should have reached a virtual impasse. Even as Mahler was creating his complex sonorities, many composers were beginning to be aware that a top-heavy weight of orchestral instruments does not in itself guarantee grandeur of expression. The inevitable reaction, once begun, could not be stopped, and by the closing years of the century the tenets of Impressionism would quietly undermine the gargantuan structure of the Romantic orchestra.

There remain to be considered, however, several more composers who persevered in the late Romantic tradition: Bruckner, Liszt, Sibelius, and, above all, Richard Strauss. Certain other composers who began their creative careers in the mainstream of Romanticism but took other paths as their styles matured—Scriabin and Schoenberg, for example—will be dealt with in other chapters.

Mahler and Anton Bruckner (1824–1896) are often linked together in musicological discussion, like Siamese twins from the same compositional womb. Yet they practiced very different instrumentational approaches, reflecting their quite different professions. Mahler heard orchestral sound as a conductor, Bruckner as a church organist. Furthermore, Bruckner conceived and executed his tonal masses in much the same manner that Gabrieli's elaborate seventeenth-century polyphony contrasted voices, brass instruments, and organ. In Bruckner's orchestral works this antiphony, or alternation by choirs, led to his pitting brasses against woodwinds, to having strings answering brasses, woodwinds and brasses echoing strings. (See, for instance, the first movement of the Ninth Symphony of 1894 [104].)

This procedure has an obvious prototype in the organ, with its several keyboards and pedals. From Bach's time to Bruckner's even the most humble church organist had capitalized on the possibility of creating musical contrast through the use of different manuals with dissimilar registration. The organist Bruckner, then, instinctively adapted this method to his treatment of the symphonic orchestra. Moreover, the exigencies of organ technique are doubtless the source of the frequent long and static pedal-points in all of Bruckner's orchestral scores.

Bruckner also departed from the Wagner-Mahler-Strauss circle by his disinclination for huge theatrical or programmatic canvases; occasionally he handled his orchestra with surprising restraint and economy. Above all, his large brass choir achieved a very different emotional effect from that of his confreres. Frequently there are organlike sustained effects of great impressiveness, as in the Ninth Symphony (Example 45), introvert in character as opposed to the more extrovert brass instruments of Mahler or Strauss. In Bruckner's incessant orchestral climaxes, on the other hand, the brasses may be uncompromisingly loud without actually achieving the overwhelming emotional intensity of many climactic moments in Mahler's orchestral works.

Technically speaking, this lack of dramatic effect may be due to the fact that no instrument in Bruckner's orchestra is placed in adequate relief. In the slow movement of the Ninth Symphony, for instance, a quartet of Wagnerian tubas (played by the hornists) should rightfully produce a deep, velvety sound. Yet the music is so thickly scored that the tuba color seems—in the words of Edward Lockspeiser— "to be squeezed out like toothpaste." The auditor hears only a never-ending stream of heterogeneous orchestral sound, a tonal impasto that eventually makes for monotony.

Perhaps because of his obvious devotion to the Wagnerian sound-ideal, without allowing for desirable differences in his own musical personality, Bruckner sensed that he had not always achieved in his orchestration the ultimate potential of the complex Romantic orchestra. This may possibly explain why, apparently alone among the significant late Romantic composers, Bruckner made many revisions of his major works, including the nine symphonies. What is more, the final printed versions sometimes differed sharply from the revised manuscripts. Apparently, in an excess of humility the composer allowed his publishers to retouch his instrumentation, making it more "Wagnerian" and hence more palatable, in their opinion, to the musical public.

This was a cruel disservice to Bruckner, for the *Urtext* scoring is frequently thinner and commendably more transparent than that of the published version, with its excessive interchoir doubling. This illustrates that a composer of compelling originality must believe in his genetic idea

EXAMPLE 45

Anton Bruckner: from Symphony No. 9, 1st movement

and trust his own musical instincts for its orchestral investiture; other-wise, he cannot achieve his full potential as composer.

Franz Liszt (1811–1886) must be included in the Wagner axis as a nearly exact contemporary of that master and as a staunch practitioner of his orchestral methodology. He was not, however, a strikingly original instrumentator, even though all his scores are imbued with a surface brilliance. In practice Liszt remained a transitional voice between Berlioz, with the early Romantic programmatic aspects of music, and Wagner, in whom the late Romantic trend was synthesized.

To an era of growing orchestral innovations Liszt contributed only a few noteworthy devices. In his tone-poem *Mazeppa* (1850), for in-stance, he cleverly imitated the snorting of horses with the use of col legno strings (Example 46). And in his *Mephisto Waltz* (No. 1 [1862]) **(105)** he became the first composer to call for harp glissandi. This characteristic device, which made its bow in Liszt's score on the ubiquitous diminished-seventh chord, was all too quickly cheapened as the common property of all second-rate orchestrators. Liszt also frequently used the delicate, simulated bell-sounds of harp harmonics, especially effective in the programmatic *Faust* Symphony (1854) **(106)**.[9]

Possessing neither the fresh and innovative brilliance of Berlioz nor the spiritual profundity of Wagner, Liszt's orchestral scoring is still agreeably rich and sonorous. At its worst, Liszt's orchestration is ex-travagant and rhetorical; at its best it contains elements of warmth and color that are in welcome contrast to the dull and turgid scores of many lesser lights of the period.

Jean Sibelius (1865–1957), though he lived the greater part of his life in the present century, belongs to the pantheon of late Romantic composers. True, the *Four Legends, Finlandia,* and the First Symphony were all completed in 1899, and his last major work, *Tapiola,* is dated 1925. These twenty-six years of composition, however, might just as well have belonged to the nineteenth century rather than the twentieth, for all that Sibelius's instrumentation responded to the revolutionary tides then surging toward the musical shore.

The crucial three years from 1912 to 1915 alone saw the advent of Debussy's *Jeux,* Charles Ives's *Concord Sonata,* the *Scythian Suite* of Prokofiev, Ravel's *Daphnis et Chloé,* Schoenberg's *Pierrot Lunaire, Le Sacre du Printemps* by Stravinsky, and Webern's *Six Pieces for Orchestra.* Yet in this period Sibelius offered the world his Fifth Symphony (1914–15), and the two tone-poems *The Bard* (1913) and *The Oceanides* (1914) –works all couched in the vocabulary of the preceding century. Despite a few tentative touches of Impressionism in *The Oceanides,* they largely

110

EXAMPLE 46
Franz Liszt: from *Mazeppa*, p. 47

*) Zwei einzelne Violinen.

employ—albeit in a very personal way—the instrumentational palette of Tchaikovsky and Brahms.

The characteristic colors of a Sibelius score are sombre, and stem from his penchant for the darker instrumental hues—low oboes, deep bassoons, closely spaced violas, cellos, and double basses; for the grey masses of low-pitched instrumental combinations of all kinds. No composer, it is safe to say, ever showed in his work a more marked preference for the special qualities of sound at the lower end of the sonic spectrum. Here, the strings are uniformly rich and vibrant at *forte* and mellow at *piano;* in the woodwinds the tone becomes weighted with gloom or tinged with mystery, while in the brasses it is thick, even turgid. Oboes on their bottom notes are acrid and nasal, a peculiar sound that manifestly fascinated Sibelius. Low clarinets are hollow and sepulchral, and low bassoons are murky or grim. Deep flutes may be warm or, in the proper context, as ominous as muted trumpets. All these qualities Sibelius exploited to the full, for they are an integral part of his technique of orchestration. It is little wonder, with the dominance of these hues, that the music of Sibelius affects the listener with gravity and melancholy.

To this characteristic thickness of orchestral texture, so favored by Brahms also, Sibelius grafted great emotional intensity. A typical instance is the very opening of the Fourth Symphony (1911) which, for all its surface reminiscence of Tchaikovsky's "Pathétique" Symphony, is unique in concept and aural effect.

The closing portion of *Tapiola* (107) offers a good example of the technical means Sibelius often employed for a cumulative emotional effect. Here the composer begins a long, steadily mounting crescendo in divided tremolando strings which carry the music into fuller harmonies, like the petals of a gigantic flower opening to the sun. And in the mythic *Swan of Tuonela* (1893) even the habitually dark Sibelian realm is illuminated by enchantment as the poignant English horn solo floats over the divided strings, "col legno tremolo," like delicate flapping wings (Example 47).

The late critic Olin Downes noted a similar characteristic in the early tone-poem *En Saga* (1892) (108): "Nothing that has appeared in modern instrumentation is simpler or more suggestive to the imagination than the ending when the solo clarinet is heard as from afar over pulsing harmonies of the muted strings, reinforced by faint rolls of the cymbals, and the indomitable rhythm of a war-dance persists until the music passes into silence" (*International Cyclopedia of Music and Musicians*).

From the time of *Tapiola* until his death in 1957, Sibelius wrote no further orchestral music of which we have knowledge, and there is con-

EXAMPLE 47
Jean Sibelius: from *The Swan of Tuonela*, p. 14

siderable doubt that he even made preliminary sketches for an eighth symphony. When this author tried to draw him out on the subject during several visits to his home in 1939, Sibelius was polite, but firmly evasive. Perhaps he had sensed that the self-imposed restraint and austerity of his style, which was in striking contrast to the prodigal effects of Mahler and Strauss, would be even less relevant beyond the late Romantic era. Sharing with Tchaikovsky and Rimsky-Korsakov an abhorrence of orchestral complexity, Sibelius, ironically enough, outlived the last great Romantic composer of the nineteenth century, Strauss—who in turn outlived his own prodigious gifts without being aware of the loss.

Richard Strauss (1864–1949), for all his frequent atrocious sentimentality, distressing prolixity, and vulgar mannerisms, yet remains one of the most astounding technicians of the symphonic and operatic orchestra in all musical history. This *Wunderkind* from Munich, whose instrumentational pyrotechnics in his early tone-poems had quite dazzled their first audiences, was a virtuoso of the orchestra second to none. As Verdi represented the culmination of a long line of Italian composers of opera, so Strauss was the epitome of the Romantic approach to the orchestra.

In his early period Strauss subscribed without question to the Wagnerian tenet of complete harmonic profile in each principal section of the orchestra. But as his music became more contrapuntal, and harmonic filler-parts gave way to genuine polyphony, Strauss's orchestration grew correspondingly more complex and intense. On melodic voices that required unusual prominence the composer would mass many instruments of different hues, not for the sake of timbral contrast but mainly for necessary balance and added power.

The indisputable brilliance of the Strauss orchestral ensemble, it goes without saying, shines from the virtuosic parts being played in every single chair. And from the time of the early *Tod und Verklärung* (1889) to that of the trio of operas—*Salome* (1905), *Elektra* (1909), and *Der Rosenkavalier* (1911)—universally regarded as the composer's masterworks, Strauss's instrumentation proliferated in the use of coloristic devices. The winds, for instance, frequently resort to flutter-tonguing (the notorious "bleating sheep" in *Don Quixote* [1897] [**109**], as an example), and to single-note tongued tremolos and to glissandos; the brass are often muted, in *fortissimo* as well as in *piano* passages; harps and glockenspiel occasionally are required to play tremolo chords (*bisbigliando,* in harp terminology), and the string instruments constantly employ every technical device known at the time.

But the remarkable fact is that one is seldom conscious of these devices and effects as such; their presence in the orchestral sonic web is

114

entirely consistent with the dramatic requirements of Strauss's expression. No better proof can be offered than the several magical moments in *Der Rosenkavalier* when the "Presentation of the rose" motive floats out above the sustained orchestral background in delicately articulated flutes, celesta, harps, and solo violins (Example 48).

No late Romantic composer ever plumbed the possibilities of the woodwind choir more tellingly than did Strauss. He had an instinctive feeling for the unique potential of each instrument—see the quietly ecstatic oboe solo in *Don Juan* (1889) (110), for instance, or the squealing D-clarinet in *Till Eulenspiegels lustige Streiche* (1895) (111). And as a section, the woodwinds have nowhere been treated more imaginatively than in the sardonic "critics" section of *Ein Heldenleben* (1898) (112) or throughout the opera *Die Frau ohne Schatten* (1919) (113) (especially in the strident "falcon" motive).

Above all, it is largely to Strauss that we owe the immense freedom shown today in brass scoring; the agility and flexibility evidenced by horns, trumpets, and trombones—even tubas—in traversing passages one would think technically possible only for woodwinds or strings, is a hallmark of Strauss's orchestral style. These virtuosic demands were first made in *Till Eulenspiegels lustige Streiche*—the solo horn on the very first page, for instance—and continued with *Ein Heldenleben* (114) (the entire "battle" section) and the *Symphonia Domestica* (1903), among the long list of Strauss scores written at the turn of the century.

Strauss's percussion writing was never less than effective, if it was in no way remarkable for the time. The pseudo-Oriental percussive flavor of Salome's "Dance of the Seven Veils" (115), for instance, is dramatically apt, though completely predictable. The ratchet in *Till Eulenspiegels lustige Streiche* and the wind machine in both *Don Quixote* and the *Alpensymphonie* (1915) are adroit color additions to the composer's instrumental resources; their initial shock value, however, has largely been dissipated during the intervening years by the twentieth-century predilection for such exotica as *ondes* Martenot, sirens, and "lion's roar" in the percussion family.

It has often been said that the string writing in a Strauss score looks like the solo part of a concerto. Certainly all four members of the string choir are given technical problems that formerly would have been found only in a display piece for violin, viola, or violoncello. Even the double basses are released from their usual earth-bound position to soar with the cellos and violas into the sonic stratosphere. (See, for example, the opening measures of *Ein Heldenleben,* or certain passages in *Don Juan* [116] and the *Symphonia Domestica* [117].)

In particular, the viola parts frequently encountered in Strauss

115

EXAMPLE 48
Richard Strauss: from *Der Rosenkavalier* (Act 2), p. 519

would no doubt have brought cold shivers to the string virtuosi of Corelli's day (as in *Also sprach Zarathustra* [1896] **[118]**, for instance). And even Nicolò Paganini, flamboyant showman of the nineteenth century, seldom wrote solo violin passages more fearsomely difficult than those assigned the entire section on many a page of a Strauss score.

To the very end of his life Strauss never forfeited the right to the tribute paid him early in his career by the critic James Huneker: "The greatest technical master of the orchestra. . . ." It is a tribute often reiterated, although unconsciously, in the ritual warm-up of symphony orchestras the world over; among the pleasant anticipatory tunings of the instrumentalists the audience is almost certain to hear the bravura horn call of *Till Eulenspiegels lustige Streiche* (119), the high bleat of the tuba from *Don Quixote* (120), or the saccharine violin solos from *Ein Heldenleben* (121) and *Also sprach Zarathustra* (122). No sincerer homage can be paid the composer by the instrumentalist.

Despite the extent of this survey, it has not been possible to comment on the work of every orchestral composer of the late nineteenth century. We have given no specific attention to the contributions of Antonin Dvořák, Edvard Grieg, Bedřich Smetana, Vincent d'Indy, Leoš Janáček, Carl Nielsen, Engelbert Humperdinck, Hans Pfitzner, Max Reger, Max Bruch, Ferruccio Busoni, Sir Edward Elgar, or Edward MacDowell. But these composers and others unnamed, though admirable in varying degrees of orchestrational skill and imagination, were basically followers rather than innovators. Each was largely content to use the orchestra, symphonic and operatic, as he found it, with no perceptible modification of the modus operandi of the great masters of orchestral style.

Even so, it is evident that there can be no easy summation of late Romantic instrumentational practice; the end of the nineteenth century produced almost as many variants of orchestral style as there were composers. By no means can we say that Tchaikovsky and Mahler, for example, shared a common approach to orchestral sonority, or that Wagner and Brahms subscribed to parallel concepts of instrumental usage, or that Bruckner and Rimsky-Korsakov treated their orchestras in an identical manner. The Russian nationalists went one way, the French symphonists another, and the Italian opera composers still another. And more than ever before, such individualists as Mahler and Sibelius went each his own personal way, regardless of current fashions in orchestral sonority and effect.

Nonetheless, there are certain observable trends now generally associated with the culmination of nineteenth-century Romanticism. The woodwind choir, for instance, expanded gradually from the pairs of instruments employed from Beethoven through Brahms to a complement of three, four, and even five instruments within each basic sub-family. It is important to keep in mind that no new timbres were added to the section, but only additional members in the four existing categories. At the apex of numerical requirement (in the scores of Mahler, Strauss, and early Schoenberg) the woodwind choir normally consisted of: piccolo and three flutes (or a second piccolo); three oboes and English horn; three clarinets (including a small instrument in D or E-flat) and bass clarinet; and three bassoons and contrabassoon. The occasional use of alto flute, bass oboe, heckelphone, basset horn, saxophone, and sarrusophone did not add any new voice to the basic colors, but merely enlarged or intensified those already present.

In the brass choir a similar numerical expansion took place; four horns became the minimum requirement, and six and even eight instruments were often demanded by the late Romantic composers. Three each of trumpets and trombones were standard resources, with a fourth player by no means uncommon; one tuba usually sufficed, although both Mahler and Strauss had no hesitation in scoring for two instruments, a tenor and bass. Thus the brass section comprised, as did the woodwind, four basic timbres; the special and only occasional use of cornets, bass trumpet, Wagnerian tubas, and the like, merely duplicated the already existing brass colors.

New sounds in the orchestral palette came solely by way of the percussion section. The bass drum, cymbals, triangle, and glockenspiel were not, of course, newcomers to the orchestra, as all had been used as far back as the early eighteenth century. More of an innovation was the requisition of tam-tam, gong, xylophone, tambourine, castanets, and such oddities as the ratchet, cowbells, and the wind machine—to name but a few of the more exotic percussion variants grafted onto the standard section. Two harps and a celesta were commonly utilized, and at least four timpani. The organ was included on occasion, in works designed for both the theater and for the concert hall, but piano and harpsichord do not appear among the special requirements of the period.

To match the now overwhelming weight and variety of massed wind-brass-percussion sonority, it was essential that the strings be similarly expanded in number of players. Thus the late Romantic orchestra balanced its sixteen to eighteen woodwinds, eleven to eighteen brasses, five or six percussion players, and two or more harpists, with a string choir comprised of some sixty performers: sixteen to eighteen first violins, fourteen to sixteen second violins, ten to twelve each of violas and violoncellos, and eight to ten double basses. At its maximum strength, then, the Romantic orchestra could provide the composer with a grand total of about one hundred ten instrumentalists, each capable of outlining a separate melodic or harmonic voice or contributing to the essential rhythmic propulsion.

In a book on the orchestra published at the height of the late Romantic period, the author, Louis Adolphe Coerne, stated: "Orchestration in its present development would seem to have reached its highest possible attainment of effectiveness and virtuosity. The problem of the future, therefore, deals not so much with material increase of orchestral resource, as with what manner of thought and music the orchestra is destined to portray." [10]

Music, according to the Romantics, was designed "to reflect the loftiest sentiments of the composer's soul," as Coerne rather fancifully phrased it. This idealistic and Victorian sentiment, however, is not apropos of the musical aesthetics of the twentieth century; though it admirably expresses the intentions of the Romantic composers, it will not serve in assessing the aspirations of the Impressionists, the Expressionists, the Neoclassicists—or any of the other divergent contemporary philosophies of musical expression. And whereas the Romantic composers, from Beethoven through Richard Strauss, seldom wrote for other than the authentic Romantic orchestra, the composers most closely identified with the various twentieth-century styles, from Impressionism to Avant-gardism, often orchestrated for ensembles not characteristic of their more familiar instrumentational styles. Thus many of the composers yet to be discussed will appear in several stylistic categories. Such evidence of creative multiple personality, however, is merely an accepted fact of life in the music of our century.

Notes

1. The relationship between sensation intensity and stimulus intensity is known as Weber's Law (after Wilhelm Eduard Weber): "The increase of stimulus necessary to produce the minimum perceptible increase of sensation is proportional to the pre-existing stimulus." From this law Gustav Theodor Fechner developed the following equation: S (sensation magnitude or loudness) $= C \log E$ (stimulus intensity). This is now referred to as the Weber-Fechner law.

2. At its first performance in 1910, under Mahler's direction, the orchestra numbered 146 players. In addition, there were two mixed choruses of 250 each, a children's choir of 350, and seven soloists.

3. An inexplicable error occurs in the Philharmonia edition of the *Parsifal* Prelude, in which the German word for kettledrum, *Pauke*, is translated as "cymbal" in both French and Italian.

4. Seven, if one counts as authentic the incomplete sketches orchestrated by the Russian composer S. Bogatyryev, labeled as Symphony No. 7.

5. Tchaikovsky's *Dance of the Sugarplum Fairy* from the *Nutcracker* Ballet was the first orchestral appearance of the celesta, invented in 1886 by the French instrument designer, Victor Mustel.

STYLE AND ORCHESTRATION

6. The opening of Franz Schubert's Symphony No. 8 ("Unfinished") presents much the same problem: the cellos and double basses are written in unison (sounding in octaves) for four measures until the low D and C-sharp force the basses an octave higher in notation. Today the double basses play the same written notes as the cellos throughout the passage.

7. The popular, though erroneous, belief that Franck was the first composer to use the English horn in a symphony should be firmly laid to rest. Haydn had called for two English horns in his Symphony No. 22 in E-flat Major, "The Philosopher," composed in 1764.

8. This is a device attributed to the early nineteenth-century French opera composer, Étienne Méhul.

9. The first-known instance of harp harmonics in an orchestral score occurred in the *opéra comique, La Dame Blanche* (1825), by the French composer François Boieldieu.

10. Coerne, Louis Adolphe. *The Evolution of Modern Orchestration* (1908).

5

The Impressionist Orchestra

. . . a muffled, softly undulating orchestra, that seems wrapped in wool . . . .

Louis Alfred Bruneau,
La Musique Française

To most musical historians, the twentieth century began on December 23, 1894, with the premiere of *Prélude à l'Après-midi d'un Faune* by Claude Debussy (1862–1918). This unique nine-minute work for reduced orchestra, with its unparalled subtlety, imagination, and refinement of expression, was to shape the course of our century as did no other single musical entity. It signals the breakdown not only of the giganticism of late nineteenth-century orchestration but also of the whole complex of traditional musical material: melody, harmony, rhythm, and form.

Before *L'Après-midi d'un Faune,* symphonic music was essentially the Germanic, French, and Russian world of Romanticism. After the debut of Debussy's pioneer work, the familiar shores were inundated by many shifting waves, the first surge being the fundamentally Gallic movement known in all the arts as Impressionism.[1] What happened to harmony, to rhythm, to traditional forms as they emerged from this rebirth is the province of the theory historian; our concern here is how this movement transformed the symphonic and operatic orchestra.

The rise of the Impressionist orchestra was not so much a total revolt against the Romantic movement as it was a new manifestation of elements intrinsic in authentic Romanticism: tone-painting, an emphasis on mood and atmosphere, and an innate feeling for lyrical and poetic expression. Our long perspective makes it clear that the rebellion aimed simply to strip away the artistic abuses of the late Romantics rather than to destroy the essence of the Romantic aesthetic. None of the Impressionists—Debussy or Ravel, Griffes or Delius, Falla or Respighi, for example—wholly abandoned the large orchestra of the end of the century. By no stretch of the imagination can *La Mer* (1905), *Daphnis et Chloé* (1911), or *The Pines of Rome* (1924) be regarded as scored for small ensembles. But the traditional symphonic and operatic orchestra in the hands of these, and other, composers found a new voice because it had transformed its intentions, aiming first of all at abandonment of "wasteful and ridiculous excesses" (William Hazlitt), and of other decadent aspects of Romanticism.

In the fundamental revulsion against grand pathos and rhetorical stance, the Impressionists turned to tenuosity and subtlety; *Sturm und Drang* and overblown passion gave way to the refined and the reticent. Ideas, associations, and familiar colors and sounds were suspended in a sensual atmosphere, amorphous and enervating. Hedonists by inclination, many Impressionist composers were drawn to exquisite shadings that could never have survived the thicket, heavy-handed techniques of their predecessors. In contrast, then, to Romantic overstatement, the new Impressionists exploited the technique of understatement. They avoided the explicit, the tangible, the intense, preferring to suggest the indefinable emotion, the diaphanous, the gossamer. This they realized by way of an orchestra "shimmering in a thousand colors, achieving a remarkable crescendo of sensuous effects by the subtlest of means, without recourse to violent colors, harmonies, or dynamics" (Paul Henry Lang).

Thus the Romantic orchestra, however traditional its visual aspect on the concert platform or in the theatre pit, became a transformed instrument in the performance of Impressionist scores. How it was transmuted, and how variously, we can only compass by detailed individual studies of the principal composers of the movement. At this threshold of the music of our century, the task of separating composers into one camp or another in matters of orchestrational style becomes well-nigh impossible. After Debussy the complete catalogue of most composers exhibits a wide range of instrumentational styles and techniques—and fluctations in basic musical philosophy.

THE IMPRESSIONIST ORCHESTRA

If Ravel, for example, was the Impressionist par excellence in the *Rapsodie Espagnole* (1907), was he not the patrician Classicist in *Le Tombeau de Couperin* (1919)? Respighi's popular *The Pines of Rome* is orchestrally Impressionistic in its two inner movements, but is close to unabashed Romanticism in its outer sections. The *Elegia* movement of Bartók's last orchestral work, the *Concerto for Orchestra* (1943), subscribes to Debussy's orchestral and harmonic precepts, while the flanking sections pay homage to the Neoromantics of his own time. The simple truth is that composers of this century have come more and more to intermix disparate stylistic elements in highly individual amalgams. And nowhere is this admixture more evident than in their music for orchestra.

In the works of Claude Debussy, however, we have a unified summary of the distinctive attributes of Impressionist instrumentation. Nothing in the early training of the young "Claude de France"—except, perhaps, his rebelliousness regarding dogma—leads us to anticipate his radical departures from the obvious exemplars of his time, Wagner and Brahms. Yet how new, after the symphonic complexity of those Romantics, were the cool, vaporous, and gently fragmented measures of his one opera, *Pelléas et Mélisande* (1892–1902), the *Trois Nocturnes* (1899), and *Ibéria* (1912; second of the *Images pour Orchestre*). For just as Beethoven in an earlier epoch liberated the orchestra from the conventions and restrictions of the Classicists, so Debussy freed symphonic instrumentation from the excesses of Romanticism.

"Where Wagner would have repeated and enlarged," Herbert Weinstock observes, "Debussy blurred and hinted; where Wagner would have gathered a towering climax, Debussy shifted a color from one end of the gamut to the other." Thus, a new approach to instrumental color was the primary hallmark of the orchestral Impressionist. As progenitor of the new aesthetic, Debussy deliberately abandoned the sonoric impasto that characterized the scoring of Brahms and Bruckner, and consistently strove for translucent instrumental sound.

At the same time, Debussy explored prophetically the delicate gradations of timbre and shading available within the compass of a single instrument. Before the era of Impressionism, few orchestral composers had capitalized on the subtle blends of tonal character available in, for instance, the total range of the flute, which, timbrally speaking, is not the same instrument in its lowest and highest tessituras. After Debussy, the Expressionists—Schoenberg, Berg, Webern, and their disciples in turn—carried this concept to the ultimate limit. Eventually, left without further recourse in the normal timbres of conventional instruments and the human voice, many experimental composers of today have expanded the tonal gamut by entering the realms of electronically generated sound.

123

STYLE AND ORCHESTRATION

Debussy's abhorrence of thick textures has led occasionally to the misconception that his orchestration was exclusively amorphic and subdued. But the composer of *La Mer, Jeux* (1912), and *Le Martyre de Saint Sébastien* (1911) clearly appreciated a massive orchestral palette—when he required it. For the total gamut of expressive demands he had a unique command of the requisite technique to convey exactly what he wished to say. When Debussy wrote that in *Fêtes* (second of the three orchestral *Nocturnes*) he visualized "luminous dust participating in the universal rhythm," that magical effect became a musical possibility, not just fanciful speculation.

It is profitable, then, to examine Debussy's exact approach to the score page, where his remarkable technique began with a new view of the relationship of the orchestral choirs. The Classicists, the early Romantics, and—to a degree—the late Romanticists, regarded the orchestra as a nucleus of stringed instruments to which were added the complementary and contrasting sections of woodwinds, brasses, and percussion. Debussy's premise, on the other hand, was a basic core of woodwind instruments to which were adjoined strings, brasses, and percussion. The woodwinds were the focal point of his orchestral thought, and his primary melodists. But instead of conventional unison and octave doubling, he often adopted an innovative procedure that might be called *overlapping*. Single instruments, or single timbres, carried overlapping and intricately interwoven strands, usually against a background of muted string sonority, with delicate touches of harp, celesta, and subdued percussion.

This overlapping technique is clearly demonstrated, as one example, in a passage from *Jeux* (123), in which the oboe and English horn, doubled by bassoon, alternate a swirling melodic figure. And in *La Mer* the procedure is applied between the woodwinds as a group and the divided violins (Example 49).

From other available illustrations of Debussy's felicity with the winds we must note only two. The concluding pages from the second movement of *Ibéria* (*Les Parfums de la Nuit*) (124) show the composer's fondness for the velvety lower register of the flute, here in unusual combination with the nasal sweetness of a solo oboe an octave above. And, finally, the intriguing color value of soft, bubbling trills in the massed woodwind instruments is nowhere more cunningly employed than in *Jeux* (Example 50). The smudged harmonies and intentionally blurred melodic outlines of this music are the quintessence of the composer's orchestrational technique.

Debussy's brasses seldom appear in a conventional guise. His horns are more often muted than not, and even when open they are called upon

EXAMPLE 49
Claude Debussy: from *La Mer*, p. 62

EXAMPLE 50
Debussy: from *Jeux*, p. 42

Copyright 1914, Durand et Cie. Used by permission of the publisher. Elkan-Vogel, Inc. sole representative, United States.

126

to play very softly—as a harmonic unit, and as a solo voice (see Example 49). When the trumpet is utilized as a melodic voice, it is frequently placed in its middle-to-lower range rather than in the brilliant, and more conventional, upper register. Both the early symphonic suite, *Printemps* (1887) (125), and *Sirènes* (the final portion of the three *Nocturnes* [126]), demonstrate this technique.

The familiar stentorian voice of the trombone also has little place in the Debussyan modus operandi. Instead, muted trombones, usually closely grouped, may add a sinister harmonic texture to the orchestration, as in many passages in *La Mer*. The tuba, which appears in very few of the composer's scores, is almost invariably restricted to low pedal effects in place of, or in support of, the sarrusophone or double basses.

The full brass choir, seldom heard open-toned and *forte,* is a comparative rarity when it appears in the concluding pages of both *La Mer* (127) and the music to the mystery drama of D'Annunzio, *Le Martyre de Saint Sébastien* (128). More frequently, the instruments are used separately, in solo or as a harmonic voice, or in small family groups, almost as an extension of woodwind timbre.

It was Debussy who uncovered the full potential of the percussion instruments, using them not so much for dynamic intensity or rhythmic emphasis as for their delicate and distinctive color attributes. No better example can be cited than the single magical stroke of the triangle at the apex of the harp glissando in *La Mer* (129)—a sound like spray flung from the crest of a wave. It shows what an unforgettable effect can be derived from the simplest of means.

In all of Debussy's scores there are innumerable passages in which the suspended cymbal or bass drum sustain almost imperceptible rolls, played with soft-headed mallets, as underpinning to subtly shifting colors in the other sections. Notable examples of this practice may be seen in *Gigues* (1909) (130), in *Rondes de Printemps* (1908) (131), and in *La Mer* (132). In the opening measures of *Les Parfums de la Nuit* from *Ibéria* (133), the clouded ictus of a single low xylophone stroke, together with the faint trembling of tambourine and exotic color-wash of celesta, embodies the very essence of Debussy's subtle insight into the hitherto unsuspected potentialities of the percussive voices. This entire movement, as a matter of fact, is so definitive a synthesis of Impressionist elements that—even more than the more forward-looking *Jeux*—it may be regarded as the high point of Debussy's style.

The harp, confined by such composers as Berlioz, Wagner, and Liszt, to conventional arpeggios and chords, revealed its essential nobility in the hands of Debussy and Ravel. There are few orchestral pages of either composer that do not exhibit imaginative and supremely effective requisition of the instrument: the translucent sweep of chord glissandos; the tenuous, celestalike tones of harmonics (as in Examples 50 and 51); or the arpeggios cascading gently upwards in *La Mer* (Example 49) that simultaneously provide harmony, figuration, and rhythmic motion. Other devices peculiar to the harp, such as the guitar-like effect produced by playing low on the strings (*près de la table*) and the muffled, pizzicato-simulating device of *sons étouffés*, were likewise used by Debussy, and by Ravel in turn, with the greatest restraint and effectiveness.

Debussy's strings, though not the center of focus in his orchestral canvas, employed a vast range of coloristic devices. This is vividly illustrated in a passage from *Le Martyre de Saint Sébastien*, calling for no less than six different aspects of string technique (Example 51). First of all, mutes are employed for all the strings, including the double basses. Second, the first and second violins are divided into three parts each, a common enough practice in Impressionist scoring, but extended further here by reducing the players to only a few desks on each part. Then, two types of tremolo are used: bow tremolo at the point of the bow for the violins, and finger tremolo in the cellos and double basses. And, finally, artificial harmonics are given to the violas, which double the figure played tremolo in the violins. All in all, this one brief passage is a veritable textbook of Impressionist instrumentation for the strings.

A similar predilection for extensively divided strings is apparent in many other Debussy scores, particularly in *Nuages*, the first of the three *Nocturnes*. These multiple voices function solely for sonority's sake, and not for the quasi-polyphonic lines used by Wagner and Strauss. Characteristic, too, is Debussy's general avoidance of having his strings play in a "black and white" manner. Instead, they are often muted, and they may be directed to play over the fingerboard (*sur la touche*) in order to intensify the pale, wispy timbre demanded by the composer. The directive to play close to the instrument's bridge (*sur le chevalet*) is also frequently encountered in Debussy's scores, an effect that imparts a cold and glassy edge to the string tone. Routine sound-production is also obviated by often using the two forms of tremolo—bow and finger—and by various shades of pizzicato, such as the strummed chords, *quasi Guitara*, in *Ibéria* (Example 52), an effect that stems directly from Rimsky-Korsakov's earlier *Capriccio Espagnol* (See Example 37, p. 87).

In other Debussy works we might also note the unorthodox spacings and doublings of string thematic strands, which seldom continue for long in any one pattern but tend to be fragmentary and elusive. Combined with extensive divisi, frequent solo parts for each section leader (includ-

EXAMPLE 51
Debussy: from *Le Martyre de Saint Sébastien*, p. 64

129

EXAMPLE 52
Debussy: from *Ibéria*, p. 88

ing the double bass), and harmonics for all sections, they produce a net result that is a versicolored web of sound serving as a cushiony background to sharp slivers of woodwind or brass timbre, the whole edged with iridescent shimmering in the percussion, harps, and celesta.

This new conceptual usage of the strings has in the intervening years influenced many composers of widely different aesthetics and compositional methodologies, as will be evident in the discussions on later pages. Historically, however, it is now quite clear that pure Impressionism—for all the post-Debussy shakeup of nineteenth-century practices—was fundamentally a one-composer phenomenon. Though Debussy's compositional style and his revisualized approach to instrumentation spread from Poland to Brazil, they seldom penetrated orchestral scores devoid of other influences. Most certainly this is true in the magnificent output of Debussy's compatriot Maurice Ravel (1875–1937).

So sensitive was Ravel to color, exoticism, and the chiaroscuro of orchestral play that he has often been identified as a pure Impressionist; mixed with his feeling for Debussyan textures, however, was a striking empathy for Spanish folk rhythms and American jazz. More important, every Ravel composition embodies the preciseness and logic, the restraint and delicate formal balance of the instinctive Classicist. His most patently Impressionist works still preserve a clear outer form and a taut inner structure, employing Impressionist means for Classical ends. Ravel's harmonies are intuitively crisper than those favored by Debussy, his sonorities more pungent, his aural environment more dissonant. And added to all this is a fascinating terseness and a highly cultivated sense of irony.

Above all, Ravel must be considered the exponent par excellence of craftsmanship for its own sake, for his orchestration is virtuosic in every sense—though far removed from the stridencies of either Berlioz or Strauss. Its great demands on the technical abilities and musical insight of the performer are well illustrated in a typical passage from his apotheosis of the dance, *La Valse* (1920), shown in Example 53. But no orchestral composer ever knew—or wrote—more precisely what he could expect from each instrument; Ravel's expertise and patrician finesse is the very antithesis of the empirical fumblings of lesser instrumentators. As the French critic Émile Vuillermoz once said: "There are several ways of performing Debussy's music; but there is only one way of playing Ravel's." This never-failing realization of orchestrational cause and effect is the despair of the embryonic instrumentator—and his eternal inspiration.

So effortless was his orchestral virtuosity that Ravel could score an

EXAMPLE 53
Ravel: from *La Valse*, p. 128

early piano work (1912; the *Alborado de Gracioso* of 1905) as if the music were originally conceived in terms of the full symphony orchestra. His *Ma Mère l'Oye* (1915), on the other hand, is an equally dazzling transformation employing the utmost economy of instrumental resource. This orchestration of the composer's children's pieces for piano (1908) shows what can be accomplished with limited means, providing both composer and orchestrator are of Ravel's calibre.

At the opposite pole, insofar as resources are concerned, is Ravel's undisputed masterwork, the ballet *Daphnis et Chloé* (1909–1912). This perfect blending of musical invention and orchestral technique reaches the same creative heights the *Symphonie Fantastique* achieved some eighty years before, and which *Le Sacre du Printemps* would display at its riotous premiere one year later. Even the sensuous charms of the *Rapsodie Espagnole* (1907), the hypnotic virtuosity of *Boléro* (1928), and the sonoric combustibility of the two piano concertos (1930, 1931) pale before the radiance and luminosity of *Daphnis et Chloé*.

Ravel's instrumentation in this ballet is notable on many counts, among his innovations being the resurrection of the alto flute. This expressive woodwind had been used by Rimsky-Korsakov in several of his operas, and it was to show up later in Stravinsky's *Le Sacre du Printemps,* in Prokofiev's *Scythian Suite* of 1914, and in Gustave Holst's suite, *The Planets* (1916).[2] Ravel also called for *eoliphone* (wind machine) and *jeu de timbre* (a keyed glockenspiel). But the magic of his instrumentation does not lie in the special instruments he calls for but in his incredible command of these total resources.

To cite endless examples of Ravel's orchestrational arcanum in *Daphnis et Chloé* is a great temptation, but four references will suffice. One is the electrifying effect of a solo horn climbing three octaves from its lowest to highest F, *piano* and *decrescendo!* At this same moment the two flutes and alto flute have a gently undulating chordal passage in harmonics, which is followed by a delicate upward sweep of combined pizzicato arpeggiatos and arco glissandos in strings, and short bursts of harp glissandos (Example 54). Equally memorable is the beginning of the *Nocturne* (134) section, with its veiled bitonal harmonies in the muted strings, *sur la touche,* and distant-sounding solos of flute, muted horn, and clarinet. Later in this section the blaze of the full orchestra is dramatically followed by the menacing snarl of low brasses, the effect heightened by the whistling wind machine and string and harp glissandos (135). Finally, no one who has ever heard it can forget the churning sweep of the four trumpets in the final general dance—a moment of unique excitement (136).

EXAMPLE 54
Ravel: from *Daphnis et Chloé*, p. 55

THE IMPRESSIONIST ORCHESTRA

Any valid discussion of Ravel's orchestrational style must include his comic one-act opera, *L'Heure Espagnole* (1907), and the lyrical fantasy, *L'Enfant et les Sortilèges* (1920–25). Both works mirror his uncanny sense of orchestral color and exotic atmosphere. *L'Heure Espagnole,* famous for its opening "clock" music, is of further significance as Ravel's first work to employ full orchestra. Among the many individual touches in this early score is the use of string glissandi on the natural harmonic series.[3] Other string effects, such as arco and pizzicato glissandos, introduced in this Ravel opera, were later to be exploited as staples of Béla Bartók's orchestral palette.

The orchestration of *L'Enfant et les Sortilèges* is considerably leaner than that of the earlier opera, though Ravel required some rather elaborate resources for his setting of the Colette fairy tale. Of particular interest is the percussion apparatus demanded: in addition to the customary resources there are *crotales* (antique cymbals), cheese-grater, rattle, whip, wind machine, and *Luthéal* piano. (This last is a piano designed to make a lute-like tone. In the event that the instrument is not readily available, Ravel specifies that an ordinary upright piano with pieces of paper placed between the strings may be used.) The composer asks that the cheese-grater be played with a metal triangle stick, and that in case a wind machine should be unavailable the effect be approximated by rubbing a wire brush over the head of a bass drum.

Among other piquant effects in this fantastical score are the flute and piccolo harmonics—a familiar Ravel fingerprint—and the "sliding" flute played with exaggerated vibrato (137). For the opening and closing pages Ravel, with a sense of daring few composers have matched, wrote for the two oboes in their highest tessitura, coupled with the disembodied tone of a solo double-bass on natural harmonics. And the celebrated— once notorious—cat duet (138) is worthy of close scrutiny to observe how dexterously Ravel paralleled the vocal meowing with an instrumental counterpart.[4]

As wide-ranging a source-book on orchestration as *L'Enfant et les Sortilèges* is Ravel's extraordinary orchestral version (1922) of Modest Mussorgsky's *Pictures at an Exhibition* (1874). Most fortunately, the published study score includes the original piano part, making readily accessible the transformation of the original keyboard material. The young orchestrator—once past the elementary problems of range memorization, knowledge of basic instrumental techniques, and superficial acquaintance with standard orchestral combinations—could do no better by way of advanced study than to analyze in detail the remarkable scoring of this tour de force of orchestration. The technical mastery displayed by the orchestral version is no less Ravel's for the paradox that the stylistic ambience is wholly Russian.

Inevitably, there were carping critics to counterbalance the general admiration for Ravel's orchestrational skill. One sarcastic commentary appeared barely three years before his death: "Although Ravel's official biography does not mention it, I feel sure that at the age of three he swallowed a musical snuff-box, and at nine he must have been frightened by a bear. To both phenomena he offers repeated testimony: He is constantly tinkling high on the harps and celesta, or is growling low in the bassoons and double basses." [5]

Ravel himself, however, was his own most uncompromising critic. "In art," he once said, "nothing is left to chance." He once proposed to his inner circle of friends that he would like to compile a manual of orchestration that would cite what he considered to be errors of judgment in his scores. Unlike Rimsky-Korsakov, who quoted from his own works in the *Principles of Orchestration* mainly those passages that came off brilliantly, Ravel wished to show instances where he felt he had failed to achieve his purpose. This humility and assumption of total responsibility ought to be an object lesson to all composers and orchestrators.

Three Parisian contemporaries of Debussy and Ravel—Dukas, Roussel, and Schmitt—were, in certain of their compositions, closer than Ravel to the pure Impressionist prototype. Paul Dukas (1865–1935) is generally classified as an Impressionist on the basis of two well-known orchestral works. The opening and closing measures of the familiar *L'Apprenti Sorcier* (more accurately translated as "The Apprentice Sorcerer" than as "The Sorcerer's Apprentice") are Debussyan to an extreme, as is the overall atmosphere of the "poème dansé" *La Péri* of 1912. The pervasive Impressionistic technique of these two compositions was not, however, a feature of the few remaining works in Dukas's long but somewhat unproductive career. Neither his overture *Polyeucte* (1891) nor the *Symphonie en Ut Majeur* (1895–96) was in the least tinged with Debussyism; in fact, the heavy chromatic hand of Wagner was far more discernible here than any other outward influence. This Germanic leaning was even more pronounced in the composer's sole opera, *Ariane et Barbe-Bleue* (1907), an unsuccessful attempt to combine the worlds of Wagnerian drama and of French opera.

Albert Roussel (1869–1937), far more succinct and lean in his musical textures than either Dukas or Florent Schmitt (see below), infused Impressionism with a slightly mordant quality. Closest to the aesthetic and technique of Debussy are his three *Évocations* (1910–11) and certain aspects of the 1912 ballet, *Le Festin de l'Araignée* (Example 55). Less manifestly Impressionist, though full of sensuous orchestral

EXAMPLE 55
Albert Roussel: from *Le Festin de l'Araignée*, p. 30

137

textures, is the brilliant ballet score, *Bacchus et Ariane* (1930), which has always enjoyed great popularity in the form of two concert suites.

The remainder of Roussel's considerable output disavowed Impressionism in favor of the growing trend toward Neoclassicism. The four symphonies (1904–1935), the *Suite en Fa* (1926), and the Piano Concerto of 1927 all point the way to the new musical precepts then being laid down by Stravinsky.

Both Roussel and Florent Schmitt (1870–1958) visited the Orient, and both came under the spell of exotic Eastern cultures. Both translated their impressions into their own music, using many Debussyan techniques —Roussel in the aforementioned *Évocations* and in his opera-ballet based on Hindu lore, *Padmâvatî* (1914–1918), Schmitt in his orchestral *La Tragedie de Salomé* (1907). Debussy himself, of course, had already created the precedent for this type of compositional assimilation; he metamorphosed his personal reactions to Balinese and Javanese music in a number of works, notably in several of the *Préludes* for piano.

Schmitt's *Salomé* was not based on the Oscar Wilde drama, as was Strauss's opera, but on a text by the French poet Robert d'Humières, and its Oriental exoticism was enhanced by music of great vividness and tonal luxuriance. Melodically and harmonically it is far closer to Strauss than to Impressionism, but in its orchestration it is an accurate reflection of the Debussyan style.

Included among Schmitt's other Impressionist-oriented scores are the symphonic episodes, *Antoine et Cléopâtre* (1919–20), the tone-poems *Mirages* (1920–21) and *Rêves* (1913–15), and the three orchestral suites that the composer termed "illustrations" of pages from Gustave Flaubert's *Salammbô* (1925). The Impressionist elements are outweighed, however, by the many Straussian passages; as with much of the music of the Englishman Arnold Bax (see below), for example, the admixture in Schmitt is more convincing in theory than in practice.

Even today the music of many French composers bears the impress of Debussyism, despite universal awareness of the limitations of the technique. Impressionism appears—if sporadically—in certain of the works of the older composers (Ibert, Milhaud, and Poulenc, for example) and in some of the scores of the middle generation (Françaix, Jolivet, Martinet, Messiaen, and—to a more limited extent—Pierre Boulez). All of these composers, regardless of basic differences in their concepts of orchestrational style, have at one time or another approached the symphonic and operatic orchestra from a quasi-Impressionist viewpoint. At these moments each has sought to shape the orchestra into an instrument of infinite color gradation, of subtle sonority, in a constantly shifting complex of tonal and rhythmic elements in which, as Mallarmé said, "there is nothing but illusion."

Of the three elder statesmen of contemporary French music, Jacques Ibert (1890–1962) has most frequently exhibited obvious aspects of Impressionism. Such works as *Persée et Andromède* (1921), the popular *Escales* of 1922 (see Example 56), and *Féerique* (1925) rely heavily on the general orchestral procedures of Debussy's *La Mer* and *Ibéria. Escales* in particular reveals a stylistic affinity with *Ibéria,* and it is notably analogous in spirit to Ravel's *Rapsodie Espagnole.* Ibert was haunted by the atmosphere of Valencia; Ravel, by all of Spain. In addition, both composers injected exotic Arabic elements into their music—Ibert, a native dance in his evocation of Tunis; Ravel, the *malagueña* of Moorish origin. But even more significant than these extraneous elements were the analogous orchestrational methods that shaped this unparalleled trilogy-by-three-composers.

Ibert's *Suite Symphonique* (1932) achieved a definite Impressionist aura with an ensemble of very modest proportions. *The Mosque of Paris* (139) section of this six-movement composition (based on the composer's incidental music for Jules Romains's play *Donongo*) is, incidentally, an amusing musical steal from the central movement of *Escales* (140). Composers of the twentieth century evidently crib from their own works as shamelessly as did the Baroque masters.

In his ballet *Diane de Poitiers* (1934), Ibert called for an oboe d'amore and a basset horn (alto clarinet) along with the standard complement of woodwind instruments. Though these two instruments are normally considered obsolete, having dropped out of the orchestral picture after the Baroque and Classical periods, they were consciously deployed in Ibert's score for their very special tone-quality. In view of Saint-Saëns' bugle in *La Jeunesse d'Hercule,* Bizet's alto saxophone in the *L'Arlésienne* music, Ravel's *Luthéal* piano in *L'Enfant et les Sortilèges*— not to mention the contrabass clarinet in Arnold Schoenberg's *Five Pieces for Orchestra*—Ibert's requirement cannot be considered exceptional.

Darius Milhaud (1892–1974) has a catalogue of music the vastness of which impedes an accurate assessment of his cardinal aesthetic. One can find traces of Impressionist technique in the two *Suites Symphoniques* (1913; 1919), and in the charming *Concertino de Printemps* (1934) for violin and small orchestra. But the technique, instead of appearing in undiluted form, only takes its place among more pronounced Neoclassical and Neoromantic elements. The amalgam thus produced is sometimes more, sometimes less, successful—which is, of course, characteristic of Milhaud's entire oeuvre.

EXAMPLE 56
Jacques Ibert: from *Escales*, p. 34

His preoccupation with percussion instruments, first demonstrated in his early—and masterful—*Les Choéphores* (1915–16), is easily visible in all his later scores, whatever their stylistic bent. But Milhaud has always honored their traditional rhythmic functions more than their coloristic capabilities. This point in itself would seem to remove much of his writing from the realm of Impressionism, which, as we have seen, concentrates on the more nebulous aspects of percussive sound rather than its clangorous propensities.

Vocal lyricism and harmonic sweetness—these are the paramount stylistic factors that shaped the music of Francis Poulenc (1899–1963). A slim margin of Debussyan Impressionism does appear in brief sections of *Les Animaux Modèles* (1949), for instance, in the ballet *Les Biches* (1923), and in the cantata *Sechéresses* (1952). In the deliciously wicked little opera *Les Mamelles de Tirésias* (1940), however, his effortless technique is employed in unmerciful mimicry of familiar and hackneyed Debussyisms, as well as of the perfumed operatic styles of Jules Massenet and Puccini.

There is little of the style and texture of Debussy's kind of Impressionism in Poulenc's other works, including the operas *Dialogues des Carmelites* (1955) and *La Voix Humaine* (1958), of the *Gloria* of 1961 for chorus and orchestra. An obvious addiction to Neoclassical procedures, instead, colors the orchestral forces in these compositions, and the *Gloria* in particular is full of Stravinskyan touches, but without any sacrifice of Poulenc's penchant for ingratiating harmony and melodic charm.

The music of Olivier Messiaen (1908–   ), said John Cage, ". . . like a changeable silk, shows now aspects of the Orient, now of the medieval world, and now of twentieth-century impressionism." This amalgamated style, so accurately described by Cage, Messiaen attributes in his *Technique de mon langage musical* to the primary influences on his expression of Debussy (specifically *Pelléas et Mélisande*), Hindu ragas, Gregorian liturgy (the composer is an ardent Catholic), and bird songs. One might suppose that the infusion of such diverse inspirations would result in exoticism of a very pronounced sort. The exoticism, however, is so heavily conditioned by an Impressionist viewpoint that it becomes absorbed into a Debussyan musical fabric.

In his symphonic poem *Les Offrandes Oubliées* (1930) and the religious meditation *L'Ascension* (1932) Messiaen's aesthetic is close to that of Debussy's *Le Martyre de Saint Sébastien*. The *Trois Petites Liturgies de la Présense Divine* (1944) expresses religious mysticism through a later expansion of this style, and employs Balinese sonorities. Here the orchestration, basically prismatic in aural effect, relies on the gamelan device of heterophony—an endless variation of small melodic cells (usually bird-calls) and highly charged harmonies. In using this technique Messiaen shares a viewpoint with that other musical mystic, Alexander Scriabin, whose music also relied heavily on harmonic voluptuousness and melodic fragmentation. From a purely technical standpoint. Messiaen's score demonstrates how cunningly he understands the color potential of vibraphone and *ondes* Martenot, two newcomers to the orchestra of the twentieth century. Their strong, almost obtrusive, timbres contribute greatly to the sensuous qualities of the instrumentation.

The ultimate application of Messiaen's ornithological obsession took place in *Oiseaux Exotiques* (1955), a work for piano solo and a small wind-and-percussion orchestra, which consists of fourteen minutes of unrelieved twittering (Example 57). According to the composer the music is "highly colored; it contains all the colors of the rainbow . . ." But even this work, in spite of its extravagant single-mindedness, is more palatable to the sensitive listener than the 1948 *Turangalila-Symphonie,* in which the many compositional influences are stacked one upon the other until the whole edifice threatens to disintegrate and bury the hapless listener under its ruins.

To some musicians, more tolerant than critical, Messiaen's music creates an analogy in sound to the visual spirit of George Rouault's art. Others, repelled to some degree by the sticky religiosity of the composer's aesthetic, are more inclined to agree with the critic Roland-Manuel: "Music has been too hard-put to rid itself of the obscure nonsense of art-religion and the contrivance of the exotically picturesque for us to wax enthusiastic over finding these elements reunited in the work of a composer who has such a large and devoted band of disciples."

Among the other middle-generation French composers, Jean-Louis Martinet (1916–) demonstrated certain Impressionist inclinations in his three-part symphonic poem *Orphée* (1945) and the symphonic sketches, *La Trilogie des Prométhées* (1947). Interestingly enough, the latter work also contains a passage (141) that might well have come directly from the final pages of Stravinsky's *Le Sacre du Printemps* (142).

André Jolivet (1905–1975), a colorist par excellence, often elicits from his orchestra the same sensuous appeal to be found in Debussy and Ravel. The concluding pages of his unusual *Concerto pour Ondes Martenot* (1952) are very close to pure Impressionism, and obvious Debussyisms also mark the style of the 1950 Piano Concerto and the *Cinq Danses Rituelles* (1939). Philosophically, however, Jolivet is inclined to a wider compositional field. "Music," he says, "must be a sonorous manifestation in direct relation to the universal cosmic system." With influences as

EXAMPLE 57
Olivier Messiaen: from *Oiseaux Exotiques*, p. 69

★ Ici, les 2 cors doivent s'entendre à travers tout l'orchestre : ce sont eux qui donnent la couleur "majeure".

U.E. 13007 LW

diverse as Berg, Messiaen, and Varèse bearing upon his writing, Jolivet's music has more in it of the primitive than the sophisticated; more of die-hard Romantic programmaticism than of Impressionist vagueness.

Properly speaking, the music of France's outstanding avant-gardist, Pierre Boulez (1926–   ), combines the sonoric values of Impressionism with the formalism of the Expressionist aesthetic. Though he professes to abhor sensuous timbre for its own sake, it was inevitable that—as Messiaen's most illustrious pupil—Boulez should inherit his mentor's passion for gamelan-like sounds. A marked kinship with Debussy is revealed by his subtle differentiation of instrumental timbres in his few orchestral scores—*La Visage Nuptial* for solo voices, chorus, and orchestra (1952), *Le Soleil des Eaux* for soloists, men's chorus, and orchestra (1948–58), *Poésie pour Pouvoir* (1958) for two orchestras, *Pli selon Pli* for voice and orchestra (1962), and *Figures-Doubles-Prismes* for orchestra alone (1968). In spite of the remarkable luminosity in all of Boulez's instrumental works, by no stretch of the imagination can he be said to be an imitator of the Debussyan style. His is a far more intellectual concept, and the rigorous discipline of his compositional technique precludes any undiluted transference of Impressionist elements to his own music.

Among the English composers influenced by Impressionism, Frederick Delius (1862–1934) was the first to adopt some of the more obvious techniques. A refined and sensitive poet rather than an epic bard, Delius was more drawn to sensuous sound than to dramatic exposition. His love of color for its own sake, both in his harmonies and in his orchestration, was comparable to that of Debussy and, in turn, Scriabin. Yet in such representative scores as the 1902 *Appalachia* the Impressionist poetic environment was overshadowed by Wagnerian chromaticism. This stylistic paradox was further obfuscated on occasion by a quasi-folklorist approach that would seem to place Delius squarely in the camp of English nationalist composers. But the musical language of *Brigg Fair* (1907), *On Hearing the First Cuckoo in Spring* (1912), the *North Country Sketches* (1914), and the opera *A Village Romeo and Juliet* (1909), was far more German and Parisian than British, despite the frequent use of folklike material.

Like the German Romantics, Delius favored a large orchestra as a rule and, generally speaking, used it in much the same manner. His woodwinds are often grouped in fours, and certain of his works call for six horns: *Paris: The Song of a Great City* (1899), for instance, and *Brigg Fair* and *A Dance Rhapsody No. 1,* both dating from 1908. The latter work also requires a bass oboe in addition to the English horn, with an important solo for this rare member of the orchestra. Like Debussy, Delius also preferred the sarrusophone to the more standard contrabassoon, possibly because of its more refined timbre. Also worthy of comment, though not an instrumental effect, is an innovation in *Eventyr* (1917) **(143)**, which called for a single, explosive shout from twenty male voices stationed backstage.

In large part, the rambling structure and amorphous nature of most of Delius's compositions may be explained in part by his impatience with conventional techniques and compositional disciplines. Certainly the rather turgid meanderings of simple folk-material in *Appalachia* and the heavy-handed dance rhythms in *Paris* (despite its colorful orchestration) are a long way from the pristine ambience of Impressionism. And the composer's most mature works, the choral-orchestral *Sea Drift* (1903) and the 1905 *Mass of Life* (inordinately long and weighted down with Wagnerisms) , carry none of the obvious hallmarks of Debussyan style. Delius, therefore, must be considered as occupying a peripheral position among the composers drawn to Impressionism.

The influence of Debussy on Arnold Bax (1883–1953) was even shallower than on Delius. In such works as his *The Garden of Fand* (1916) —a somewhat Celtic version of *La Mer*—and the two 1917 tone-poems, *November Woods* and *Tintagel,* we are conscious of a curious kind of Straussian Romanticism overlaying orchestration of a typically Debussyan shimmer and evanescence. But the banality and general heaviness of much of Bax's music mitigates the effectiveness of any Impressionist elements present.

Bax's more notable contemporaries, Gustav Holst and Vaughan Williams, also came somewhat under the spell of Debussy's art. Both, however, eventually renounced Impressionism for a more personal and nationalistic mode of expression. Ralph Vaughan Williams (1872–1958) , it is true, retained more conspicuously the Impressionist manner of orchestration in his later work, even after he had turned to his native folk material for inspiration. Nonetheless, Impressionism was never a dominating influence in his style, even when it was consciously utilized, as in the *Sinfonia Antartica* (1952), creating a tonal landscape of great beauty.

Traces of Debussyism are, however, more clearly indicated in the early *Norfolk Rhapsody No. 1* (1906) , in certain parts of the Symphony No. 1 (the "Sea"; 1914) , and in almost the whole of the *Pastoral Symphony* (No. 3; 1922) . Indeed, the latter work might be considered an Anglicized—if rather extended—version of *L'Après-midi d'un Faune.* But as these works just mentioned constitute only a small part of the composer's total output, it would not be accurate to say that Vaughan Williams was deeply influenced by the tenets of French Impressionism.

Gustav Holst (1874–1934) on occasion combined the techniques of the Impressionist with a strong exotic reflection of his intense interest in Hindu culture. He composed two operas based on episodes from Hindu literature, *Sita* (1906) and *Sāvitri* (1908), and an orchestral suite of North African influence, *Beni Mora* (1910). His best-known work, the suite *The Planets* (1914–16), is sporadically Impressionist in its elaborate orchestration, despite its complexity and the huge array of instruments demanded. These include the alto flute (*not* the bass flute—see footnote 2), bass oboe, two tubas, six kettledrums, and organ. The flavoring of Debussyan instrumentation is most pronounced in the movements entitled *Venus, Saturn,* and *Neptune;* the remaining sections owe perhaps more to Edward Elgar's mode of scoring than to that of Debussy or Ravel.

Only the final pages of Holst's *Egdon Heath* (1928) may be said to contain traces of Impressionism, and no discernible elements are to be found in such typically "English" works as *A Somerset Rhapsody* (1910) or the ballet score, *The Perfect Fool* (1923). The syntax of Debussyism was notably transitory in Holst's music, and it was not long before he asserted his national heritage in such compositions as the *St. Paul's Suite* for string orchestra (1921), the *Fugal Concerto* (1923), and the undeniably English opera, *At the Boar's Head* (1925). Both Holst and Vaughan Williams, then, were occasional, rather than confirmed, Impressionists—an observation that applies to quite a few of the composers discussed in this chapter.

The work of the Russian composer Alexander Scriabin (1872–1915), although he was not an Impressionist per se, must be considered within the context of this orchestral style because in his later works his procedures often paralleled those initiated by Debussy. The basis of his orchestration, however, was compounded of Wagner with overtones of both Strauss and Mahler. The large orchestral forces, the massive and apocalyptic sonorities, the chromatic convolutions of melody and harmony, all stemmed directly from the precepts of the post-Wagnerian Romantics. Yet at the same time the kaleidoscopic play of color and light and the sensuous delight in varying sound-textures seem to vividly follow the Impressionist syntax of Debussy.

From Wagner, Scriabin learned the principle of "harmonic counterpoint"—the creation of secondary melodic strands that in reality are only figurations of a basic chordal progression. But allied to the methods of the French Impressionists were his propensity for sequential repetitions, his frequent ostinato figures, and a highly fragmentary delineation of melodic line. All these aspects of Scriabin's commingled style are amply illustrated on almost any page from *Prométhée: Le Poème du Feu* (1909–1910) or from the more frequently performed *Le Poème de l'Extase*

(1907–1908); the score page shown from the latter (Example 58) is especially Debussyan in feeling.

A logical extension of Scriabin's penchant for tone color was his conviction that an unmistakable affinity existed between musical tones and the visible color spectrum. His grandiloquent *Prométhée* is dedicated to this thesis; the score prescribes the use of a "color organ" to mirror aural sensations with visual effects. Scriabin's projected *Mysterium,* which he did not live to complete, would have attempted a synthesis of all the sensory perceptions save one—sound, sight, smell, and touch—omitting only taste.

To ensure the exact projection of his emotional concepts, Scriabin laced his scores with elaborate subjective directions—in French rather than Russian or the conventional Italian. Although French was both a diplomatic and a "social" language among the Russian aristocracy, Scriabin was alone among the contemporary Russian composers in selecting its graphic sensuality for musical directives. These highly personalized designations of instrumental quality or explicit mood (*avec une volupté de plus en plus extatique*), reminiscent of Mahler's practice, are almost as important to an effective realization of Scriabin's intentions as the notes themselves. Certainly, they account in large measure for the supercharged, almost drunkenly emotional atmosphere of much of Scriabin's music in performance.

No technical details, however, can contribute as much to our understanding of Scriabin as does a knowledge of his religious prepossessions. As with Messiaen, a spiritual and artistic synthesis became the overriding motivation of his later creative life, shaping a musical style of highly charged harmonies, evanescent rhythms, and mystical coloration. And like Wagner's cosmos, Scriabin's world was the product of incredible egomania; unlike the great German master, however, Scriabin exerted very little lasting influence on the music of the twentieth century, despite a current revival of interest in his work.

Several other non-French composers, widely separated both geographically and stylistically, owed orchestral Impressionism a substantial debt; among them were Respighi, Falla, Szymanowski, Villa-Lobos, and Griffes. Ottorino Respighi (1879–1936), most notable of the Italian Neoimpressionists, studied for some time with Rimsky-Korsakov, but his instrumentation shows a greater influence of the precepts and technique of "Claude de France." The French sense of delicate coloration, expanding Respighi's innate Italian lyricism, resulted in the immensely effective tonal and orchestral language of the trilogy: *The Fountains of Rome* (1917), *The Pines of Rome* (1924), and *Roman Festivals* (1929).

EXAMPLE 58
Alexander Scriabin: from *Le Poème de L'Extase,* p. 36

THE IMPRESSIONIST ORCHESTRA

If in the third work Respighi was frequently vulgar and tedious, he was, conversely, a sensitive tone-poet in the other two. *The Pines of the Janiculum* movement, in particular, is one of the most atmospheric nocturnal evocations in the modern repertoire (Example 59). This same movement also opened a new era in orchestrational concept and practice with the use of a phonograph recording to reproduce the nightingale's actual song (144)—an effect basic to his programmatic intentions.

It goes without saying that the composer was castigated for this imaginative stroke, but today, with modern composers freely using the tape recorder as an instrument in the orchestra, Respighi's musical "crime" seems mild indeed. Novel instrumental effects, whether extracurricular or not, usually draw fire from purists who suspect all extramusical material, regardless of its motivation. Beethoven's storm in the "Pastoral" Symphony; Strauss's bleating sheep in *Don Quixote;* Honegger's locomotive in *Pacific 231*—each in turn has brought down the wrath and critical scorn of the unenlightened. But if such special devices contribute artistically to the overall effectiveness of the composer's music, who has the right to forbid their use?

Respighi also successfully applied his Italianate Impressionism to the symphonic impressions, *Church Windows* (1926–27), the *Brazilian Impressions* of 1927, and the *Botticelli Triptych* of the same year. Though he failed to achieve the perfect synthesis of musical content and masterful orchestration that distinguished the scores of Debussy and Ravel, Respighi's ear for color-nuance and his high sensitivity to delicate textures and sonorous masses have guaranteed that his music has not fallen into disfavor with concert audiences.

Manuel de Falla (1876–1946) was Spain's outstanding composer in the first half of the twentieth century, and in content and spirit his music is purely Andalusian. But in his orchestration Falla was often Impressionist—fastidious and succinct like Ravel, yet indebted to Debussy in nearly every one of his major works. In point of fact, the first of Falla's four *Homenajes* ("Homages") for orchestra bears the inscription: *Pour le Tombeau de Debussy* (1920).

Falla's Impressionism probably reached its high point in the two popular ballets, *El Amor Brujo* (1915) and *El Sombrero de Tres Picos* (1919), and in the non-concerto composition for piano and orchestra, *Noches en los Jardines de España* (1915–16). Indisputably Spanish in their musical materials, the three works are indelibly French in their orchestral techniques; the quotation from the latter score (Example 60) might easily have come from Debussy's pen. Even the "Spanishness" of this music was an element common to the two composers, as Falla testi-

EXAMPLE 59
Ottorino Respighi: from *The Pines of Rome*, p. 62–63

EXAMPLE 60
Manuel de Falla: from *Noches en los Jardines de España*, p. 21

fied by his approbation of the authenticity of Debussy's *Ibéria* and of those piano *Préludes* based on Spanish subjects. Thus the exchange of influences was mutually beneficial to both composers, Falla acquiring from France, Debussy from Spain.

Following the writing of his ballets, Falla abandoned the essentially limiting style of Impressionism for a more concise and intellectual Neoclassicism. The new austerity was evident in his *Master Pedro's Puppet Show* (1919) and the *Harpsichord Concerto* (1923–26), and continued into his final work, the uncompleted oratorio *La Atlantida* (1927–) — if there are any remnants of Debussyism in its orchestration, they are successfully camouflaged.

Karol Szymanowski (1882–1937) was—like Bax, Respighi, and Falla (in his younger days) —a Romantic Impressionist. His early music was Straussian in its dramatic flavor; the composer then turned to the late harmonic style of Scriabin, coupled with the barbaric splendor of Rimsky-Korsakov's instrumentation in shaping his evolving expression. Szymanowski's fascination with Debussy's methods, which followed his immersion in Russian methodology, is vividly reflected in the first Violin Concerto (1917), the neoprimitive ballet *Harnasie* (1926), and the *Symphonie Concertante* for piano and orchestra (1932).

In these works Szymanowski metamorphosed French Impressionist methods to suit his individual requirements, in which a natural feeling for Polish folk elements was never far from the surface. As with all those who avidly embraced the Debussyan aesthetic, "it was no longer the full chords, the massed sonorities of the gigantic orchestra that interested the Impressionist composer, but the soft, strange, muted sonorities, produced not by reducing the enormous orchestral apparatus of the post-Wagner period, but by handling it with the utmost delicacy." [6]

The notably eclectic Brazilian composer, Heitor Villa-Lobos (1881–1960), retained elements of Impressionism in nearly all of his major works for orchestra. Even his Neoclassical essays, in particular the series *Bachianas Brasileiras,* show an unmistakable Impressionism in their orchestrational procedures. A relatively mild exposition of the composer's Impressionist leanings is represented by the clever *The Little Train of the Caipira* (1930), one of the movements of *Bachianas Brasileiras No. 2.* Much closer to the undiluted Debussyan atmosphere are many pages in the exotic-primitive tone-poem *Uirapurú* (1917), a score that contains the best and the worst of Villa-Lobos.

Many of the composer's series of *Chôros* (those that employ orchestral forces) and such indigenously inspired compositions as *Danses Africaines* (1916), *Amazonas* (1917), and *Erosion: The Origin of the Ama-*

zon (1950) demonstrate the same mixed marriage of the exotic-primitive with pure Debussyism. If love of color, feeling for atmosphere, and nebulous expression constitute the paramount ethos of the instinctive Impressionist, then Villa-Lobos surely qualifies for inclusion in the pantheon of Impressionist composers.

The United States has not produced any notable Impressionists other than Charles Tomlinson Griffes (1884–1920) and Charles Martin Loeffler (1861–1935). The Alsatian-born Loeffler, however, hardly qualifies as an American composer, despite his long association with the Boston musical scene. Nor, in the light of his rather characterless echoing of Debussyisms, was he anything but a transitory Impressionist.

Griffes was our only major composer to become a thoroughgoing Impressionist; of this we are sure despite the pitifully small legacy of orchestral works for any evaluation of his instrumental procedures. There is but one major score for large orchestra, the remarkable tone-poem based on Coleridge's haunting mystical vision, *The Pleasure Dome of Kubla Khan* (1920). There is one minor score, the charming *Poem* for flute and orchestra, with its attenuated Orientalism. And, finally, there is Griffes's own orchestration of his often-played piano piece, *The White Peacock* (1915). Yet in just these three works appears an abundance of the devices that thread the fabric of Debussy's music: gliding, muted string sonorities, delicate and faintly exotic touches of soft percussion, sensuous harp glissandi, fugacious, swirling woodwind figures, and blurred swashes of brass color.

In *The Pleasure Dome of Kubla Khan*, Griffes created not only the *pièce de résistance* of American Impressionism but also an exemplar of Impressionism's most fastidious world-wide standards. Taking as his inspiration the lines that describe the "stately . . . the sunny pleasure-dome with caves of ice . . .," the composer let his imagination have free rein with a subject pregnant with Impressionist possibilities, and the resulting score is an almost perfect blend of barbarism and sensuality (Example 61).

To the lengthy list of early twentieth-century composers for whom Impressionism was a major influence we can add a wide gamut, from Puccini to Stravinsky, who were fleetingly touched at certain stages in their careers by some aspect of the Debussyan style.

Puccini, whose theatrical sense was essentially foreign to musical understatement, embodied, however, Impressionist parallel harmonies in *The Girl of the Golden West* (1907–1910), and there are faint touches of Debussy here and there in *Turandot*. Certain Debussyan elements may be found in Zoltán Kodály's *Háry János Suite* (1926), in both the

EXAMPLE 61
Charles Tomlinson Griffes: from *The Pleasure Dome of Kubla Khan*, p. 23

STYLE AND ORCHESTRATION

Marosszék and *Galanta Dances* (1930; 1933), and in the "Peacock" Variations of 1939. Ernest Bloch, though essentially a Romantic, recalls Impressionist orchestral technique in portions of the *Evocations* (1937), in a random page or two from *Schelomo* (1936), and at times in the *Three Jewish Poems* (1918).

In the highly individual catalogue of Béla Bartók's music there are occasional references to Impressionism, although the aesthetic was never a dominating one in the composer's oeuvre. These traces may be found in the First Suite for orchestra (1905), in the first of the *Deux Images* (1910), and throughout the opera *Bluebeard's Castle* (1911). Also, the *Elegia* movement of Bartók's last major orchestral score, the *Concerto for Orchestra* (1943), reflects a Debussyan ambience.

And in Igor Stravinsky's immense output we find the imprint of Impressionist orchestration on the early scherzo, *Fireworks* (1908), on *The Firebird* ballet score of 1910, on parts of *Petrouchka* (1911), on the opening measures of the second part of *Le Sacre du Printemps* (1913), and on the exotic *Chant du Rossignol,* dating from 1917.

This is not to imply that any of these composers slavishly imitated Debussy, even briefly, or that they methodically utilized the techniques of French Impressionism in their treatment of the orchestra. Each composer in turn transmuted the style, however fleetingly it was appropriated, to his own individual use; each in time relinquished Impressionism as his personal convictions ripened and his artistic expression matured. Pure Impressionism, then, is largely a subliminal influence in the orchestrational styles of the early- to mid-twentieth-century composer. Amalgamated, however, with aspects of the Romanticism from which it once rebelled, it has produced one of the most powerful of contemporary instrumentational techniques—Expressionism. This in its turn will be explored in the chapter to follow.

The foregoing survey should have made clear both the musical attitudes and the specific orchestral techniques of the authentic Impressionist. To review quickly the characteristic sound environment created by these composers and the means by which they achieved it: in the scores of Debussy and his closest disciples the woodwinds were the cardinal instrumental voices, taking precedence even over the strings in outlining melody. They were used in their non-brilliant registers as a rule, the softer qualities and lower tessituras being favored. All of the woodwind members functioned as melodists, with the exception of the bass clarinet and contrabassoon (or sarrusophone). When employed in a harmonic context, the instruments were usually grouped homogeneously, with a smooth blend of sonority as the prime criterion.

THE IMPRESSIONIST ORCHESTRA

The brass choir in Impressionist scoring was seldom employed for conventional dynamic strength, and was (with the exception of the tuba) in fact muted more often than not. The horns frequently appeared as part of a woodwind sonority; a solo horn was often used melodically, but rarely were all four instruments doubled. Trumpets were almost invariably muted, especially when used in solo, and seldom duplicated each other's parts. Customarily, the trombones and tuba acted as harmonic rather than as melodic members of the section. Though not so frequently muted as horns and trumpets, they were usually required to play at the lower end of the dynamic scale.

Among the percussion instruments utilized by the Impressionists, those of soft and delicate quality were the most favored. The suspended cymbal, gong, bass drum—all were in constant requisition, but played upon by soft mallets as a rule. The timpani were usually used more for their muffled and coloristic contributions than for their dynamic potential. The higher-pitched percussion (glockenspiel, xylophone, and triangle, together with celesta and harps) were basic to the Impressionist palette; again, it was the element of timbre, of radiant or diaphanous color, that was exploited in orchestral usage.

Finally, the strings appeared more frequently as sonoric elements in the orchestral whole than as traditional melodists. They were almost constantly divided into many voices, used as components of vertical sonorities rather than for horizontal thematic strands. Their unique color properties—achieved by using mutes and by playing tremolo, *sur la touche, au chevalet,* and on harmonics—were requisitioned by the Impressionist composers almost more than their normal and unadorned manner of performance.

As an entity, the Impressionist orchestra was made to gleam with a luminous and shimmering iridescence. Now glassy, now faintly clouded, now crystalline, now huskily blurred and veiled—the play of instrumental colors was like quicksilver. The listener was caught up in a wash of varicolored sounds, and enmeshed in a web of kaleidoscopic transparency; the senses were soothed, the imagination quickened, the emotions warmly caressed. Though not to everyone's taste, and possessing liabilities as well as indisputable strengths, the orchestra of the Impressionists remains one of the glories of modern music.

Notes

1. A parallel transformation occurred simultaneously in both painting and literature, and French composers quickly appropriated the term from their painter

compatriots. Debussy himself was annoyed by the term, which he felt was misused by musicians. Correct or not, however, "Impressionism" is the convenient generic term that has persisted.

2. Holst, along with many other English composers and writers on music (Adam Carse, for one) persisted in calling the alto flute a *bass* flute. These are actually two different instruments, with dissimilar ranges and transpositions. The alto flute in G, not the C bass flute, is to be used in Holst's work.

3. Igor Stravinsky usually receives the credit for having invented this striking color effect in his ballet *The Firebird* (1910), but this universally admired—and subsequently extensively imitated—effect first appeared in the 1907 score of Ravel's opera.

4. A comparison of this passage with another feline portrait—Tchaikovsky's *Pas de Caractère* in the *Sleeping Beauty* ballet score (1889)—may reveal why Tchaikovsky's cats are mundane, while Ravel's are endowed with magic.

5. Robinson, Edward. "The Naïve Ravel," *American Mercury* 26, no. 101, May 1932.

6. Lang, Paul Henry. *Music in Western Civilization* (New York: Norton, 1941).

6

The Expressionist Orchestra

It is well to remember that art . . . reflects the attitudes of the individuals that produce it.

Roger Sessions,
The Musical Experience

Orchestral Expressionism, like orchestral Impressionism, was a logical twentieth-century sequel to the Romantic instrumentation of the late nineteenth century. There was, however, no sudden surgical excision of all that had gone overripe in Romanticism; both Impressionist and Expressionist composers created their new sound and tonal values on the base of the ensemble they inherited. But in time, because of the extraordinary influence of Anton Webern, even the symphonic ensemble became attenuated, and a chamber-music concept came to permeate the musical expression of the period.

Both new "isms" borrowed their names from the world of painting and had, as well, many emotional parallels with movements in contemporary literature. Both utilized new compositional techniques that lie outside the province of this volume except where they are inextricable from the composer's manipulation of instruments. And both styles set a premium on orchestral color.

STYLE AND ORCHESTRATION

On their intentions in the use of color, however, the two paths diverged. Impressionism shaped its artistic expression through sensual reactions to a universe consciously perceived; Expressionism, on the other hand, voiced the fears, desires, and tensions arising in the subconscious mind. The more external aspect of Impressionism thus found its antipode in the internal, psychological approach of Expressionism. "Whether in painting, poetry, or music," Paul Collaer observes, "French impressionism consists of the penetration of the outside world; the subtle play of nuances is captured through abstraction from the particular. The artist stands face to face with nature without thinking of himself. . . . The German [Expressionist] also opens himself to nature, but he chooses only those harmonies that suit his psychic state of the moment" (*A History of Modern Music*).

This raison d'être of Expressionism—so lucid in retrospect—sounds simple because it is stated *a posteriori*. The style of orchestrational Expressionism evolved, of course, from the life-work of Schoenberg, Berg, and Webern toward a total synthesis that is still functional among certain late twentieth-century composers.

Arnold Schoenberg (1874–1951) began his compositional career strongly in the tradition of Wagner, Strauss, and Mahler. The early string sextet, *Verklärte Nacht* (1899), was a direct product of the late Romantic wave. In the symphonic field the composer—who was so predisposed by the massive instrumentational styles of *Tristan und Isolde*, of *Tod und Verklärung*, and of Mahler's "Resurrection" Symphony (No. 2)—at first fabricated his own complex and overburdened scores: the *Gurre-Lieder* of 1901 and the symphonic poem *Pelleas und Melisande* (1902).

On the basis of these early works, Schoenberg might reasonably have been expected to continue the creation of overblown Romantic music. Instead, he realized (even if his contemporaries did not) that he must extricate himself from the impasse toward which the style was leading him. As systematically as Debussy had renounced the tepid French Romanticism exemplified by Massenet and Gounod, so Schoenberg mutated his Romantic harmonies into atonalism and then into dodecaphonism, and his decadent instrumentational style into a new concept of delineation.

It is significant that Schoenberg's first radical departures from his early manner took place in his first string quartet (1904) and in the *Kammersymphonie*, Op. 9 (1906). As Aaron Copland has pointed out, the choice of medium foreshadowed "the use of the orchestra as if it were a large ensemble of chamber-music players, with the notion of giving each tone in the harmonic complex its solo color. . . ." This chamber-music

160

element was to permeate far beyond the work of Schoenberg and his followers into the music of the later Neoclassicists, and on to the avant-garde of today. In the intervening decades it infiltrated the instrumental approach of Webern's *Five Pieces for Orchestra* (1913), Stravinsky's *Renard* (1917) and *Ragtime* (1918), Milhaud's *Le Boeuf sur le Toit* (1919), Copland's *Music for the Theatre* (1925), Hindemith's *Kammermusik* series (1925–27), Stockhausen's *Kontrapunkte* (1953) —and a host of other equally strange bedfellows.

The apogee of Schoenberg's chamber-music approach was his 1912 *Pierrot Lunaire*. This revolutionary work calls for soprano voice, employed largely in *Sprechstimme,* accompanied by five solo instruments—an ensemble with many parallels to Stravinsky's 1918 *L'Histoire du Soldat* for narrator and seven instrumentalists. Though the actual resources differ, each composer selected a tonal gamut essentially covering the various orchestral sections. Stravinsky's winds are clarinet and bassoon; Schoenberg's are flute (alternating with piccolo) and clarinet (alternating with bass clarinet). For strings, Stravinsky chose violin and double bass; Schoenberg, violin (alternating with viola) and cello. *L'Histoire du Soldat* uses one percussionist; *Pierrot Lunaire,* the piano.

The orchestral works of Schoenberg, however, contain little of the chamber-music ambience. In the remarkable *Five Pieces for Orchestra* (1909; revised 1949), Wagnerian and Straussian mannerisms still exist, but what leaps decades ahead is the revelation of the composer's unique sense of *Klangfarbe,* or tone color. The third piece—*Changing Colors* (later entitled *Summer Morning on a Lake*)—has color agglomerations that go far beyond even the virtuoso Impressionist palette in Debussy's *Jeux,* and there are pointillist elements prophetic of Webern's much-imitated later style (Example 62).

To achieve this new relationship of timbre, the conductor's score gives explicit directions to avoid accented entrances, thus forcing aural concentration on the changes in instrumental color alone. The overwhelming success of the scoring is described by one of Schoenberg's disciples, Erwin Stein: "The subtly changing colors on a lake's lightly rippled surface are painted by changing orchestral timbres of a five-part chord. The instruments sustaining the chord give way to others of a slightly different color. . . . In this way a climax of changing colors is built up, which quickly recedes until the original pace returns. Delicate short passages of other instruments occasionally shade the colors of the quasi-sustained chord—shadows of passing birds, as it were. . . . A very delicate balance has to be maintained; and only a sensitive mind [allied] with acute ears will discern and enjoy the interplay of softly shaded tone colors" (*Orpheus in New Guises*).

161

EXAMPLE 62
Arnold Schoenberg: from *Five Pieces for Orchestra*, p. 33

THE EXPRESSIONIST ORCHESTRA

Nothing of Schoenberg's after this first full-scale Expressionist score went beyond the orchestrational elements outlined in the last of the *Five Pieces for Orchestra*. Here rich instrumental lines are conditioned by a great and constant variety of expression, rather than by the impulse to experiment with exotic color for its own sake. Just as the human voice constantly alters its inflection, even in casual speech, so the best of Schoenberg's orchestration endlessly varies the color of the melodic strands of his musical fabric.

Following the writing of this pioneering work, the composer embodied the same highly charged orchestrational elements in two large concert works for voice and orchestra: the monodrama *Erwartung* (1909) and *Die glückliche Hand* (1913), a drama based on the composer's own libretto. As well as demonstrating an immense skill in orchestral deployment, *Erwartung* probably represents the quintessence of Schoenberg's Expressionism; one must approach this score in the same frame of mind required for the viewing of the paintings of Edvard Munch.

Later compositions—the *Variations for Orchestra* (1928), the *Accompaniment to a Cinema Scene* (1930), the concertos for violin (1936) and for piano (1942), and the uncompleted opera, *Moses und Aaron* (1932–)—are cut from more or less the same orchestral cloth. Elements of innovation appear largely in the compositional, rather than instrumentational, aspects of these works, and the development of Schoenberg's dodecaphonic technique is not the province of this particular study. Moreover, many young composers today might well be reminded that Schoenberg's fundamental aim was simply to compose better and better music, developing both his instrumentation and his compositional style only to this end. "The question of the twelve tones," he said, "is my own affair." Intransigent defenders of serial music—and of Neoclassicism, of electronic music, of aleatoric procedures, or what you will—might do well to put first, as did Arnold Schoenberg, the caliber of the music itself.

Schoenberg's disciple Anton Webern (1884–1945) now looms as one of the most pervasive influences in contemporary musical thought. His compositions are few—until 1961 thought to be only thirty-one, of which only six were for full orchestra or enlarged chamber ensemble.[1] What is more, his expressive gamut was extremely circumscribed, especially when compared to the totality of Bartók's, Stravinsky's, or Hindemith's work. In the face of this attenuation, Webern's work might logically have constituted an artistic cul-de-sac. Yet today, those composers inclined to Expressionist persuasion may respect Schoenberg and Berg, but they are more inclined to write in the Webern manner.

STYLE AND ORCHESTRATION

Like his two compatriots, Webern combined the psychological implications of Expressionism with a coloristic approach, but he went far beyond them to achieve an almost total atomization of musical means. The scores of his later works for orchestra—the *Five Pieces for Orchestra* (1913), the *Symphonie* (1928), the *Concerto* (for nine instruments; 1934), and the *Variations* (1940)—demonstrate even to the eye a musical conception light-years away from the late Romantic era. A new aural epoch is evident in the pointillistic leaps from instrument to instrument on a single thematic line, the visual bareness of the page, the restricted instrumental resources, and the calculated moments of complete silence (Example 63).

Webern's fragmentized color, the orchestrational counterpart of a compositional technique that fragmented harmony, melody, counterpoint, and rhythm, will be further treated in the general summary of this chapter. The visual bareness and the restricted instrumental resources are products of a search for the ultimate transparency—the conscious reduction of musical materials to a skeletal minimum. There are quite literally no dense tonal masses in Webern's later works; after the Op. 1 *Passacaglia* there are not even any tutti passages.

One can hardly call Webern's method "orchestration" in the accepted sense of that word; though his scores call for more instruments than would be found in the average chamber ensemble, there are seldom enough for his "orchestra" to fill out even the Classical patterns of the eighteenth century. Since only one or two pitches are usually called for at one time, only one or two instruments play at any given moment. When instruments do unite, it is rarely in combinations of more than two or three. Unison and octave doublings are almost nonexistent; rarefaction takes the place of weightiness, and compression substitutes for tonal expansion and development.

Often the Webern manner includes composed silences. This "no-sound," very different from the simple absence of sound, may be considered a logical extension of Webern's distillation process. It is equally the result of his strong sense that (while painting and sculpture are arts existing in two or three dimensions) music exists solely in the fourth dimension—time. Our impression of a piece of music is the sum of sounds (or sound-groups) heard singly between silences of varying durations. Yet Webern was the first composer in musical history to compose these silences deliberately in the framework of time, or "continuum of temporality," in which all music exists.

Color fragmentation, transparency, silence—all suggest the ultimate in distillation; in Philip Hale's words, "dabs of pale colors expressive of the inaudible." In method and result they are the antithesis of the

164

EXAMPLE 63
Anton Webern: from *Symphonie,* p. 14

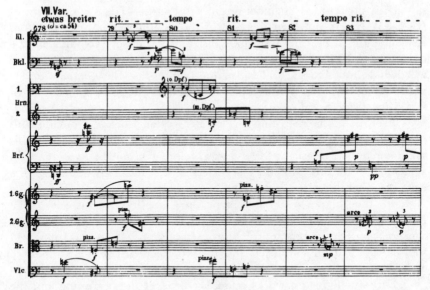

gigantic orchestral apparatus of Schoenberg's *Gurre-Lieder* or *Pelleas und Melisande.* No music of the past ever attempted so to compress the basic stuff of musical composition—so ruthlessly to strip away all apparent nonessentials, and so starkly to reduce the expressive elements of music.

Yet between the great art of this patent simplicity and the responsiveness of the average listener lies, unfortunately, a chasm difficult to bridge. Beyond even the challenge of the composer's serial technique are the other demands on the listener's participation; the impact of isolated sounds framed by silences, for instance, depends upon the hearer's receiving those sounds in his mind, turning them over, reflecting on, and then associating them. Few listeners are inclined to be so strenuously involved in the creative process; hence Webern's fragmented forms appeal largely to the circle of initiates.

With the music of Alban Berg (1885–1935), the most lyric of the Middle European Expressionists, a more immediate appreciative response is possible. As great a master of form and material as either Schoenberg or Webern, as imbued as they with the revolutionary spirit, Berg possessed an inner glow and spirituality very different from the aloofness that often stands between the listener and the music of Webern and Schoenberg.

Still, these three composers had more than the twelve-tone technique

165

in common. Like the others, Berg was an adroit manipulator, when it suited his purpose, of chamber-music procedures. His *Kammerkonzert* (1923–25) is very much in the vein of the *Kammersymphonie, Op. 9* of Schoenberg, and uses the restrained instrumentation of Webern's mature orchestral works. Considering the limitations of its resources—nine woodwinds, four brasses, and violin and piano solo—the *Kammerkonzert* produces an amazing gamut of sound, and must be reckoned one of Berg's most significant creations.

Even in his larger compositions Berg often isolated from the full orchestra a core group of varied instruments, at one moment pitting this small ensemble against the large one, at another using the two groups in agreement. In this way Berg transferred the intimate qualities of a chamber work from the concert hall to the dramatic stage. But unlike Webern, the composer did not favor these qualities exclusively. The *Drei Orchesterstücke* (1914), the *Fünf Orchesterlieder* (1912) and the concert aria for soprano and orchestra, *Der Wein* (1929), and the 1935 Violin Concerto all employed the full complement of the symphonic orchestra.

Berg's two greatest works came, however, at the beginning and the end of his mature career. The opera *Wozzeck* (1914–21) must surely be accounted Berg's masterwork; in power, original conception, and orchestration it is rivaled by few twentieth-century compositions. Like Stravinsky's *Le Sacre du Printemps,* Berg's score is the consummate expression of a personal style, and in each item of instrumentation appears the inevitable guise of a unique creative idea.

Certainly no music of our century is more atmospheric and more emotionally compelling than *Wozzeck*. The ultimate in Expressionist orchestration, without doubt, frames the chilling moment when the demented Wozzeck wades into the pond to recover the knife he used to kill Marie. As he sinks into the water, the orchestra plays a steadily rising and overlapping passage of densely constructed chords, like slowly widening ripples on the surface of the water (Example 64). In itself, this device is obvious; in effect, it is shattering. It is eloquent proof of Berg's artistry that at the moment of listening we are unaware of the technical methods used to achieve this effect, just as during the progress of the entire opera we are unconscious that Berg has set this traumatic drama in a series of strict musical forms.

On close examination, however, it is clear that Berg consciously developed many characteristic technical devices for musical ends. Both *Wozzeck* (145) and his last opera, *Lulu* (1935–) (146), demonstrate one of his most individual procedures: his chords are frequently constructed in a horizontal rather than a vertical manner, with the component members of the sonority entering one by one rather than attacking their notes simultaneously. Usually these staggered entrances are assigned to non-homogeneous instrumental timbres; occasionally the chord notes have similar or closely allied colors.

For his unfinished *Lulu,* Berg added alto saxophone, vibraphone, and piano to an otherwise traditional late nineteenth-century ensemble. The leering voice of the saxophone, memorialized in Stravinsky's aphorism as a "juvenile delinquent personality," is singularly appropriate to the decadent atmosphere of this score. Here, too, the vibraphone part is especially apt, if one can disassociate its oily and tremulous sound from the routine treatment it receives by TV and film composers.

Other notable aspects of the *Lulu* orchestration have been cited by René Leibowitz: "The orchestra—smaller and simpler than that of *Wozzeck*—clearly serves to maintain a 'unity of sonority.' Certain personages of the drama are partially characterized by an instrumental tone-color which persists throughout the work; changes in dynamic and orchestral character completely differentiate passages of similar thematic material; the distinction between the accompanying functions and the dominating functions is more sharply drawn here than in *Wozzeck;* the principal law appears to be the direct and plastic expression of the vocal parts, which Berg underlines with an orchestration of exemplary transparency" (*Schoenberg and His School*).

The aesthetic canons of Schoenberg, of Webern, and of Berg persist to some degree in the scores of many composers of Expressionist persuasion. For example, the Americans George Perle, Wallingford Riegger, George Rochberg, Roger Sessions, Ben Weber, and Stefan Wolpe; the Austrian-American Ernst Křenek; the Italian Luigi Dallapiccola; the Japanese Yoritsune Matsudaira and Toshiro Mayuzumi—all have orchestrated in a style directly linked to the procedures of one or another of the Viennese triumvirate. Occasionally, too, composers not notably Expressionist in their aesthetic adopt aspects of this orchestrational technique. Elliott Carter's 1955 *Variations for Orchestra,* for instance, gives every external indication of following the instrumentational style of Berg and Schoenberg; the composer's musical concept, however, is more a fusion of Neoclassical and Neoromantic elements than outright Expressionism (Example 65).

Considered as a whole, the orchestrational technique of the Expressionist composer exhibits a fascinating crossbreeding of Late Romantic and Impressionist elements. From the Romantic orchestra Schoenberg and Berg inherited, and never totally abandoned, a penchant

EXAMPLE 64
Alban Berg: from *Wozzeck* (Act 3, Scene 4) pp. 458–59

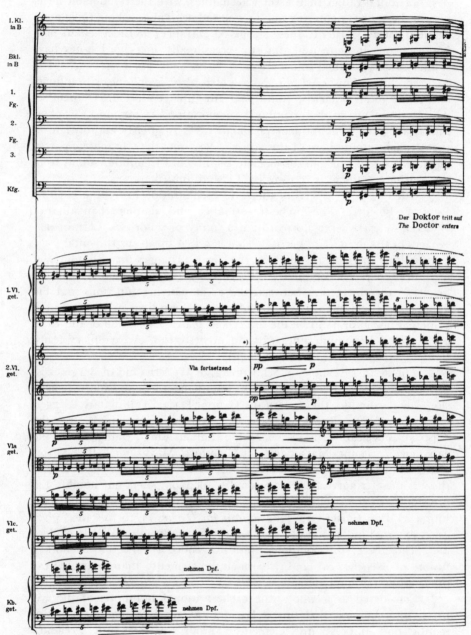

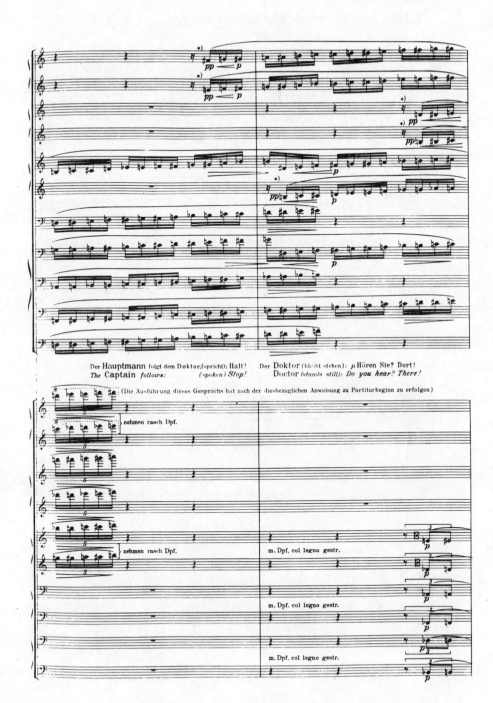

Der **Hauptmann** folgt dem Doktor,(spricht): Halt!   Der **Doktor** (bleibt stehen): *p* Hören Sie? Dort!
The **Captain** *follows:*   *(spoken) Stop!*   Doctor *(stands still): Do you hear? There!*

(Die Ausführung dieses Gesprächs hat nach der diesbezüglichen Anweisung zu Partiturbeginn zu erfolgen)

EXAMPLE 65
Elliott Carter: from *Variations for Orchestra,* p. 45

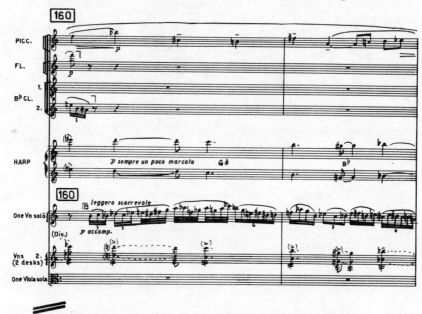

for large instrumental forces; Webern's link in this respect is merely the commonly shared empathy for emotional intensity. From Impressionism the Expressionists appropriated the sensuousness and the flair for color and dynamic nuance characteristic of Debussy and Ravel. To these elements they added the extreme extension of the techniques of fragmentation; in their hands aural pointillism became one of the most significant innovations of twentieth-century instrumentation.[2]

"If Impressionism is an integrating movement," Nicolas Slonimsky observes, "then Expressionism is a differentiating movement. Thus in instrumentation Expressionism individualizes each instrument, bringing to light the subtlest points of orchestral color." This process begins with the transformation of the thematic line by scattering the notes freely, from high to low to middle range, from instrument to instrument. Melodic elements are thus powdered into a fine grain of isolated single pitches, instead of being carried through on the level of a single orchestral voice.

Chords, which Romantics and Impressionists both outlined in an essentially homogeneous manner, the Expressionists present in deliberately mixed timbres. Each note of many of their vertical sonorities, in fact, is given to a different-colored instrument. In this way individualization of instruments replaces conventional doublings, groupings by choir, or the affinitive massing of orchestral combinations. (See Example 63, p. 165 for instance.) This pointillist chord technique often obscures the formal structure of the music, acting as a camouflage behind which structural details may pass unnoticed.

As the primary emphasis is on the linear in dodecaphonic scores, the twelve-tone composer will subdivide the string section to obtain contrapuntal outlines instead of to build rich chords. He will thus create separate strands of thematic voices rather than pure coloristic effects, such as we might sometimes find in Bartók. Yet here, again, the approach stems from the basic fragmentation technique, for color is employed not so much to establish a line as to diversify it. The orchestrator here seldom carries through the horizontal strand in a single instrument; after a measure or two—even a beat or two—one instrument will be replaced by another timbre, which in turn is superseded by yet another instrumental hue.

The tonal variety thus produced is frequently bewildering. Unity of design and kinship of color give way to infinite diversity; cohesion is sacrificed to abstraction, or to such fractured images as one sees in some paintings of the Cubists. But too constant a change of color can become almost as monotonous as unyielding sameness. Neither Schoenberg, Webern, nor their many proponents, have irrefutably proved that the art of music benefits from such extreme measures. In reacting against the excesses of certain late Romantic practices, the Expressionists have produced only a different kind of creative intemperance—just as they have but substituted one set of elaborate compositional rules for another in abandoning tonality and harmonic progression to follow the dictates of the twelve-tone technique.

One must admire, however, the ingenuity with which the Expressionist orchestrator exploits the almost infinite color permutations available in the strings alone. The scoring of Schoenberg, Berg, and Webern offers an almost endless kaleidoscope of string timbral nuances; these composers have made every known manner of striking, plucking, or bowing the strings a standard procedure in their music. And not even the Impressionists with their refined sense of color more fully exploited one of the most sonically intriguing of all string devices—the series of overtones (natural and artificial harmonics), with all their arcane hieroglyphics of notation.[3]

String mutes in Expressionist orchestration are a standard, rather than exceptional, practice. Often they are required for only a single note or two, or for a few measures; frequently muted and unmuted instruments are combined in a passage, producing two colors simultaneously. Other string devices constantly requisitioned by the Expressionists range from the edgy glassiness of pitches played on or very close to the instrument's bridge to the breathless, rather fluty quality of notes played high over the fingerboard.

Finally, the Expressionists make innovational use of the device of col legno, the technique by which the string is struck with the wood (back) of the bow rather than stroked with the customary bowhair. In these highly individualized applications, the bow is drawn across the strings in the manner of ordinary bowing (col legno tratto), or it is bounced on the string in rhythmic fashion (col legno battuto), in the same manner as saltando bowing. This latter effect, essentially percussive in nature, is analogous to short, dry strokes on the xylophone, woodblocks, or bongos.[4]

Pure woodwind timbre, so integral a part of the Neoclassical orchestral concept (discussed in detail in the next chapter), has almost no place in the orchestration of Schoenberg or of the many peripheral Expressionists. It exists, of course, in Webern's scores, but appears so fleetingly in his fragmented lines that there is little perception of individual timbre. Moreover, Webern does not use the woodwind instruments so much for their own special qualities as for their function as heterogeneous voices added to his instrumental resources.

THE EXPRESSIONIST ORCHESTRA

When the Expressionists' woodwinds are entrusted with anything like an extended melodic line, they are apt to double one another at the unison or, more rarely, at the octave. In the choice of such combinations they are likely to be unconventional by previous instrumentational standards. Flute and bassoon, oboe and bass clarinet, piccolo and clarinet—these are but a few of the unexpected unison couplings favored by Schoenberg and his followers. The most prevalent composite woodwind color is that of flute, oboe, and clarinet in unison. The admixture of the three voices results in no one familiar sound, but a new tone with elements of all three timbres.

Further to diversify the available timbres, Expressionists exploit every variation of woodwind and brass tonal quality made possible by altered articulation, phrasing, or tone production. Foremost among the available devices is flutter-tonguing; its peculiar, fuzzy effect, like a whirring machine-noise, admirably complements the nasal sound of the strings playing sul ponticello.

Glissandi in both the woodwinds and brasses, commonly utilized by the Expressionists, are an inheritance from Strauss and Mahler. But it was Schoenberg who first required the trombones to employ this striking effect in symphonic music, thereby adding to the science of instrumentation one more device of dubious potential. If we give Franz Liszt rueful thanks for the ubiquitous harp glissando, we must credit Schoenberg with this other orchestral effect subsequently painfully misused by many a hack arranger and third-rate composer.

Mutes, in Expressionist scoring, are called for as extensively in the brasses as in the strings. It is significant that in only five out of Webern's fourteen works calling for brass instruments do they play unmuted, and then only for very brief passages. Muting the brass, however, was no longer thought of exclusively as a softening agent in Expressionist orchestral textures; mutes were frequently used in *forte* passages to produce a very piercing and plangent timbre. Because the muted sound of brasses is by now as commonplace as the natural, open tone of the instruments, it can be logically contended that another staple color has been added to the orchestra, symphonic or operatic. Since mutes radically change the basic brass tone, the modern composer therefore has on call two different kinds of horns, trumpets, trombones, and tuba.[5]

The percussion, of all the instruments of the orchestra, are the least utilized by the early Expressionists (Berg's *Wozzeck* and *Lulu,* and Webern's *Six Pieces for Orchestra* are notable exceptions). Perhaps the intense emphasis on color devices indigenous to the melodic instruments, in addition to the fundamental linear approach of the dodecaphonists,

173

obviated the conventional usage of the percussion section. Whatever the reason, even Schoenberg used the timpani, and the other percussion, sparingly.

When the composer of Expressionist persuasion does employ percussion voices he usually chooses almost exclusively melodic or colorative components; seldom are his percussive instruments purely rhythmic factors in his orchestration, as we would find in the scores of Stravinsky and Bartók, for instance. This means that the keyed instruments—xylophone, glockenspiel, and vibraphone—are the most favored, being capable of contributing both melodic elements and distinctive color flashes to the orchestration. It is significant that of the nonpitched percussion, the low-voiced instruments—bass drum, tam-tam, gong—are most commonly used. The brightness of the triangle, the dry crispness of the snare drum, the related rustle of the tambourine, the click of the castanets—these are seldom compatible with the sonorous images of the Expressionist orchestrators.

The harp was only occasionally employed by Schoenberg (notably in the *Five Pieces for Orchestra* and in the *Variations*) and not, it must be stated, in a particularly grateful manner. He wrote many four- and five-note chords for the instrument in the higher register, marked by the composer: "harmonics if possible" (147). Anyone conversant with harp technique knows that this is a physical impossibility; only the left hand can play two to four harmonics simultaneously (the right hand only one), and those only on adjacent strings.

Even granting a very flexible pedal technique to the orchestral harpists of our day, the pedal changes required in both Schoenberg's and Berg's harp parts are excessive, even when not downright impossible (as in numerous passages in *Wozzeck* [148], for example). The chromaticism of Webern's harp writing is more easily navigated, thanks to his pointillistic manner; the harpist has more time to negotiate the pedal changes, as the instrument is required to play only scattered notes, separated by ample rests.[6]

Of the keyboard instruments, the celesta is the most often utilized; the piano appears only occasionally and the harpsichord rarely as orchestrational adjuncts. Perhaps the fact that German-built celestas are equipped with an extra lower octave accounts for the great prominence the instrument enjoys in such scores as Schoenberg's *Five Pieces for Orchestra*, Webern's *Variations for Orchestra*, and Berg's two operas. Besides, its tenuous and rather throaty sound in the bottom register admirably complements and enhances the flute-like tones of string harmonics. These two timbres, when used together or in imitation of each

174

other, are ideal for the withdrawn, veiled effect of much of the Expressionist's sonoric world.

To this gamut of conventional instruments unconventionally treated, the Expressionist added such untraditional instruments as the mandolin and guitar. While Mahler had previously scored for both instruments, Schoenberg and Webern gave them a unique Expressionist guise, soloistic and fragmentary. Instances of their utilization may be found in Schoenberg's *Serenade* (1923) and in Webern's *Five Pieces for Orchestra, Zwei Lieder* (1928), *Das Augenlicht* of 1935, and the Cantata No. 1 (1939). Oddly enough, Berg did not make use of either instrument in any of his works. (It should cause no surprise to the seasoned musical observer to find the mandolin showing up in several of Stravinsky's dodecaphonic scores.) Unconventional as is the handling of mandolin and guitar in the Webern and Schoenberg works, their lute-like tones are eminently fitted to the aphoristic expression of these scores.

One final, and very significant, hallmark of the Expressionist's orchestrational technique is the use of extreme registers in all pitched instruments. Schoenbergian instrumentators draw extensively on the peculiar sound of the trombone pedal notes, a particularly nasty effect that must be heard to be believed. Berg's score to *Wozzeck* (149) brings to light a striking example of contra-D for the bass trombone, a note that is considered excessively low even for the tuba. Horns and trumpets are likewise frequently used at the bottom and at the very top of their compass, and woodwinds and strings are also exploited at their ultimate limits of pitch. The strained and unnatural effect of low instruments placed in a high tessitura and, conversely, of high-pitched instruments playing at the bottom of their compass imparts extreme tension to orchestral sound and texture, a tension wholly in tune with the emotional ambience of the Expressionist score.

It must not be supposed, nevertheless, that all of these orchestral devices are the exclusive province of Expressionist orchestrators. They were extensively used by the Impressionists, although in different contexts; they exist as well in Neoromantic compositions, though on a more infrequent basis, and they are sometimes found in the orchestral works of the Neoclassicists. And needless to say, they appear with great frequency in the orchestrations of the avant-garde. But the exploitation of these timbral devices has a highly specialized function in Expressionist instrumentation. Extreme registers, mutes, flutter-tonguing, col legno, and all other devices basic to Expressionist orchestration, serve—indeed exist— as substitutes for the traditional guideposts abandoned by their compositional philosophy.

STYLE AND ORCHESTRATION

The basic premise may be stated in this way: if a composer's exposition and development of his generic material no longer depends upon the former anchors of tonality, harmonic progression, and classical structures to give his music coherence, then he must rely upon other factors to achieve the same end. For the Expressionist this meant an intensified application of tonal color and instrumental timbre, a wide dynamic gamut, fastidiously indicated nuances and articulations, and individual note-texture. These new elements—or more accurately, old elements newly used—create the required logic, cohesiveness, and final artistic justification of the music. When this thesis is thoroughly understood, the apparent mysteries of Expressionist orchestration do not seem quite so enigmatic.

The precepts of Expressionism, including its instrumental investiture, assuredly have enduring validity. Midway between the values of Impressionism and Romanticism, Expressionism has created many exciting and provocative instrumental sonorities. The Expressionist has, in addition, canonized in the science of instrumentation the special technique of pointillism—an expressive device now firmly entrenched in the styles of many widely diversified composers, from the "far right" to the "far left." If the concepts of total serialization and unmitigated atonality should in time become casualties in the constant ebb and flow of stylistic doctrines (and there are already signs that this is indeed happening), Expressionist orchestration surely has the substance to survive.

Notes

1. In 1961 several additional early Webern manuscripts were rediscovered by the musicologist Hans Moldenhauer. These included a ballad for voice and orchestra, *Siegfrieds Schwert* (1903), and a full-scale, typically post-Wagnerian orchestra work, *Im Sommerwind* (1904), subtitled *Idylle fur grosses Orchester (nach einer Dichtung Bruno Willes)*.

2. Orchestral fragmentation, or pointillism, is somewhat allied to a medieval vocal technique known as *hocket,* in which the different voices alternately sang and rested. It began to emerge as an instrumentational procedure only in the late scores of Debussy, and was named after the palette pointillism of Seurat and the divided colors of Monet.

3. The fastidious orchestrator should make certain that his notation is precise and unambiguous, for many pitches in the stringed instruments can be produced as harmonics in several different ways, each with a subtly different tone-color. Such precision need not, however, duplicate the redundancy of Schoenberg's notation for harmonics: the fingered fundamental, plus the diamond symbol for the player's fourth finger on the string node, plus the tiny o sign, plus the actual pitch that will sound, plus the German directive *flageolet!*

4. The extensive use of col legno in contemporary orchestration has induced

some players to cheat a bit by executing this device with the side of the bow—half hair and half wood. While this protects the varnish on their valuable bows, the effect produced is not the same as the sound of the string struck with the bow-stick alone. Considering the frequency and importance of this timbral device, string players should sensibly possess two bows—a good one for normal requirements and an inexpensive one specifically for col legno requisition. After all, if brass players today have to supply themselves with at least three or four different mute types, and percussion players with any number of variegated sticks and mallets, why should not the string player equip himself for contrasting arco and col legno performance?

5. Today's heavy reliance on muted sound, both in brass and stringed instruments, has created something of an unforeseen problem in concert performance. The listener can be so fascinated with the constant putting on and taking off of mutes that he hardly hears the music. Whether such visual distraction makes the listener more— or less—receptive to the musical ideas can, of course, be seriously argued.

6. This use of the harp as a melodic rather than as a chordal, or purely decorative, instrument provides one area at least in which the Expressionists and Stravinsky (in his Neoclassical and later dodecaphonic periods) have a point of orchestrational contact.

7

The Neoclassical Orchestra

Orchestration has become a source of enjoyment independent of the music . . . . We have had enough of this orchestral dappling and these thick sonorities; one is tired of being saturated with timbres, and wants no more of all this overfeeding. . . ."

Igor Stravinsky,
An Autobiography

In a universe where every weight has its equipoise, it was inevitable that orchestras of more modest size and resources should make a comeback in the twentieth century. The Impressionist first manipulated the late Romantic orchestra in such a way as to transform its sound-atmosphere without greatly reducing its size. But the Expressionists, also starting from the premise of the large symphonic ensemble, inclined more and more to chamber-sized groups, culminating in the attrition that marked the Webern style.

Economic factors after World War I also diverted musical creativity into the pattern of the reduced orchestral body. In the widespread poverty of the post-war era the immense orchestras of *Gurre-Lieder, Daphnis et Chloé,* and *Le Sacre du Printemps* were financially prohibitive; resources once bestowed on orchestral support had to be diverted to more immediate needs. Symphonic and operatic orchestras, to keep alive at all, fell back on the basic nucleus of the Classical period, with woodwind and brass instruments in pairs, modest percussion, and a reduced body of strings. And by the time of partial economic recovery, when money considerations had begun to recede in importance, many composers were writing for this stripped-down orchestra by preference.

The obvious aural advantages of a restricted orchestral ensemble, achieving ingratiating transparency by an austere economy of means, were in every case an appealing reaction against overblown Romanticism and against the vagueness and architectural looseness of Impressionism as well. Most especially, those composers inclined to trenchant expression gravitated by choice in the direction of brief forms, concise exposition, and smaller ensembles. They brought to their music the meticulous approach of the essayist (the Classicist) in preference to the bold manner of the dramatist (the Romanticist). And so began a significant cleavage of musical expression that even today influences all new music that is not patently experimental.

The first major Neoclassical work was Serge Prokofiev's 1917 Symphony No. 1, "Classical", and the composer's familiar notes for this deservedly popular score are a prophetic statement of the aims of the authentic Neoclassicist: "It seemed to me that if Haydn had lived into this century, he would have retained his own style of writing while absorbing certain things from newer music. I wanted to write the kind of symphony that would have such a style." Prokofiev did not, however —despite the immense success of this refreshing essay in eighteenth-century elegance and restraint—write any further works of this character.

The 1923 *Octet* of Igor Stravinsky (1882–1971), on the other hand, initiated the indomitable force of his Neoclassic period, and signified a complete reshaping of his musical style. Nonetheless, the composer's renunciation of the orchestral splendors of *The Firebird, Petrouchka,* and *Le Sacre du Printemps* in favor of an austere palette was no sudden volte-face. An orderly evolution from these highly colored sonorities in the Rimsky-Korsakov tradition had already become evident in several transitional works using drastically reduced resources. *L'Histoire du Soldat* and *Ragtime* appeared in 1918, *Pulcinella* and the *Symphonies of Wind Instruments* in 1920, and the two *Suites* for small orchestra from 1921 to 1926. In these compositions a new concept of diatonic writing (pandiatonicism), logical linearity, and a rather impersonal application of instrumental color already foreshadowed a Neoclassical expression.

In the *Octet* (scored for flute, clarinet, two bassoons, two trumpets, and two trombones) the transformation was clearly and finally outlined. Here the composer let natural contrast in instrumental volume define the musical architecture objectively, without resort to other dynamics than *forte* and *piano*. A taut, cool, and transparent kind of orchestration with pure timbres—as during the early Classical period—took precedence over massed heterogeneous effects. The glowing aura of the ballets had given way to a lean, hard, and clipped manner that became both Stravinsky's personal hallmark and the musical signature of the international school of Neoclassical expression.

The immediate shock-impact of the new style was equaled only by the composer's salty pronunciamento: "I consider that music is by its very nature essentially powerless to express anything at all." We are not meant, of course, to take this polemic at face value. But what Stravinsky indubitably wished to convey is a terse summation of the intellectual character of his Neoclassicism. For him—as for his numerous adherents who rebelled against Romanticism, Impressionism, and Expressionism with almost equal intensity—tonal architecture was at this period the equivalent of emotional content. Indeed, one can say that these Neoclassicists rejected passion per se for the abstract fervor of ideas; their creative postulate was thus to "seduce by reasoned argument." Manner and style, then, take precedence over feeling; the way musical ideas are stated and developed assumes a greater importance than the generic ideas themselves.

It is natural that some listeners were baffled, even repelled, by Stravinsky's "new sound" in the *Concerto for Piano and Winds* (1924), *Oedipus Rex* (1927), the ballet *Le Baiser de la Fée* of 1928, and the *Dumbarton Oaks Concerto* (1938). Yet however thin and restrained the new orchestral style might seem, the composer's approach to tone color was still virtuosic. "His stunning effects," Aaron Copland explains, "are mostly arrived at through a careful choice of unhackneyed instrumental combinations, balanced and juxtaposed in such a way as to keep their separate tonal values clearly distinguishable in the orchestral mass. . . . Once again, as with Mahler, the orchestra plays 'without pedal.' It produced a hard, crackling sonority unlike anything to be heard in previous music" (*Our New Music*).

In this Neoclassical concept of timbre, Stravinsky detached his ensemble sound from the aura of Impressionist and Romantic deployment, and especially from the Expressionist's conception of *Klangfarben*. For while the Expressionists, like the Romantics, had a predilection for constant mixing of tone colors, Stravinsky leaned toward the essential simplicity of texture that is a distinguishing factor of all Classicism. He preferred to use pure, primary timbres rather than tonal mixtures, as is particularly notable in his treatment of the woodwind instruments.

Typical of Stravinsky's approach to woodwind timbre is the second

180

part of his 1930 *Symphony of Psalms* (**150**). Here the third statement of the fugue subject, first given to oboe and answered conventionally by the higher flute, is then given to a low flute, rather than to English horn or bassoon—the logical choice of a more traditional composer. Furthermore, the succeeding six-measure episode is assigned to the monochrome of piccolo and four flutes rather than to a more differentiated instrumental combination.

In his wind scoring Stravinsky abrogated the standard color devices of the Impressionists and Expressionists—flutter-tonguing, glissandos, raised bells, and the like—in favor of a technique of distinctive articulation new in the history of instrumentation. Briefly stated, this is the doubling of similar instruments using opposing types of articulation. For example, two flutes will be joined in unison on a melodic passage; the first flute will play even, legato notes, while the second flute will produce the same pitches staccato, or double-tongued, or with cross-accenting, or interspersed with rests—as in the quotation from the 1934 *Perséphone* (Example 66). A marked distinction in timbre is thus achieved, yet the aural effect is more subtle than exaggerated. Other clear instances of such contrasting wind articulations appear throughout the *Symphony of Psalms* (**151**) and in *Orpheus* (1947) (**152**).

This device is not exclusive with Stravinsky's Neoclassical scores, however. It appeared even earlier in *Le Sacre du Printemps* (**153**), in *Chant du Rossignol* (1917) (**154**), and in the later dodecaphonic *Agon* (1957) (**155**). In effect this practice corresponds to the way in which varying string sounds can be combined— arco with pizzicato, tremolo with nontremolo, harmonics with natural tones, sul tasto with sul ponticello, and so on. Such contrasting articulation and technical application is an unmistakable characteristic of Stravinsky's orchestrational style.

Stravinsky usually preferred the unadorned, natural tone of the brass instruments; muted brasses are as rare in his Neoclassical scores as they are commonplace with the Impressionists and Expressionists. Moreover, he wrote for these instruments generally in their middle, rather than their extreme, ranges. In particular, the composer showed a recurring predilection for the trombone used as a solo melodic member, entrusted with scrappy, rather angular themes somewhat percussive in nature and frequently grotesque. *Agon* (**156**), whose orchestration is strongly Neoclassical (even though the work is compositionally dodecaphonic) contains notable examples of this type of writing for trombone.

This conception of the instrument, quite counter to its traditional function in the Romantic orchestra, may be considered a typical reaction of the 1920s against most nineteenth-century principles of orchestral practice. A kind of instrumentational perversion—in which brasses are assigned typical string or woodwind passages, strings are used percussively, and woodwinds achieve the importance previously the domain of strings —is a frequent technical manifestation of this twentieth-century rebellion.

In his use of the percussion, Stravinsky was surprisingly conservative in the scores dating from the early twenties up to the late sixties (his final works). This is in emphatic contrast to the massive array of percussion required in *Le Sacre du Printemps* and *Les Noces* (1914–23), and to its crucial importance in such works as *L'Histoire du Soldat*. Perhaps the lavish exploitation of the barbaric qualities of percussion in his earlier scores surfeited the composer's interest in this particular area of percussive sound. Whatever the reason, the crash of cymbals and tam-tam, the stylized rustle of tambourine, and the bright ictus of triangle are virtually nonexistent in Stravinsky's later orchestral compositions. Instead, the timpani—in company with the harp and piano—assumed almost the entire burden of his percussion requirements.

But even the timpani, though listed under the instrumental requirements, are infrequently used in the course of many Stravinsky scores. For example, in the *Ode* (1943) they play in only five measures in the entire work, in *Threni* (1958) in only twenty-one, while *Agon* utilizes them in but three out of its fifteen sections. Other late Stravinsky scores, from *Canticum Sacrum* (1955) to *Variations: Aldous Huxley in Memoriam* (1963–64), dispense altogether with kettledrums. On the other hand, Stravinsky's last major work, the *Requiem Canticles* (1964–66) requires two timpanists.

Noteworthy was Stravinsky's extensive use of the piano as a member of the percussion section, even as a substitute for the timpani. Typical of this concept is a passage from *Symphony of Psalms* (pp. 87ff in the miniature score); here both piano and harp serve as reinforcements of the timpani ostinato. The same kind of treatment is also illustrated in *Oedipus Rex* (1927) **(157)** and in *Threni* **(158)**.

The incisive and brittle sound of the piano in its upper register is cunningly combined with strings (alternately arco and pizzicato) in the first movement of the *Symphony in Three Movements* (1945), shown in Example 67. A less original composer (granting he could have conceived this passage in the first place) might rather have used a fuller orchestral palette, laced with harp, xylophone, and glockenspiel accents.[1]

Stravinsky's occasional percussion resources also included the mandolin—a favorite of both Schoenberg and Webern—which furnished delicate percussive touches in *Agon*. The harpsichord, absent from other of his works, was made to assume a major instrumental role in the composer's opera, *The Rake's Progress* (1948–51). Except for the fact that

EXAMPLE 66
Igor Stravinsky: from *Perséphone*, p. 76

EXAMPLE 67
Stravinsky: from *Symphony in Three Movements*, p. 10

Stravinsky used no trombones in his opera, the orchestral resources are identical with those required for Mozart's *Don Giovanni.*

Surprisingly enough, Stravinsky frequently utilized the harp in his Neoclassical scores and in his later twelve-tone essays as well. Though the harp would not appear an apt orchestral color for the emotionally reticent ambience of Neoclassicism, the instrument assumes a highly important position in such stylistically diversified works as the *Divertimento* (1934; revised 1949), *Perséphone* (the only Stravinsky score to call for two harps), *Orpheus, Canticum Sacrum, Agon, Threni,* and *Movements for Piano and Orchestra* (1959).

Stravinsky's harp, however, in his Neoclassical works abandoned the traditional arpeggios and glissandi to serve as a chordal and melodic instrument, functioning very like a harpsichord. Bleak, somewhat acidulous chords, played *sec* ("dry"; played close to the soundboard) require the harpist quite literally to "pinch" the strings, insuring the ultimate in desiccated sound. Elsewhere the harp was required to play melodic passages of a pandiatonic nature, as though it were a keyboard instrument (as in *Orpheus* [159], for instance), or to substitute for the piano in reinforcing timpani or pizzicato bass lines, as in the scores of *Perséphone* (160) and *Threni* (161).

In all of Stravinsky's Neoclassical scores, with the possible exception of *Apollon Musagète* (1927), the strings are somewhat impersonal, avoiding the warmth and richness of texture that are so much a part of Romantic and Expressionist string writing. Only in the six-part string orchestra of *Apollon,* his classical Greek ballet (literally, "Apollo, Leader of the Muses") was he "much attracted by the idea of writing music in which everything should revolve about the melodic principle. And then the pleasure of immersing oneself again in the multisonorous euphony of strings and making it penetrate even the furthest fibers of the polyphonic web! And how could the unadorned design of the classical dance be better expressed than by the flow of melody as it expands in the sustained psalmody of strings?" (*An Autobiography*).

Elsewhere in this period, however, the composer went so far as to omit the strings altogether in his piano concerto, and to dispense with violins and violas in the *Symphony of Psalms*—ostensibly to avoid the implication of sentimentality associated with these instruments.[2]

Stravinsky's string writing is also notable for the special pains he took with precise notational demands. Always meticulous in this area, he frequently indicated both position and string to be used by the players, as well as the required fingering for awkward passages; wherever essential, he carefully marked up- and down-bow signs, and bowing slurs and accents, and in general left no room for doubt in the performer's mind. In this respect, at least, composers of all stylistic affiliations would do well to emulate Stravinsky in this very basic aspect of an orchestrator's labors.[3]

That the Neoclassical scores of Stravinsky are impeccable, musically and notationally, comes as no surprise to anyone conversant with the music of our time. During the past fifty years the world has learned not to be amazed by anything concerning this composer—even his late conversion to dodecaphonism. Though the "new" Stravinsky, who imposed on the rarefied techniques of Webern his own personal brand of the serial technique, may lack the universal appeal of the old, the agility and resilience of his mental processes commands admiration.

The parameters of Stravinsky's special Neoclassicism are as pervasive and forceful as any other technique of twentieth-century composition. The Neoclassical spirit, if not its specific style, has influenced a wide range of composers, many of whom have shown a preference for more Romantic expression. Ernest Bloch's Concerto Grosso No. 1 (1935), Falla's Harpsichord Concerto of 1926, Hindemith's *Kammermusik* series (1921–28), Poulenc's 1928 *Concert Champêtre*, Roussel's *Suite en Fa* (1926), and several of the *Bachianas Brasileiras* suites of Villa-Lobos (1930–1947)—all these works pay homage to the aesthetic and style of Stravinsky's *Octet* and its "back to Bach" outlook.

Many composers of the twenties and thirties, it is true, fell into the Neoclassical movement not out of strong and compelling conviction but rather by default. They were not necessarily Classical in their musical thinking, but they were anti-Romantic, anti-Impressionist, or anti-Expressionist. Inclined to some aspect of the new movement—its innate sophistication, its cultivated taste for the patent simplicity of the archaic and the primitive, its thin textures and transparency of style—they were more drawn to the Neoclassical milieu than to any other compositional trend of the times. Such composers as Poulenc and Milhaud are perfect examples of what we might call the "vicarious Classicist."

Others, like Prokofiev—whose "Classical" Symphony we have mentioned—had only a transient *affaire d'amour* with the Neoclassic spirit, only to turn thereafter to a more personal orchestral manner. The rubrics of Stravinsky's Neoclassicism, for instance, affected only the early *Kammermusik* of Paul Hindemith, and his later *Theme and Variations: The Four Temperaments* (1944). Though he consistently employed Neobaroque forms—the passacaglia, fugue, concerto grosso—Hindemith's natural antipathy to orchestral thinness of texture and to pure tone-color made him the spiritual opposite of the Neoclassical Stravinsky. The rich sonorities of *Mathis der Maler* (1934) and *Die Harmonie der Welt*

(1951), for instance, demonstrate his inherent Teutonic Romanticism that must be dealt with in the following chapter.

Maurice Ravel, too, though his characteristic orchestration is undeniably Impressionist, showed affinity to the new classicism in his refinement of style. Only two of his orchestral works, however, display the reticent instrumental means typical of the Neoclassical approach. One is *Le Tombeau de Couperin* (1917), mentioned in the previous chapter, which was originally written for piano and later orchestrated by Ravel. The other work is the Concerto in G for piano and orchestra (1931), which neatly juxtaposes the rhythmic propulsion of Stravinsky, the versicolored scintillations of the Impressionist, and tingling jazz elements. Despite the sonorous instrumental complement, the effect of the work is of a sophisticated brittleness characteristic of the Neoclassical orchestra.

In the United States, Stravinsky's 1939 lectures at Harvard University, coming at the height of his new period, helped to extend the geographic horizons of the Neoclassic style. Many of the young composers who flocked around Stravinsky at this time were already predisposed to his style by virtue of having studied with Nadia Boulanger in Cambridge or in France. As a result, several eminently successful works in the Neoclassical manner soon emanated from these contacts; among them were Harold Shapero's *Symphony for Classical Orchestra* (1946), Irving Fine's *Toccata Concertante* (1947), Arthur Berger's *Ideas of Order* (1951), and certain works of Aaron Copland, Walter Piston, and Samuel Barber.

Copland's two early works for orchestra—the *Dance Symphony* of 1925 (actually a reworking of his ballet, *Grohg*, of 1923) and the *Symphony for Organ and Orchestra* (1924) (later, in 1928, to become in revised form his First Symphony)—are indubitably Neoclassical in spirit and substance. The same stylistic austerity also pervades the *Short Symphony* of 1933, later to be reshaped by the composer as a sextet for clarinet, piano, and string quartet.[4]

Two scores by Walter Piston likewise demonstrate a clear-cut Neoclassical approach to the orchestra, along with his usual transparent, patrician compositional style: the *Concerto for Orchestra* (1934) and the delightful *Concertino* for piano and orchestra (1937). Piston's later works, however, including the eight symphonies, subscribe to fuller instrumental sonorities and a more robust style.

Samuel Barber's *Capricorn Concerto* (1944) is a prime example of the tangential influence of the Neoclassical style. Charming as the music is, this American reflection of the spirit of Stravinsky's *Dumbarton Oaks Concerto* is uncharacteristic of its composer's well-established Romantic aesthetic. The more expansive instrumental palette of Barber's major works, as well as those of Copland and Piston, will be dealt with in the succeeding chapter.

Even in such an unlikely locale as Mexico, some aspects of Neoclassicism have joined in unlikely alliance with Indian-Spanish or other indigenous materials. A surprisingly reticent, anti-Romantic sound comes from the large orchestra required for the *Sinfonia de Antígona* (1933) of Carlos Chávez—this despite its alto flute, heckelphone, and large array of native percussion instruments. Even the composer's Fourth Symphony (1952), subtitled *Romantica,* is more a demonstration of musical linearity—Classicism, in other words—than a piling up of vertical sonoric blocks in approved Romantic fashion.

Other Mexican composers—Blas Galindo, Pablo Moncayo, and Jimenez Mabarak, for instance, embraced Neoclassicism with enthusiasm. From such indigenous expressions as Galindo's *Sones de Mariachi* (1940) and Moncayo's *Huapango* (1941), these composers turned to conscientious imitations of Stravinsky's *Octet* period. Though undeniably skillful, these works lack the essential quality of personal expression, always a patent danger when an artist imposes an alien aesthetic and technique on an inherently contradictory style.

Galindo's *Sinfonia* No. 1 (1956), successfully introduced at the 1957 Caracas Festival, is a perfect example of the kind of creative eclecticism that defies national identification. For all its obvious merits, the symphony is not "Mexican," but a Hindemithian amalgam of Romantic orchestration and Neoclassical polyphony that conceivably could have been written by an Englishman, a Pole, or an Italian, for the language it speaks is international.

No useful purpose would be served by further listing the adherents to Neoclassicism in other centers of the musical world—unless it were to give us "some idea of how many musical oysters have to be opened in order to find one pearl," as Adam Carse remarked. Wherever these composers live and work, they have a basic similarity of philosophy and technique, and achieve a remarkable unanimity of effect. Given the precepts of Neoclassicism, it is easy to hazard how these composers choose to treat the symphonic or operatic orchestra. Mozart and Haydn, even at times the Baroque Handel and Bach, return as the instrumentational ideal; Romantic compositions (except, perhaps, for the early works of Beethoven) are bypassed as models in a refreshing quest for orchestral simplicity and leanness.

The Neoclassical orchestra usually employs fairly limited resources, comparable in numbers of players if not in actual makeup to the eighteenth-century pattern. For architectural clarity, the approach to the instruments is essentially soloistic; even when united they create a texture that is open, well-defined, and contrapuntal. Voice doublings are at a minimum and chord spacings are commendably transparent. The overall impression of the orchestral sound is lean and succinct.

In their concepts of orchestral color the Neoclassicists, unlike the Impressionists and Expressionists, abrogate the exotic, the flamboyant, the extreme. Their credo calls for stricter control of materials and starker use of primary instrumental timbres than was customary with the late Romantic composers. Pure color, with an absolute minimum of instrumental doubling, becomes once more the stylistic ideal. The "palette" orchestration of the Impressionists, who used color for its own sake, now finds its antithesis in the Neoclassic concept of a contrapuntal, or "terraced," instrumentation using contrasting colors to insure melodic independence in a polyphonic context.

Above all, in Neoclassicism style triumphs over matter; composers subscribing to this technique obviously prefer refinement of idea and statement to the emotionalism of the Romantic, the tenuousness of the Impressionist, or the tension of the Expressionist. They sometimes appear, as a consequence, to abandon the admirable equilibrium of formal design and emotional content possessed by the early Classical composers, who were, of course, their first models. Everything in the Neoclassical works of Stravinsky and of his many followers is cool, detached, impersonal, and, usually, immensely skillful. If they touch the mind before touching the heart, so be it. In our complex world, so full of inconsistencies and contradictions, there is assuredly ample room for many different musical philosophies. Those stubborn individualists, the composers, can surely be counted on to keep them alive and flourishing.

Notes

1. This passage from Stravinsky's symphony inevitably invites comparison with an orchestrationally parallel section in Béla Bartók's *Music for Strings, Percussion and Celesta,* composed nine years prior to the *Symphony in Three Movements* (see Example 69, p. 200).

2. Stravinsky cannot (and did not) claim credit for pioneering the conception of string choir minus violins. The first known instance of this device is the 1806 opera of Étienne Méhul, *Uthal.* In contemporary times, Hindemith's viola concerto (*Kammermusik* No. 5, 1927), and Karl Amadeus Hartmann's Fifth Symphony (1952) both dispensed with the higher strings.

3. In view of Stravinsky's meticulous care, one wonders whether the nonexistent low A written for the oboe in the third of the *Quatre Études pour Orchestre* (1928-30)

was a momentary indiscretion on his part or merely an engraver's typographical sin. The latter is more likely, as Stravinsky's other published scores from this particular period are riddled with similar careless notational errors.

4. For a fascinating and fruitful musical experience, one should compare the two versions of this Copland work by listening to the orchestral version while following the sextet score, or vice versa. Few important compositions in the musical repertory offer such an opportunity for analytical comparison; the insight gained into the composer's musical thinking genuinely rewards such analysis.

The Neoromantic Orchestra

Style, the crown and flower of technique, if bereft of invigorating imagination disintegrates into fashion. Routine and fashion—there are the worst snarls that can entangle the creative mind.

Paul Hindemith,
A Composer's World

Though the ponderous and the opaque in orchestration are generally unfashionable today, the potential of full orchestral resources yet claims the allegiance of many a twentieth-century composer. Sharing a common viewpoint of the orchestra, these Neoromantic composers still display in their instrumentation a strong predilection for the sound-ideal that shaped the music dramas of Richard Wagner, the grandiose symphonies of Gustav Mahler, and the tone-poems of Richard Strauss.

A similarity of approach to the orchestra and a common conception of its immense sonoric capabilities, however, do not guarantee correlative musical materials. We are faced with a basic contradiction between the essential nature of much contemporary music and the specific instrumental means employed for its realization. Composers closely akin in compositional technique may often be totally unrelated in orchestrational style. In content the music of the Neoromantics and of the Expressionists frequently intermingles; in style of presentation elements of Impression-ism and even of Neoclassicism sometimes color the expressions of the Neoromantic composers. In the process a good deal of one style rubs off on another, and demarcation lines between differing, even contradic-tory, aesthetics often become dim. Yet, whatever the interaction of stylistic elements, the basic orchestral concepts of all these differing view-points remain far apart.

The return to the orchestra as a massive and heterogeneous instru-mental combination, rather than an enlarged chamber ensemble, sug-gests a reexamination of the full resources of the late twentieth-century symphonic-operatic orchestra. Despite the wide range of stylistic ap-proaches over the years discussed in the preceding chapters, the orchestra itself has not changed as much as one might think from the ensemble that served Beethoven in his last five symphonies. Now, as then, the orchestra consists of but four generic choirs: woodwind, brass, percussion, and string. Within three of these groups there have been only numerical additions, with new members of the family types brought in, during the past century and a quarter. Only in the percussion section have new colors—hence new instruments— been added.

In the modern orchestra the woodwind choir still comprises the four fundamental timbres available to Haydn and Mozart—flute, oboe, clar-inet, and bassoon. Each of these four family members has today certain complemental "extras": piccolo and alto flute; English horn (very rarely, bass oboe or heckelphone) ; small E-flat or D clarinet and bass clarinet (occasionally, alto clarinet and contrabass clarinet) ; and contrabassoon or sarrusophone. Even the saxophone (an instrumental voice that suggested to poet-novelist Robert Penn Warren a sound "like the slow, sweet re-gurgitation of sorghum molasses") takes its place tonally with the bas-soons.

Among the brass instruments we have had the same four colors of horn, trumpet, trombone, and tuba since the mid-nineteenth century (the period of Berlioz). Of the occasional additions to the brass choir (unlike the woodwinds, all on a nonpermanent basis), the cornet is but another tonal version of the trumpet, and the baritone only an altered horn or tuba. Primarily a band instrument, the baritone has been used with any degree of consistency in the symphonic orchestra only by the American Roy Harris. The more rarely used bass trumpet, flugelhorn, contrabass trombone, and the various Wagnerian tubas are, of course, only exten-sions of existing brass colors.

In the string section of the orchestra of today no additions at all have been made since the rise of the early Classical orchestra. Obviously, a far larger number of string players than was employed by Mozart, Haydn, and the other Classicists is common to our concert orchestras today; modern salary schedules, however, usually make prohibitive the number of string players demanded by Strauss and Mahler. Generally speaking, though symphony orchestras vary widely in number of personnel, the major ensembles of Europe, the Americas, Australia, and Japan, possess string sections comprising from twelve to eighteen each of first and second violins, from eight to twelve each of violas and cellos, and from six to twelve double basses. It is, of course, axiomatic that the more string players there are at his disposal the happier is the Neoromantic composer; the solid richness of the strings is one of the most valuable aspects of his orchestrational palette.

The only orchestral section that can boast of a truly phenomenal physical growth and musical development in the past century is the percussion. Both in types of instruments required and in the extent and manner of their use the accretion of this part of the orchestra has been astounding. From a modest nucleus of two timpani, plus the occasionally used bass drum, cymbals, and triangle (mostly in compositions for the theater), to a grouping of some fifteen or twenty assorted wood, metal, and membranous instruments (requiring from three to eight players), the percussion has evolved into an orchestra within an orchestra. This expansion, which began in the early nineteenth century (with Berlioz, Meyerbeer, and others), reached its zenith by the era of late Romanticism at the turn of the century. Today, in the late twentieth century, the concept of the "percussion orchestra" is an essential aspect of Neoromantic, Exotic, and avant-garde orchestral expression.

The new concept of this instrumental family is far more sophisticated than an emphasis on sheer numbers; it concerns the coloristic aspects of the various instruments and their ability to enhance the more subtle elements of the composer's expression. Until the present era it was sufficient for standard instrumentation texts (Berlioz-Strauss, Rimsky-Korsakov, Prout, Widor, Forsyth, and others) to group the percussion instruments into two broad categories: those of definite pitch (such as timpani, glockenspiel, bells), and those of indefinite pitch (bass drum, gong, tambourine, and so on). In the light of contemporary usage, however, these simple classifications no longer suffice. Indeed, they are both misleading and inaccurate, for each pitched instrument has its own unique timbre, and even unpitched instruments can give an aural illusion of relative pitch in certain contexts.

Above all, it has been during the present century that orchestrators have made the most varied and sensitive use of percussion color potential.

STYLE AND ORCHESTRATION

In fact, one might go so far as to say that this orchestral section has long since assumed a role comparable to that held by the brasses in the nineteenth century and by the woodwinds in the eighteenth. The strings are still sovereign, at least in the Neoromantic orchestra, but the percussion assuredly has for some time enjoyed equal status with woodwinds and brasses.

This particularized twentieth-century orchestra, then—an obvious descendant of the symphonic ensemble of 150 years ago—is the sound-medium of the Neoromantic orchestrator. Its distinctive manner, the stamp of its personalized instrumentation, is a pattern established cumulatively by the key figures in this vital area of compositional technique. Only by ranging over the entire Western world and its masters of orchestration can we demonstrate in the end a common denominator—the inherent factor of purpose and of method that unites patently irreconcilable instrumentational approaches.

Certainly the two major fabricators of the Neoromantic orchestrational style, Bartók and Hindemith, would appear diametrically opposite in personality, training, and musical temperament. Béla Bartók (1881–1945), as if in direct refutation of Stravinsky's enigmatic pronouncement on musical expressiveness, once said: "I cannot conceive of music that expresses nothing." The Romantic tenet that musical and emotional expression are synonymous pervades the entire gamut of his writing. In compositions with national roots (such as the 1923 *Dance Suite*), with an exotic motivation (like *The Miraculous Mandarin* ballet of 1919), or in more abstract expressions such as the concertos for piano and for violin, the flexible orchestration of each is unfailingly appropriate to the composer's creative thought.

From first to last Bartók's orchestration is essentially Romantic in its sound and emotional impact, though not invariably dependent on massive instrumental forces. Exceptionally large orchestras appear only in the 1910 *Deux Images,* the opera *Bluebeard's Castle* (1911), the *Four Orchestral Pieces* of 1912, the danced pantomime *The Wooden Prince* (1917), and *The Miraculous Mandarin.* On the other hand, the *Deux Portraits* (1908) and the *Dance Suite* and the *Concerto for Orchestra* (1944), as well as the several concertos for solo instruments, all utilize ensembles of moderate size. Furthermore, two major Bartók works concentrate on the potentialities of the string orchestra.

But whether Bartók's orchestra is large or small, it is entirely free of the stigmas of nineteenth-century Romanticism—muddiness and opacity. For all his stabbing rhythms and harmonic acerbity, Bartók's late works are almost Mozartean in their clarity. Despite its power and

194

sonorous weight, his orchestration manages always to combine a subtle instinct for color with textural transparency.

The most conspicuous single aspect of Bartók's instrumentation is his extraordinary use of the percussion section. Somewhat slighted by the post-Expressionists and distinctly neglected by Stravinsky in his Neoclassical and dodecaphonic periods, the percussion contribute enormously to the impact of Bartók's way with the orchestra. This emphatic percussion ambience was the natural outcome of the composer's inclination towards pungent harmonies and asymmetrical rhythms; the more subtle permutations of percussive sound, however, are Bartók's individual contributions to the "Bible" of modern percussion scoring.

He often indicated precisely, for instance, the kind of mallet or beater to be used at every point in his score; furthermore, he would request a particular kind of attack upon the drums, cymbals, or gong to achieve exactly the effect he wished. The *Sonata* [Concerto] *for Two Pianos and Percussion* (1937) abounds with specific directives to the players: the suspended cymbal is to be struck with a snare-drum stick on the dome of the plate (which gives quite a different sound from a stroke on the rim) ; the cymbal is to be vibrated with two soft timpani sticks, beginning on the dome and gradually moving outward to the rim—or, elsewhere, the exact reverse; the bass drum is to be struck with a heavy wooden stick (rather than the ordinary, soft-headed beater) at the edge of the membrane; the timpanist is instructed to use hard felt sticks and to execute a roll beginning at the very rim of the head, then moving to the dead center of the membrane (thus changing the tone quality, and even the pitch, from a tight, high sound to a normal, clear timbre and then to a dull, almost toneless thudding) .

With characteristic creativity Bartók also seized on the timely invention of the pedal timpani, designed for quick pitch-changes that made possible a chromatic bass-line. Going much further in conceptual usage, Bartók expanded this new device to include two forms of pedal glissando: the pitch is altered by the pedal while the player rolls on the drumhead, or the pedal raises or lowers the pitch immediately following a sharp stroke (see the *Music for Strings, Percussion and Celesta* [162], for instance) . It seems significant that Expressionists and Neoclassicists alike rarely employ this unique percussion device; even Hindemith in his most Romantic moments notably refrained from requesting pedal glissandi. Nonetheless, the technique has become a staple for most Neoromantics, and a valuable (though sometimes overindulged) addition to contemporary instrumentational resources.

All these ingenious percussive devices, however, are no more extramusical contrivances in Bartók's orchestration than the standard use of mutes in brass and stringed instruments, or of woodwind and string harmonics. Like the more routine pizzicato and col legno in strings, or double- and triple-tonguing articulations in wind instruments, they are completely valid in imparting color-values to the composer's full orchestral textures. By sensing their musical potential and using them with sensitivity, Bartók has immeasurably increased the available permutations of percussive sound in the modern orchestra.

Even the piano, celesta, and harp as used by Bartók may be regarded as members of the percussion ensemble. The piano, given the greatest prominence in nearly all of the cited Bartók works, is exploited for a variety of timbral propensities. In its lower register it frequently assumes a gong- and drum-like character (as in Example 68, p. 199); in its upper range, combined with pizzicato strings (see Example 69, p. 200)[1] or with harp or celesta, the piano tone is transformed into a new kind of bell timbre, scintillating and hypnotic.

The celesta appears frequently in Bartók's scores as a muted pianistic sonority (see the fourth movement of the *Dance Suite* [163]). It plays a prominent, almost soloistic, part in the sonic texture of the *Music for Strings, Percussion and Celesta* and in *The Miraculous Mandarin* as well; in *The Wooden Prince* the celesta part actually requires two players. In the *Deux Images* and the Second Violin Concerto, the instrument has a more subsidiary role.

Bartók's harp writing, if somewhat less innovative than one might logically expect, is always completely effective. One characteristic presentation of the composer is a passage of unsupported (or lightly reinforced) arpeggiated chords suggestive of accompaniments used by bardic minstrels. Such handling of the instrument may be found in the *Deux Images* (164); the fourth movement of the Suite No. 2 (1907) (165); the opening measures of the Second Violin Concerto (166) (the one most frequently performed), and in the composer's last major orchestral work, the *Concerto for Orchestra* (167).

There are few extended passages of routine arpeggio writing in Bartók's scores, but several of his works contain instances of harp chords arpeggiated downwards, reversing the normal manner of performance. The conventional glissando appears only when indispensable to brilliant tonal outbursts. But the composer's most dramatic writing for harp is the icily glittering tone-color achieved in both the *Dance Suite* (168) and *Music for Strings, Percussion and Celesta* (169), where the harp is combined with high piano, celesta, glockenspiel, or xylophone.

Bartók seems to have made only one serious miscalculation in his demands on the harp: in the first movement of the *Concerto for Orchestra* (170) he asks for a series of rapid glissandi to be played near the sounding board with a wooden or metal stick. Should the player literally follow the composer's request, he or she could easily snap one or two of the strings or, at best, put them out of tune. Therefore the harpist, with proper concern for his expensive instrument, usually plays this passage in the normal manner with the fingers—or possibly with the fingernails.

In his general treatment of the woodwind instruments, Bartók occupies a middle ground between the Expressionists, in whose scores pure woodwind timbre is nearly nonexistent, and Stravinsky's late dodecaphonic works, where pure color is the general rule. Oddly enough, flutter-tonguing—common in the scores of Schoenberg and Berg—appears only in a few early Bartók scores. He did, however, favor the extreme woodwind ranges no less than the Expressionists—a timbral conception that was to reach its ultimate fulfillment in the orchestration of the avant-garde of the sixties.

If any single woodwind claims priority in Bartók's instrumentational schema, it is the clarinet. The warmly expressive, even sensuous, capabilities of this instrument find complete realization in Bartók's hands. And rarely, if ever, has the clarinet suggested eroticism more convincingly than in *The Miraculous Mandarin* (171) (the entire "seduction" scene, for example). The skill with which the composer treated the remaining woodwinds is well demonstrated in the second movement of the *Concerto for Orchestra* (172); here each instrumental family in turn is given a distinctive theme, beginning with bassoons, then followed by oboes, clarinets, flutes, and finally by muted trumpets. Not only does the intervallic relationship between each pair of instruments change, but the thematic characteristics alter to accommodate the timbral distinctions of each pair of instruments in turn.

Bartók's brasses tend usually to be either full-voiced or menacingly muted for dramatic effect. Especially distinctive is his concept of the brass fanfare, a persistent feature of his later orchestral works. But instead of massing chordal elements in the traditional harmonic manner, such as in Strauss's *Ein Heldenleben* or *La Péri* of Dukas, Bartók juxtaposes imitative polyphonic lines. Typical successive entries of the brass instruments playing short, angular figures may be found in abundance in the *Concerto for Orchestra* (173).

From the wide range of other brass effects, Bartók makes full use of double- and triple-tonguing patterns and is notably fond of coruscating trills. As with the woodwinds, he rarely calls for flutter-tonguing. Most frequent, however, and most provocative, is his expert manipulation of trombone glissandi.[2] In the context of *The Miraculous Mandarin* this effect is sinister (see Example 68) ; in the *Concerto for Orchestra* (third movement [174]) it is vulgarly humorous—an obvious parody of a Shostakovich mannerism.[3] The aura surrounding this technical device depends entirely on contextual harmony, dynamics, and complemental instrumental color, as Bartók so effectively demonstrated.

The ultimate measure of Bartók's genius in orchestration, however, undoubtedly lies in his extraordinary skill with the stringed instruments. Not even the Expressionists, or the Impressionists before them, more tellingly defined the modern physiognomy of these instruments. From the warmly expressive and lyrical to the brutally percussive, Bartók's string resources appear in retrospect almost limitless. His personal imprint is stamped on even the conventional procedures of chord stopping, pizzicato, harmonics, and col legno; his bold use of string glissandi, moreover (as in the *Dance Suite* and the 1940 *Divertimento for String Orchestra* has become a stylistic hallmark. To these established techniques Bartók added one notable device, the "snap" pizzicato (see Example 69). As every student of instrumentation knows, this method of plucking makes the string strike the fingerboard with such force that it rebounds with a sharp, percussive snap.

This distinctive sound, however, is only one facet of the virtuosity that marks every page of a Bartók score. In the final analysis, it is futile to attempt to account for Bartók's mastery of orchestration by noting any single device or special use of any one orchestral section. For Bartók stands today—along with Stravinsky and the great Viennese Expressionists—as an uncontested master of contemporary orchestration in all its technical and imaginative aspects. Few symphonic works in the mainstream of twentieth-century music since Bartók's time are totally exempt from his pervasive influence.

In many ways Paul Hindemith (1895–1963) was as pragmatic as Bartók was innovative, even though both composers conceived of the orchestra as a vehicle of Romantic sonority. It is not that Hindemith was largely responsible for the concept of *Gebrauchsmusik* (a term he came to detest), but that his entire output was conditioned by directness, practicality, and the love of sheer craftsmanship. No experimenter with exotic effects (despite the siren and sand-filled box in the *Kammermusik* No. 1 of 1922 [175]), no revolutionary seeker of new instrumental paths, Hindemith was an orchestrator of cool and reasoned judgment, of methodical Germanic solidity, and of an almost offhand competence.

The unfailing aplomb of this "universal musician," as he has been called, may be credited to his singular achievement of possessing a per-

EXAMPLE 68
Béla Bartók: from *The Miraculous Mandarin*, p. 296

EXAMPLE 69

Bartók: from *Music for Strings, Percussion and Celesta*, pp. 28–29

*) am Rand des Felles
**) ♦ bezeichnet ein pizz., bei welchem die Saite auf das
Griffbrett anschlägt

*) au bord de la peau
**) ♦ indique un pizzicato, auquel la corde frappe la touch.

U. E. 10888 W. Ph. V. 201

forming technique on several orchestral instruments. Hindemith had the technician's insight into instrumental potential; no composer, therefore, is more authentic in his assignments to the individual instruments. But this facility as an orchestrator occasionally degenerated into mannered and stereotyped scoring; this is particularly noticeable in his writing for wind instruments (as in the third movement of the *Concerto for Orchestra* [1925]).

In general, Hindemith's orchestral style is marked by his predilection for contrast by choirs. Whole sections of a work, let alone extended passages, will be scored for one basic choir, to be contrasted with a following passage or section given entirely to another orchestral entity.[4] Where the full orchestra plays simultaneously, Hindemith was inclined to keep the various choirs on contrasting levels, using differentiated materials. In a typical passage, drawn from his symphony, *Die Harmonie der Welt*[5] (Example 70), four distinct textures are spun out: florid figuration in the woodwinds; a powerful three-voiced melodic statement in the brasses; rhythmic emphasis and embellishment in percussion; and an imitative, flowing counter-subject in the strings. The prototype of this kind of sectional orchestration, it will be remembered, is to be found in the scores of Tchaikovsky (see Example 35, p. 84). Contrasts by alternating choirs, seen earlier in our survey in the Bruckner symphonies and an important feature of the orchestral works of William Schuman (discussed later), are unmistakably characteristic of the Hindemith oeuvre.

Considered as a whole, Hindemith's composition is uncompromisingly straightforward, entirely devoid of pretty impressions and shallow glitter. The devices integral to the Impressionist and Expressionist palettes seemed to him superficial and extraneous. Thus, one will seldom find in Hindemith sul ponticello string tremolos, or elaborate heterophony for harp, celesta, and keyed percussion; his woodwinds do little flutter-tonguing, his brasses no glissandi, and there are no patently exotic percussion devices.

Hindemith did not often require unusual instruments in his orchestra, nor did he demand more than the normal complement of woodwinds in threes. For him, four horns are standard, and two trumpets suffice in most of his scores—sometimes only two trombones as well. His percussion writing is generally "square," with his resources deployed more for obvious rhythmic support or mild embellishment than for colorful or otherwise unusual decoration. With his basic conservatism, he normally found two timpani sufficient; the *Symphonic Metamorphosis on Themes by Weber* is one of the few scores requiring four kettledrums, and only a handful of the others specify three. Many of his Neoclassically oriented,

EXAMPLE 70
Paul Hindemith: from *Die Harmonie der Welt*, p. 55

203

chamber-like works dispensed altogether with percussion instruments, timpani included (the *Concert Music* for solo viola and large chamber orchestra, for instance, or the *Concert Music for Strings and Brass,* both written in 1930).

In his harp writing Hindemith was almost austere, avoiding all the clichés of nineteenth-century usage. For example, in the *Concerto for Woodwinds, Harp and Orchestra* (1949) **(176)** the solo harp part contains only two brief glissandi, the composer almost militantly avoiding the common (and much abused) resources of the instrument. This was not, however, for lack of inventiveness; there is one solo passage in the score written without bar-lines, in free time, with the instruction that the harpist is to disregard the meter and tempo of the other instrumentalists.

Possibly the closest Hindemith ever came to an exotic effect in his orchestration is the percussion interlude in the fugal Scherzo of the popular *Symphonic Metamorphosis on Themes by Weber* **(177)**. And only once did the composer emulate Mahler's practice in assigning off-stage passages for various instruments. In the slow movement of the *Symphonia Serena* **(178)**—an unjustly neglected work—a solo violin and solo viola are drawn from the double string-orchestra utilized in this movement; one player is stationed backstage left and the other backstage right. The two soloists engage together in antiphonal play with the main body of strings, as well as between themselves, and at one point participate in a dialogue with an onstage solo violin and viola.

But for all its customary severity and no-nonsense attitude, Hindemith's instrumentation is Romantic to the core, and as richly sonorous as any orchestration of the twentieth century. The gusto with which the composer approached sheer music-making, his pure delight in musical sound as an essential of the good life, and his firm belief that music well made will, without question, move the hearer—all unfailingly indicate a composer of true Romantic persuasion. Whether the work be the early *Philharmonic Concerto* (1932), the austere ballet score, *Nobilissima Visione* (1938), the poignant requiem on Walt Whitman's text, *When Lilacs Last in the Dooryard Bloom'd* (1946), or the breezy *Sinfonietta* of 1949—Hindemith's orchestral expression is unambiguous, refreshingly direct, and emotionally satisfying.

Although both Bartók and Hindemith exerted considerable influence on mid–twentieth–century instrumentation, one cannot maintain that either composer established a "school" of orchestral style. Certain externals of their individual techniques have been incorporated, however, in the procedures of widely divergent musical personalities. Because these Neoromantic approaches to the orchestra have appeared throughout the Western world, we shall consider them by country or region, rather than chronologically.

Of the Russian adherents to the Neoromantic orchestra—which includes almost every contemporary composer—Serge Prokofiev (1891–1953) was outstanding both for his musical achievement and for his artistic integrity in the face of fluctuating totalitarian demands. Only in his Seventh Symphony (1952), his last major work, do we sense any adjustment of his creative impulses to the artistic dictates of the state. And if the final symphony is disappointing, it is far outweighed by the long list of superb compositions that preceded it.

We have already seen that the resurgence of Classicism brought into being Prokofiev's refreshing *Classical Symphony* (1918), antedating by some years even Stravinsky's initial essays in the reborn style. This tour de force of eighteenth-century form and spirit was unique in Prokofiev's career, but the melodic clarity and intrinsically polyphonic expression therein never disappeared from his writing. Even in the grandiose structures of the last three symphonies, for all their powerful dramatic expositions, this much of the Classical essence survives.

More characteristic of Prokofiev's intrinsic style, however, were the elements of bold experimentation first exemplified in the *Scythian Suite* of 1914; a virile emotion expressed in a lyric vein (as in both violin concertos and the 1936 ballet, *Romeo and Juliet*), and, most especially, his proclivity for a demoniac scherzo-like quality. This last quality, with its related motor drive and propulsive rhythms, is threaded throughout Prokofiev's music, from the ballet *Chout* (1920) to the final three symphonies (1944–52). The element of sardonic wit—"jest, laughter, and mockery," as the composer put it—is peculiarly Prokofiev's own. It was perhaps the cardinal element in his musical aesthetic, and it determined to a high degree the nature of his instrumentation.

In simplistic terms, Prokofiev thought always of the orchestra as full-bodied and sonorous, but was inclined strongly to grotesque instrumental effects. His wizardry in this area lay not so much in the use of technical devices as in his instinct for uncommon orchestral spacings and combinations. Israel Nestyev, his biographer, cites several examples from the Sixth Symphony (1947): "Prokofiev deliberately upset the usual distribution of voices, entrusting to the flutes tones which lie below the oboe and clarinet,[6] or combining the first violin with the tuba, two octaves apart.[7] At rehearsals he called particular attention to the effect of the asthmatic 'wheezing' of the French horns in the development of the first movement, and to the English horn which plays above the oboe. . . ."[8]

Strings, woodwinds, and brasses—all were frequently maneuvered into just such unorthodox vertical arrangements when Prokofiev stacked up his harmonic components. Violas and cellos seem to be as often in the violin range as in their more normal tessituras (see the 1921 Piano Concerto No. 3 [179], for example, or the Fifth Symphony [180]). The same conception is frequently applied to the woodwind instruments, with oboes and/or clarinets placed well above the flutes.

But even more a personal hallmark was Prokofiev's penchant for high brass instruments playing in a deep register, and for those of lower pitch playing at their highest level. The composer was almost inordinately fond of the sound of trumpets on their bottom notes, as displayed in numerous passages in the *Scythian Suite* (181), *Chout* (182), and the Fifth (183) and Sixth (184) symphonies. Again ordering his vertical arrangements in an unexpected way, he often put trumpets or horns (or both) below the trombones in melodic and harmonic situations alike, poising the harsh quality of low horns and trumpets against the bright and piercing sonority of high trombones.

Even in horizontal (unison) combinations Prokofiev preferred unrelated and unexpected pairings. He was also strongly drawn to the grotesque tonal quality of very high and very low instruments playing simultaneously, with nothing in between (the opening of the cantata, *Alexander Nevsky* [1939] is a prime example). Much of his instrumentation stressed this unusual acoustical bareness, and in so doing amalgamated two of the paramount factors—the experimental and the bizarre—that were central to his creative imagination.

Percussion instruments, while not always lending themselves to the odd manipulation characteristic of his approach to the other orchestral sections, still played an enormous part in Prokofiev's characteristic style. Both xylophone and glockenspiel were frequently given extended and elaborate parts, including single-note and chord tremolos and rapid glissando sweeps (as in *Chout* [185] and the *Scythian Suite*—also known as *Ala et Lolly* [186]). The castanets make an unusual appearance, considering the musical context, in the first movement of the Third Piano Concerto (187). And the varying resources of all the drum instruments, timpani included, were regularly utilized by the composer to the fullest extent.

Harps and celesta, too, were in almost constant requisition in Prokofiev's scores—in abstract works such as the symphonies and concertos no less than in the ballets and other programmatic essays. As for the piano as an orchestral instrument, not even Bartók or Stravinsky used its percussive qualities more stunningly than did Prokofiev. Instances of its use as a harmonic reinforcement, a melodic doubler (see Example

71) ,[9] or color additive are far too numerous to cite individually; they can be found in almost any one of Prokofiev's orchestral compositions.

Unlike Stravinsky, who shed his musical "Russianism" at about the time that he embraced the new Classicism, Prokofiev never abandoned his strong national ties. Nor did his younger compatriot, Dmitri Shostakovich (1906–1975) , an enormously prolific composer of great natural skill in matters of instrumentation, ever aspire to erase his ubiquitous label of "Soviet composer."

Generally speaking, Shostakovich's orchestration is obvious and uncluttered. His heavily contrapuntal music is scored with the most conventional groupings on the various melodic lines, as in the Fifth Symphony (Example 72) . There is no figuration to speak of, either of melodic strands or harmonic underpinning; the latter element in his music usually assumes the character of square-cut chordal blocks, invariably orchestrated in homogeneous colors. "Effects" are sparingly used; the composer restricts himself to occasional humorous glissandi in the strings—or, more vulgarly, in the trombones, as in his opera *Lady Macbeth of Mtsensk*.[10] Furthermore, he shuns the more exotic col legno and snap pizzicato in strings, and flutter-tonguing in winds. Even his percussion instruments are used "straight," with a minimum of color devices in evidence; harp, celesta, and piano parts are routine at best.

Nonetheless, for all his unproblematic approach to the modern orchestra, Shostakovich was to the manner born—directly in the tradition of his renowned predecessor, Tchaikovsky. And like his orchestrational ancestor, Shostakovich made mannerisms of certain techniques—such as greatly extended melodies given to a single woodwind instrument, and rhythmic ostinatos that are prolonged unmercifully. That he could rise above routine when demanded by his subject matter is stunningly illustrated in the Thirteenth Symphony, "Babi Yar" (1962; revised 1963) . Though its orchestration is still basically conservative, the music has a power and emotional immediacy conspicuously lacking in most of the composer's later compositions.

Unfortunately, all too often Shostakovich reminds us of some of the less exemplary aspects of Gustav Mahler in his love of bombast, massive instrumental display, and vehement emotional outbursts. The *scherzo* movements from Shostakovich's symphonies (with the oft-played *Polka* from his 1930 ballet *The Golden Age* as prototype) appear to be direct descendants of Mahler's ubiquitous *Ländler* passages in the symphonies. There are, moreover, further Mahlerian touches: the full chorus required in the finale of the Second Symphony (1927) , and the male soloist and chorus in the "Babi Yar" symphony; his fondness for the small E-flat

EXAMPLE 71
Serge Prokofiev: from *Scythian Suite* (*Ala et Lolly*), p. 58

EXAMPLE 72
Dmitri Shostakovich: from Symphony No. 5, p. 37

clarinet, which shows up in several of his works; the extra brasses (four horns, three trumpets, three trombones) used throughout the Seventh Symphony, "Leningrad" (1941); and, finally, the inordinate length of most of Shostakovich's full-scale works.

It is regrettable that in so many of the composer's scores these now-dated elements outweigh his technical acumen and stylistic conviction. His credo that "there can be no music without ideology" enforced a style that seems to repeat itself from one work to the next, any change being merely a matter of degree rather than of substance. The same observations, of course, may be made regarding Shostakovich's confrères, Dmitri Kabalevsky (1904–), Aram Khachaturian (1903–1978), and Tikon Khrennikov (1913–). Like Shostakovich, they treat the modern orchestra in a sonorous and generally massive manner, adding little to his basic instrumentational technique and clearing away none of his stylistic mannerisms.

In Central Europe the Neoromantic approach to the orchestra was most notably exemplified by the Austrian Ernst Toch and the Swiss Ernest Bloch (both of whom spent their final years in the United States), and by the Frenchman Arthur Honegger. Bloch (1880–1959), like Bartók, wrote music of great emotional impact, but his orchestrational models were the rhetorical stance of Franz Liszt and the grandiloquent ambience of Richard Strauss. Given Bloch's Hebraic intensity of feeling and this stylistic inclination, one would expect his scores to be studded with unusual orchestral devices. Instead, his way with the symphonic orchestra was surprisingly straightforward.

Like Hindemith, Bloch always scored in a solid and massive style, yet he avoided the sonoric exaggerations of the late Romantics and the introverted emotional aspects of the Expressionists. Bloch's orchestral choirs are mixed far more often than they are separated or alternated, and his doublings are in the main traditional. He calls for all the common devices pertaining to wind articulation, brass muting, and string coloration, and is especially fond of harmonic heterophony.

In a passage from his undoubted masterpiece, *Schelomo* (1916), typical of this technique of sonorous figuration, the pale color of low flutes merges with the dry tone of high bassoons, while at the same time a quiet murmuring in celesta and harps creates a memorable background to the violin melodic line (Example 73). Similar applications of this kind of tonal heterophony can be found in the composer's *Sacred Service* of 1932, the cello and orchestra tone-poem *Voice in the Wilderness* (1936) (188), and the somewhat Impressionistic *Evocations* (1937) (189). In every case, however, this device—a veritable hallmark of Bloch's or-

EXAMPLE 73
Ernest Bloch: from *Schelomo*, p. 63

211

chestral style—is never an end in itself, but is used to intensify a dramatic moment.

One of the most imaginative contemporary orchestrators was Ernst Toch (1887–1964), composer of four symphonies, many film scores, and a number of highly descriptive orchestral works. His writing is always tonal, even when predominately chromatic in texture, and is full of a headlong rhythmic propulsion. Though the chromaticism sometimes becomes cloying, Toch's opulent Romantic orchestration invariably creates excitement and a sense of anticipation.

Unlike Hindemith, with whom Toch shared a natural instinct for woodwind and brass potentialities, the composer had a notable flair for percussion coloration. His First Symphony (1950) calls for both marimba and vibraphone in addition to the standard instruments, and in the Third Symphony (1955) he requires a glass harmonica, tuned glass balls, and Hammond organ, as well as two players for the vibraphone. In the Second Symphony (1951) **(190)** Toch made an interesting use of the timpani pedal glissando, here treated melodically and in precise rhythm. The two players execute a steady sixteenth-note pattern while alternately depressing and raising the pedal mechanism. By so doing, they alter the pitch in a measured pulsation, creating an ascending and descending chromatic scale.

Not all of Toch's exotic effects, however, are the result of percussive devices or uncommon instrumental resources; many stem from his technical inventiveness with the established instruments. In the First Symphony, for instance, there are several string passages that depend on the visual element for their ultimate impact. Swirling figures that begin in the first desk of the second and first violins are progressively carried through the remaining stands so that the eye of the listener follows a wave of bow-motions from the front of the section to the rear, followed by the reverse procedure (shown in Example 74). The picture is analogous to the ripples made by a stone cast into a still pond, with concentric waves spreading outward from the center. This carefully calculated device depends for its visual effectiveness (its very reason for being) upon the strings being positioned in the European manner, with the two violin sections on either side of the conductor's podium. Aurally, of course, the passage would lose little were the violin sections seated side by side, as they are in most American orchestras.

Still another novel instrumental effect is created in this same symphony: in the second movement the violins and violas are to be placed on the players' knees with their f-holes facing toward the audience; they are then to be plucked like a guitar or mandolin. This same device

212

appears also in the opening movement of the Second Symphony (191).

Elsewhere in his orchestration Toch demonstrates almost inordinate fondness for constantly shifting, elaborate heterophonous chord figurations created by the higher strings divided into three or more parts each. Usually the effect is made to serve as an animated background for sharply pointed motives or longer thematic elements in the woodwinds or brasses (illustrated conspicuously in the Second Symphony). Frequently the device is extended to the keyboard instruments—celesta, piano, organ —or to the harps, as seen on many pages of the first three symphonies.

The Toch scores also favor dense, almost cluster-like tone structures in homogeneous groups of instruments—divisi strings, for instance, or muted horns and trumpets. These function as solid inner pedals, around which swirl animated arpeggio patterns or scales in winds and strings, the whole laced with flashes of percussion color.

The musical style of Arthur Honegger (1892–1955) is a fascinating compound of Classical restraint, with its emphasis on the linear, and the highly colored tonal chromaticism of the late nineteenth-century German Romantics. His expression ranged from the religious elevation of *Le Roi David* (in two versions: 1921; 1926), through such bows to musical realism as *Pacific 231* (1923) and *Rugby* (1928), to the darkly introspective Romanticism of the five symphonies (1930–1950).

Intuitively dramatic, Honegger put some of his best music into stage works, or into symphonic pieces of pronounced theatrical character. His two operas, *Judith* (1925) and *Antigone* (1927), both evolved from incidental music written for stagings of the plays. *Horace Victorieux* (1921) was originally intended as a "mimed symphony," although it ended up as a programmatic work for orchestra instead. It is, however, *Le Roi David* and the oratorio, *Jeanne d'Arc au Bûcher* (1937) that constitute the ultimate demonstration of Honegger's superb handling of complex forces—narrators, soloists, full chorus, and fairly large orchestras.

The two existing versions of *Le Roi David,* moreover, vividly illustrate how deeply a dramatic work may be conditioned by its instrumentation. Honegger's original setting made use only of wind, brass, and percussion instruments; it was, consequently, more austere than opulent in its sound-values. In the reorchestration, which adds the full body of strings, the music glows with a warmth singularly missing from the original treatment. Both presentations of Honegger's musical material, nonetheless, are Romantic to the core, with a personalized Romanticism that permeates even the more Classically controlled *Monopartita* of 1951.

Compositional factors, needless to say, entered into the Neoromantic totality of the Honegger style. There are many instances of polyharmony

EXAMPLE 74
Ernst Toch: from First Symphony, p. 156

214

used for powerful emotional purposes (the opening measures of the Fifth Symphony, *"Di Tre Re"*: 1950, for example). And, inversely, the composer never embraced the purely mechanical aspects of atonalism, which repudiation in turn affected the nature of his instrumentation: fragmentation, extreme ranges, and psychological colorings are conspicuously absent from Honegger's orchestral style. Instead, he relied heavily on full orchestral sonorities, on solid brass outlining of harmony highlighted against one-, two-, or three-octave melodic spacings in the strings or woodwinds. (The 1946 *Symphonie Liturgique* (**192**) contains many such instances.) Standard color devices—mutes, flutter-tonguing, glissandi, strings sul ponticello, and so on—are amply represented (yet never overused) in Honegger's orchestration, and luxuriant texture is the rule rather than the exception.

Harp and celesta Honegger used rather sparingly; the piano as an orchestral instrument only occasionally, mainly for its percussive qualities. Moreover, his writing for percussion is surprisingly conservative as to both types and numbers of instruments, and in a general lack of complexity regarding what they were required to do. Notable for its rarity in Honegger's instrumentation is the very effective use of the *ondes* Martenot in *Jeanne d'Arc au Bûcher*.

For passages that would ordinarily require timpani reinforcement, Honegger would often substitute the bass drum, evidently preferring this heavier, duller, unpitched sound to the clearly articulated tones of timpani. There are no kettledrums at all, for instance, in the remarkable *Prélude pour "La Tempête"* (1923) (**193**). This is a tone poem of chilling effectiveness, descriptive of Shakespeare's (and Prospero's) storm-racked island; among its many pictorial touches are the eerily whistling violin harmonics that complement rushing woodwind figures.

Honegger made frequent use in his orchestral scores of a general, as opposed to a selective, scheme of dynamics (*nuances génerales*). The necessary indications of crescendo and diminuendo are placed on the score page just above the string parts, but they apply to all instruments simultaneously. While this concept of amplitude increases the dramatic intensity of the entire instrumental body, it also automatically eliminates the subtle shadings inherent in individually applied dynamics. It is the very antithesis of Mahler's "dynamic counterpoint" (see Example 44, p. 106), so integral to his orchestrational methodology.

There have been few composers of the twentieth century more intent than Honegger on pursuing an individual path of musical expression, unhandicapped by any adherence to fashionable dogma or the constant fluctuations of style and aesthetic. Honegger may well be a somewhat lonely figure in the music of our century, but his personal integrity is respected even by those who do not subscribe to his creative tenets.

Of the other important Middle European composers of Neoromantic tendencies, Boris Blacher (1903–1975) is best known in the United States for his *Orchestral Ornaments* and *Study in Pianissimo*, both written in 1953, and the *Virtuoso Music* of 1967. Although the Romanticism in these compositions is restrained, they utilize the resources of full orchestra in robust fashion.

The style of Karl Amadeus Hartmann (1905–1963), violently dramatic and lyrically elegiac in almost equal measure, stems principally from the work of Mahler, Berg, and Bartók. Always a notable element in his resources is a full complement of percussion, including all the " 'spiels and 'phones" available to contemporary orchestrators. Celesta, harp, and piano are nearly always requisitioned, and his timpani writing (frequently for five or six drums) is consistently virtuosic.

Of the orchestral music of Wolfgang Fortner (1907–), Gottfried von Einem (1918–), and Giselher Klebe (1925–), little need be said other than that a Romantic viewpoint of instrumentation is common to all. Worthy of more detailed discussion is the work of Hans Werner Henze (1926–), an eclectic composer of opera and of symphonies and, more recently, of avant-garde experimental works.

It is in his operas rather than his symphonies that Henze most vividly demonstrates his orchestrational Romanticism. The influence of Wagnerian sonority and Messiaenic coloration makes for a fascinating blend of stylistic elements in his dramatic music, from *The Stag King* of 1955–62 to *The Bassarids* (1965; based on Euripides's *The Bacchae*). An enormous orchestra is required for the allegorical *The Stag King,* including guitar, mandolin, and accordion in the greatly expanded percussion section. *Elegy for Young Lovers* (1961), on the other hand, uses a standardized wind choir with a reduced string section; however, there is an enlarged complement of percussion instruments.

But whether enormous or more traditionally constituted, Henze's orchestra is used to delineate music of great power and expressiveness. Not without good reason is he regarded today as the logical successor to Richard Strauss in the province of German opera.

From the composers of Central Europe we turn to three Englishmen who have given new vitality to Neoromantic orchestration: Vaughan Williams, Walton, and Britten. It is refreshing to have had in this century the candor and integrity of a Ralph Vaughan Williams (1872–1958). If he has at times been overestimated in his native country, he has no less surely been underestimated elsewhere. His appeal, for all its sturdy national roots, is only superficially conditioned by his "Englishness," for his expression is too universal to be circumscribed by locale.

Much of the generous warmth of Vaughan Williams's Romantic orchestration is technically traceable to the prevalence of chordal streams —passages of parallel movement in which simple triads or more complex tonal structures move in clearly delineated instrumental patterns. Invariably these sonoric streams are orchestrated in homogeneous colors (see Example 75). By and large, there is a good deal of intrachoir doubling in the composer's instrumentational schema, a practice that imparts richness and weight to his orchestral fabric.

Vaughan Williams's individual choirs, too, have a very personal mien, though the composer was no technical inventor in the Stravinsky or Bartók manner. His characteristic string sound is a texture often achieved by the use of mutes or extensive divisi, and solo strings frequently add their individual qualities to the tonal, usually neomodal, background—as, for instance, in the slow movement of the Second Symphony, "London" (1914), and the first movement of his third symphony, the *Pastoral* (1921). Although Vaughan Williams freely used all the forms of arco and pizzicato (save the snap pizzicato), as well as tremolo at the bridge or the fingerboard, he rarely called for col legno or for harmonics.

The character of Vaughan Williams's brasses is often involved with his perceptive application of muted timbre. "We can add mutes . . . to our brass instruments," the composer once said, "which change their features so that their own mothers would not know them." Though his horns and trumpets are frequently muted, his trombones are more apt to be open, though played softly. Trills and flutter-tonguing he rarely used, and glissando effects are conspicuously absent from his scores.

In such quasi-programmatic works as his seventh symphony, *Sinfonia Antartica* (1952), Vaughan Williams was lavish with the harp, the celesta, and the higher--pitched percussion instruments. The symphony also utilizes both organ and wind machine, the latter for obvious pictorial considerations (see Example 75).[11] Although the Eighth Symphony (1956) is non-programmatic, the composer's fascination with novel instruments and unusual timbres here has uninhibited play; the last movement, in particular, utilizes every kind of metallic percussion sound. And in the Ninth Symphony (1957; his last) Vaughan Williams appropriated the flugelhorn from the military band, an instrument unjustly neglected in symphonic instrumentation.[12]

It should be stressed, however, that these novel instrumental colors

EXAMPLE 75
Ralph Vaughan Williams: from *Sinfonia Antartica*, p. 83

are always made to serve musical purposes; they are not simply imposed on the composer's orchestration like ornamental frosting on a cake. This is certainly true of Vaughan Williams's instinctive feeling for and use of the saxophone (which in Alban Berg's *Lulu* lends so odious a coloring to the music characterizing his "heroine"). Equally telling in effect, though very different in purpose, are the appearances of this instrument in *Job, A Masque for Dancing* (1930) **(194)**, wherein the saxophone cunningly reflects the smirking hypocrisy of Job's comforters. In the Sixth Symphony (1947) **(195)**, where the saxophone engages in ribald dialogue with the other winds, the listener is vividly reminded of Lawrence Durrell's pungent description in *Justine:* "The foundering plunge of saxophones crying to the night like cuckolds." In his Ninth Symphony the composer calls for a trio of saxophones. They are not expected, Vaughan Williams tells us with his accustomed dryness, "to behave like demented cats, but are allowed to be their own romantic selves." If a case must be made to bring the saxophone into the symphonic orchestra, then this is the prime exhibit in the defense.

The Romantic Vaughan Williams, neither iconoclast nor reactionary, was in his own forthright way as visionary a creative artist as either Bartók, Schoenberg, or Stravinsky. His immense creative energy never flagged until the day of his death, and few other composers of our time have demonstrated in their entire body of work a more lucid style or more uncompromising artistic integrity. As Donald Ferguson puts it, Vaughan Williams "devised no system for himself and had none to transmit to others; but he did effectively illustrate a truth too often hidden from the followers of systems—that the language of music is rooted in the understanding not merely of music as an art, but of experience which music transmutes into art" (*A History of Musical Thought*).

Sir William Walton (1902–   ), from the robust *Portsmouth Point Overture* (1925) to the 1960 Second Symphony has applied a sure and consistent hand to his orchestral approach. It is strong and it is direct. And because it makes an unequivocal impact on the listener's ear and emotions alike, Walton's music has always enjoyed great appeal.

His Romantic attitude toward orchestration pervades the wide gamut from *Façade* (1922), with its elements of the English music hall and American jazz, to the virile dramaticism of *Belshazzar's Feast* (1931), and to the formal austerity of the three string concertos and the First Symphony (1934). Though much too predictable, Walton's instrumentational style is always full-blooded; its texture places great reliance on massive combinations and powerful, fanfare-like outbursts in the brasses and percussion. Even the 1957 *Partita for Double String Orchestra,* patently motivated by the Neoclassical movement still in progress, shows in its orchestration a singular lack of reticence and textural transparency. For all its indisputable twentieth-century ingredients, Walton's work has Elgar's late Romantic penchant for almost constant interchoir doubling of melodic and harmonic strands. Usually such an approach to instrumentation spells bombast, a pitfall he has adroitly avoided—except, perhaps, in his "occasional" music: the *Crown Imperial Coronation March* (for George VI) of 1937, and the *Orb and Sceptre Coronation March* (for Elizabeth II) of 1953.

Walton's natural skill with the orchestra is amply illustrated throughout his opera *Troilus and Cressida* (1954) and in his several notable film scores. Indeed, in his "Battle of Agincourt" music for *Henry V* (1944), Walton comes very close to equaling the spine-tingling excitement of Prokofiev's "Battle on the Ice" in *Alexander Nevsky*. That Walton was assigned a number of important film scores is a tribute both to his stature as a composer and to the perspicacity of England's film producers and directors.

Benjamin Britten (1913–1976) was always so facile that it is difficult to assess his musical personality. He could orchestrate in a cool and deft neo-Stravinskyan manner, as in the chamber opera, *The Rape of Lucretia* (1946); in an introverted, almost neo-Schoenbergian style, as in *The Turn of the Screw* (1954); or with powerful dramatic impact, as in the *Sinfonia da Requiem* of 1940, the operas *Peter Grimes* (1945) and *Billy Budd* (1952), and in the eloquent *War Requiem* of 1962. He could with equal nonchalance toss off the deservedly popular *Young Person's Guide to the Orchestra* of 1946 (a veritable manual of Neoromantic instrumentation), and in such expressions as the trilogy of church parables (*Curlew River* [1964], *The Burning Fiery Furnace* [1966], *The Prodigal Son* [1968]) blend medieval and modern with consummate ease. And to cap it all, he could write a work as delicately English as the *Serenade for Tenor, Horn, and Strings* (1941)—a miracle of string, brass, and vocal felicity.

Venturesomeness was always a significant feature of Britten's orchestration; seldom did it repeat itself from one work to another. Each new composition of the composer called forth its own characteristic, even unique, instrumental complement, from the full symphonic forces of the *Sinfonia da Requiem* and the more massive operas to the selective chamber ensembles of *The Rape of Lucretia, The Turn of the Screw,* and the three church parables. Britten's 1960 opera based on Shakespeare's *A Midsummer Night's Dream* requires only twenty-eight orchestral players, employed with the greatest distinction. Here each of the three main groups of characters has its individual orchestral sound: strings and woodwinds for the earthly lovers; brasses and low woodwinds for Bottom and his fellow rustics; and for Oberon, Titania, Puck, and the other inhabitants of the fairy kingdom, only harp, celesta, and delicate percussion. In Britten's final opera, *Death in Venice* (1973), a similar linking of specific instrumental color with certain of the drama's characters is fundamental to the composer's orchestrational approach. The mimed role of the boy Tadzio, for instance, is accompanied only by a large percussion ensemble in which the vibraphone has the starring part. As Donald Mitchell observes (in his notes to the London recording), "The wholly distinctive sound and character of that music—which manages to be overpoweringly present and emphatically remote at the same time—sharply separates it from the score of which it forms a part where, of course, the 'conventional' orchestra is used." Always texturally transparent, that orchestra is employed with consummate skill, its sound stamped as indisputably personal and unique.

Britten's delightful *Spring Symphony* (1949) calls for a large orchestra (including cow horn), though the composer seldom employs his total resources. Instead, many of the rather brief sections—settings of spring poems by English writers—are scored for but a handful of instruments. Three trumpets alone, for example, accompany the vocal solo in "The Merry Cuckoo," (196) and in the aria "Waters Above (197) only the violins support the tenor line.

Furthermore, the *Spring Symphony* as a whole clearly shows Britten's predilection for pattern scoring; that is to say, a whole movement, or a lengthy section within a movement, will be orchestrated in an almost undeviating pattern of vertical and horizontal tracery. The pattern of a particular piece may never be repeated—Britten was too inventive for that—but within a single work it will be used consistently. In adhering rigidly to this orchestrational premise the composer foregoes the wide-ranging coloration and textural fragmentation which is at the core of Impressionist and Expressionist instrumental conceptions.

Although no contemporary composer was more sensitive than Britten to the need for instrumental transparency behind any vocal delineation, when voices are not a factor in his expression Britten's orchestra is fully unleashed in authentic Romantic fashion. The interludes in *Peter Grimes,* for example, not only are integral links in the advancement of the drama but vividly demonstrate the composer's natural empathy for orchestral power and richness, when and to the extent required. The ending of the storm, when the moon's rays pierce the clouds, is a superb moment in the opera and indisputable proof of Britten's ability to find just the right orchestrational garb for the drama of the moment (Example 76).

222

EXAMPLE 76
Benjamin Britten: from *Peter Grimes* (Act 1, Interlude 2), p. 157

Music by Benjamin Britten; Libretto by Montague Slater. Copyright 1945 by Boosey & Hawkes, Ltd.; Renewed 1972. Reprinted by permission of Boosey & Hawkes, Inc.

STYLE AND ORCHESTRATION

Of his self-confessed eclectic style, Britten has said, "I try to write as Stravinsky has written and Picasso has painted. They were men who freed music and painting from the tyranny of the purely personal. They passed from manner to manner as a bee passes from flower to flower. I try to do the same. Why should I lock myself inside a narrow personal idiom?" The statement is not only a succinct summation of Britten's artistic credo but implies that for him, as for all authentic composers, the techniques he used concerned only himself.

As we have seen, the composers just discussed were all involved in the widespread renaissance of the Romantic orchestral tradition in Europe. In the mid–twentieth-century, however, instrumental Neoromanticism was perhaps strongest throughout the western hemisphere. And today the serious music of the Americas embraces, in true melting-pot style, every facet of musical persuasion from the most austere Neoclassicism to the most fulsome Romanticism, from didactic serialism to outré exoticism and avant-garde experimentation. But it is possible that, until mid-century at least, the Neoromantics in the United States outnumbered all the rest; certainly much American music up to the sixties was predominantly Romantic— in musical aesthetic and in orchestrational technique. What we are pleased to call the extroverted, optimistic, and ingenuous character of the native-born American elicited from our composers a great deal of music that revels in the sheer sound and expressiveness of the symphonic orchestra. Today, however, Neoromanticism has become transmuted into a style partaking of widely divergent attitudes and compositional materials, all of which determine the nature of the composers' treatment of the traditional orchestra.

Within the large group of American Neoromantics there were many ideological shadings; despite their common approach to the orchestra, not all the composers shared an obvious agreement on musical cause and effect. There was—and still is—one substantial group with a predominantly intellectual approach, the *abstract* Romanticists if you will. Composers like Roy Harris, Walter Piston, and William Schuman have compositional styles that verge on the Neoclassic; they assign cardinal importance to the linear and formal aspects of music-making while still preferring the resources of the full orchestra. In contrast there is the quasi-programmatic approach of the *Americana* Romanticists, whose primary concern is to communicate aspects of the American heritage. This group would include Charles Ives, Douglas Moore, Virgil Thomson, and, on occasion, Aaron Copland. Finally, there is a fairly substantial body of composers who might be characterized as *authentic* Romanticists—composers whose musical tenets embrace neither the intellectual pragmatism of the abstract Romanticists nor the limiting near-chauvinistic attitudes of the Americana-ists. Instead, these composers (Samuel Barber, Paul Creston, Howard Hanson, Gian Carlo Menotti, and Robert Ward, among others) express an unabashed personal Romanticism in terms of the ensemble inherited from the late nineteenth-century.

Of the abstract Romanticists, the most indubitably Classical in spirit and compositional style was Walter Piston (1894–1976). Piston's cardinal conviction was linearity; he was almost academic in his devotion to canonic and fugal imitations and other contrapuntal devices that have always delighted the craftsman. But wedded to this disciplined style is a Neoromantic conception of the orchestra in terms of sonority and power. One is continually surprised not so much by Piston's dry wit as by the warmth and passion of a great deal of his music, notably the slow movements of his various symphonies. Here is truly the Neoromanticist speaking, yet everything is under firm control in both statement and manipulation—as fastidious, refined, and well-wrought as any Ravel score.

The full sonority of the Piston orchestra is brought about more by linear spacings and doublings than by vertical harmonic stacking. His scoring is unfailingly clean, bright, and exhilarating, and even in harmonically quiescent periods there is considerable activity from rhythmic pulsation and instrumental fluctuation. If the contrapuntal lines are sometimes severe and dry, the orchestration is never thin and desiccated; it is this particular aspect of Piston's habitude that sets him apart from the Neoclassicist instrumentators.

Like Hindemith, Piston favored his orchestral choirs on contrasting planes. In the quoted passage from Piston's Sixth Symphony of 1955 (Example 77) the woodwinds are concerned with the canonic theme in rhythmic diminution, staccato, while the brasses and percussion interject sharp bursts of harmony. At the same time the strings are engaged on a broader, legato version of the melody in canon; the orchestrational analogy to Hindemith's technique is clear (compare with Example 70, p. 203).

Piston also shared with Hindemith a pronounced antipathy to "devices"; hence his scores are almost completely devoid of flutter-tonguing, glissandi, snap-pizzicato effects, harmonics, or other exaggerated coloristic touches. His consistent avoidance of these timbral staples constitutes a kind of disdain for interposing any distraction between the composer's direct expression and the listener. Moreover, Piston's technique of instrumentation, which seldom deviated from a basic premise of clear, businesslike scoring, is entirely parallel to his decision to use absolute musical forms. It is always deft, always sure; it is invariably brilliant and transparent—

EXAMPLE 77
Walter Piston: from Symphony No. 6, p. 104

and easy to prognosticate. But when listening to Walter Piston's music we must content ourselves—as Sibelius once said about his own music—with a glass of pure water rather than one of more heady properties.

Roy Harris (1898–) has written no ballets, no operas, no film scores, no programmatic tone-poems—only those absolute and contrapuntal forms that achieve their epitome in the symphony, instrumental sonata, and string quartet. Yet his works are as "American" as anything that has come from the lesser composers of Grand Canyon suites, Indian lullabies, Creole nocturnes, or Kentucky hillbilly dances. At its best the Harris music is spacious, endlessly flowing, and powerful; the orchestration is correspondingly massive and dynamically incisive.

Both the composition and its instrumentation, however, are more traditional than one would anticipate, given the composer's uncompromising personal credo. "To talk with Harris," Henry Cowell once said, "one would gather that his music must be radical. On hearing the music, one finds it sounding quite conventional." This stylistic paradox can be explained by the fact that Harris is as much the Classicist as he is the Romanticist. Like Hindemith, Piston, Schuman, and early Copland, he prefers the abstract and polyphonic forms of music rather than more architecturally loose modes of descriptive and programmatic expression. But at the same time Harris conceives the orchestra as a medium of tonal and dynamic strength, and—even though he is unalterably opposed to colorism for its own sake—brilliant timbral potentiality. In this respect Harris is certainly not unique; many twentieth-century composers stand astride the tenets of Classicism and Romanticism without losing their artistic equilibrium.

Characteristic of Harris's orchestral style is his consistent use of the brass choir in broad, chorale-like passages. But unlike William Schuman, who also favors this device, Harris juxtaposes legato polyphonic lines in woodwind and string instruments against the brass solidity. These melodic lines are usually heavily doubled to compensate for the greater power of the brass instruments. Harris thus uses a mingling or overlapping technique rather than a more clearly differentiated antiphony. His orchestrational premise is well illustrated in a passage from the Seventh Symphony of 1952 (Example 78).

In the opinion of many commentators on the American musical scene it is Harris's Third Symphony (1938) that best typifies the composer's rugged, dramatic style and vivid orchestral manner. The five sections of this one-movement work are each characterized by Harris in terms of emotional content and instrumentational plan: the first, *Tragic,* emphasizes low string sonorities; the second, *Lyric,* is predominantly

227

EXAMPLE 78
Roy Harris: from Symphony No. 7, p. 20

given to woodwinds, horns, and strings; the third, marked *Pastoral*, concentrates on woodwind color; the fourth, *Fugue—Dramatic*, exploits brass and percussion, while the final section, *Dramatic-Tragic*, is saturated with a dark resonance reminiscent of Brahms and Sibelius.

Although Harris has never surpassed the high point reached in his Third Symphony, he has continued to grow in technical assurance and in the conviction of his personal aesthetic, and to express himself eloquently on the vocation of the modern composer. "Musical literature never has been and never will be valuable to society as a whole," he once wrote, "until it is created as an authentic and characteristic culture of and from the people it expresses." In a world of musical expression now almost completely internationalized, Harris's credo would appear to be isolated from all the rapid, radical stylistic changes now taking place throughout Europe and the Americas.

Of all the current American practitioners of orchestral art, William Schuman (1910–   ) comes closest to having a truly distinctive orchestrational style. Basically, his premise is that of "block," or sectional instrumentation. In this he has much in common with Hindemith, yet—because of Schuman's more dissonant tonal language and his frenetic rhythmic drive—there is an enormous difference in their results.

In the Schuman scores, long passages—even entire sections—are scored for but one orchestral choir. If other instruments are brought in, they are likely to be completely homogeneous in timbre. An excellent instance of this kind of instrumental thinking occurs in the opening passacaglia of the Third Symphony (1941) **(198)**, where the strings (minus double basses) have a tense, quasi-canonic passage, in which they are later joined by four trombones in closely spaced harmonies in their middle registers. No changes in this instrumental pattern take place until the fugue, given to horns and strings, breaks in somewhat later. In turn, this brass-string relationship continues until the delayed entrance of the woodwind choir, thus confirming the composer's unswerving adherence to "block" instrumentational patterns.[13]

Not always, however, does Schuman's concept of antiphony involve long passages or sections; frequently choir answers choir in rapid, almost kaleidoscopic succession. On a page excerpted from his Sixth Symphony of 1948 (Example 79), we can see biting, polytonal brass sonorities contrasted immediately with harsh chords in the strings, which in turn give way to the relative clarity and brightness of the woodwind instruments spread over four octaves; then he returns to the high, sharp strings, followed by the brasses in close-position harmony—all within the span of five measures. Innumerable instances of similar antiphonal treatment can be located in any one of the composer's other major scores.

EXAMPLE 79
William Schuman: from Symphony No. 6, p. 65

It is interesting how this conception of group answering group, choir responding to choir, recurs in the history of Western music. A salient feature of much Renaissance music, antiphony virtually disappeared until it was revitalized as an important orchestral device in the late nineteenth century. We have already seen that the technique was a major aspect of Bruckner's creativity and was frequently used by other composers, notably Tchaikovsky. In William Schuman's orchestral style the concept of antiphony is as intrinsic as his predilection for jagged, athletic rhythms, grinding polyharmonies, and extended parallel movements of chordal sonorities.

Schuman's orchestration also evidences other highly personal signatures, such as lengthy and often elaborate cadenzas for solo timpani.[14] These rhetorical outbursts are integral to the composer's personal style; so is his partiality to the shock value of snare-drum rim-shots. Few modern composers for the symphonic orchestra have exploited the clamorous potentialities of the percussion more militantly than Schuman (see, for example, the concluding pages of *Credendum* [199]). Yet he can also draw on the subtler qualities of these instruments, as witness the tautly delineated, *pianissimo* pattern given to the snare drum at the outset of the Toccata finale of the Third Symphony (200).

Although Schuman is not given to writing extended passages for a solo instrument (excepting timpani), he has on occasion written other instrumental solos of extraordinary difficulty. One of these is the passage for bass clarinet accompanying the snare-drum solo just mentioned (Third Symphony, last movement). This solo wind-part ought truly to be marked "for virtuoso players only," for it takes the instrument from the very bottom to the very top of its range in a matter of three brief beats. No one who has heard it can deny that the effect is absolutely hair-raising.

Also indisputably calculated to raise the hackles on one's neck is an earlier passage in the same symphony given to four trumpets in close formation (measures 195–207 of the fugue section). The cutting force of these four brass voices—independent but imitative—creates an effect, Vincent Persichetti says, like "that of an electric trumpet machine." The coruscation of this sound—matched only by the sweeping trumpet passage in the finale of Ravel's *Daphnis et Chloé* (201)—finds many parallels elsewhere in Schuman's panoramic orchestration. No doubt his early association with the jazz scene gave him a nonchalant attitude toward brass technique, for his demands on these instruments generally exceed those for other orchestral resources, percussion included. Singly, in family groups, or as a massed phalanx, Schuman's brasses are frequently used to punch jagged apertures in the orchestral fabric, usually backed up by the reverberant percussion.

That Schuman's orchestrational style is individual, practised, and immensely powerful cannot be denied by anyone conversant with his music. The listener may be thrilled by this orchestration or repelled by it. From its high stridency and frenetic pace the musical sensitivities may be quickened and stimulated or may suffer actual physical discomfort.

But whatever may be one's reaction to Schuman's orchestral music, it is quite impossible to remain indifferent.

To that "stubborn Yankee," Charles Ives (1874–1954), is accorded the honor, among many others, of being the first composer of authentic *Americana*. Whether or not Ives was an authentic Romanticist can be argued; iconoclast is a more realistic label for this prophetic voice in American music. Moreover, a definitive, even an accurate, analysis of Ives's orchestrational style is exceptionally difficult to achieve, owing to its somewhat serendipitous origins. So much pure experimentation went into his scores, with results unpredictable even to the composer, that no clear and consistent method of instrumentation can be extrapolated.

The four symphonies of Ives, which together with the *Three Places in New England* (1903–1914) constitute the core of his orchestral oeuvre, grow progressively in complexity of musical material and in orchestrational interest. Both the First (1896–98) and Second (1897–1902) symphonies are scored for normal-sized orchestras; the Third (1901–1904) utilizes a chamber orchestra, while the Fourth (1910–1916) calls for an enormous ensemble that includes organ, an orchestral piano (four hands), a solo piano, "Ether organ" (possibly Ives meant a Theremin), three optional saxophones, and a distant (offstage) group of violins and harps, as well as mixed chorus.

In this symphony, as in the *Three Places in New England,* Ives's instrumentational style can be characterized as one of complete independence of all instrumental parts. Rarely do two instruments do exactly the same thing, whether their part is melodic, harmonic, or figurative. The aural result is a gigantic tonal mesh in which it is literally impossible to distinguish the separate strands (Example 80).

An unusual aspect of Ives's requirements for the *Three Places in New England* is that he specifies the standard complement of instruments but does not indicate the number of each. Almost without exception, the woodwind and brass parts are written as single-line melodies or harmony notes. They could, therefore, be doubled at will, according to the conductor's discretion. Only the strings are written divisi, frequently backed up by the piano. The latter instrument plays almost continuously, contributing an elaborate heterophony to the tonal landscape.

Among the dozens of prophetic devices that are threaded throughout the work of Ives is the occasional use of orchestral tone-clusters—notably in the *Fourth of July* movement of the *Symphony: Holidays* (1913) (202).[15] Many of his compositions make significant forays into unusual instrumental resources, predating by more than half a century similar experiments by the current avant-garde. In *The Unanswered*

EXAMPLE 80
Charles Ives: from Symphony No. 4, p. 77

233

STYLE AND ORCHESTRATION

Question (1908), for instance, we find an orchestra of muted strings, four flutes, and a solo trumpet played offstage. Throughout, the strings play soft sustained harmonies while the flutes engage in a gradually increasing complexity of dissonance—futile answers to the ever-questioning phrase of the insistent trumpet. The means employed in this remarkable work are disarmingly simple, but the musical effect is quite extraordinary.

The conceptual and technical anticipations of Ives, says Peter Yates, "are not ideas which someone has since used to better advantage. . . . Ives was as aware as Schoenberg of his accomplishment; unlike Schoenberg, he had no opportunity to hear his instrumental compositions in performance. His orchestration is the work of silent knowledge, his most remarkable anticipation, which our experience validates" (*Twentieth Century Music*).

Aaron Copland (1900–), with the urbanity and sophistication of a native New Yorker, naturally gravitated both toward a stylistic use of jazz and into the rarefied climate of Neoclassicism. Far more amazing is the later mutation of his musical language from the severe disciplines of his early period to an approach that combined harmonic directness, melodic simplicity, and stylistic moderation. Furthermore, a new conceptual usage of the symphonic orchestra and an intense interest in American folk materials put Copland squarely in the camp of the composers associated with *Americana* aspects of musical expression.

This metamorphosis of Copland's style took place after his first trip to Mexico in 1932. During the four years that followed, his efforts to find an appropriate expression of his Mexican experience took shape in *El Salón México* (1936). After completing this witty piece of tourist music, Copland continued to explore the problems of synthesizing folk-like tunes and rhythms with his normally complex and subtilized technique. His success in creating this personal amalgam has been universally admired, and he has as a consequence often been regarded as the authentic voice of the American Southwest.

Few concertgoers or balletomanes in the United States today are unacquainted with *Billy the Kid* (1938), *Rodeo* (1942), or *Appalachian Spring* (1944). Untold millions have heard Copland's superb film scores for *Of Mice and Men* (1939), *Our Town* (1940), and *The Red Pony* (1948), though many have probably not remembered the composer's name. (But then most moviegoers are notoriously indifferent to the identity of anyone connected with a film except its stars.)

In terms of orchestration, Copland's special brand of American Romanticism has resulted in textures that have brilliance without deadening weight; clarity without anemia; commendable picturesqueness without freakish exoticism. Copland, like Walter Piston, favors a clear-cut style of instrumentation in which doublings are kept to a minimum except in tutti passages. All melodic or polyphonic lines, as well as the various harmonic strata, are aurally distinct, and all extraneous matter is carefully eliminated. There is, however, generally more interchoir mixing of thematic and harmonic components in Copland's scores than in those of either Piston or William Schuman; furthermore, Copland does not favor sectional antiphony, or "block" orchestration, at least to the same extent as Schuman or Hindemith.

Stylistic simplicity, litheness, and an essentially native musical tongue became fully synthesized in Copland's eloquent Third Symphony of 1946. In musical expression this work is as authentic Copland as any of the ballets or movie scores, proving that the composer can be "native" without the underpinning of story, locale, and stage action to give his expression credibility. To many musicians this symphony represents the best elements of Copland's two distinct musical personalities—the formal austerity of the creative symphonist, and the appealing directness of the mature *Americana* stylist.

Copland's orchestral timbre in this symphony evinces a preference for sharp colors and, generally, an absence of muted or veiled sonority. Like Schuman, Copland favors trenchant expression over blurred orchestral effect; the hard, clipped sound of the higher register of all the instruments has more appeal for him than the dark rumblings of the lower tonal gamut (Example 81). Like Schuman, too, he has a predilection for the piercing bite of the brass choir operating on an extremely elevated level, as in lengthy segments of *Statements* (1935) and *Music for a Great City* (1964). And, indeed, the *scherzo* movement of the Third Symphony (203) is almost a definitive essay in the exploitation of high-brass tone quality.

The composer's *Orchestral Variations* (1957) offer a rare opportunity to examine his instrumentational concepts as he transforms material originally conceived as the *Piano Variations* (1930). Unlike such a work as the *Ma Mère l'Oye* of Maurice Ravel, however, Copland's original material was not a basically pianistic concept to be later transformed into an orchestral entity. The early piano variations—militantly percussive, pointillistic, constantly alternating between loud and soft—were nonpianistic in the traditional sense. But a close study of their evolution into orchestral format clarifies Copland's dexterous use of instrumental balance and timbral contrast. One regrets, however, that the publishers did not include the original piano version beneath the orchestral score, as they did in printing Ravel's orchestration of the Mussorgsky *Pictures at an Exhibition*.

Copland's later works for orchestra, including *Connotations* (1962)

EXAMPLE 81
Aaron Copland: from Third Symphony, p. 19

236

and *Inscape* (1967), are tonally oriented serial essays that use the orchestra from the viewpoint of the Romanticist rather than the Expressionist. Stylistically, they are a far cry from the *Americana* aspects of the composer's middle period, and from the warmly Romantic atmosphere of his opera, *The Tender Land* (1954). Yet one would have no hesitation in identifying the orchestrational ambience of the later scores as Coplandesque.

"In general," Copland has said, "I belong to the category of instrumentator whose orchestral framework and detail is carefully planned so as to carry out more faithfully the expressive purpose inherent in the entirely completed ground plan of the work" *(Music and Imagination)*. It may be that Copland tends consciously to adjust his instrumental colors after the work is composed, rather than at the precise moment of conception. But one suspects that this deferred choice of instrumental timbres is still intuitive, and that Copland at the very moment of writing down his generic ideas knows his precise scheme of orchestration, even though its outward realization may come later. But whatever the approach, or by whatever means Copland arrives at his distinctive orchestral style, his results are eminently right and satisfying to the listener.

To glimpse the wide range of viewpoints among the large group of—for want of a better term—"authentic" Romanticists in the United States, one need only compare a page of orchestration by Samuel Barber with one by Paul Creston, or one by Howard Hanson with one by Gian Carlo Menotti. Where the cardinal tenet of the abstract Romantics— Piston, Harris, and Schuman—is linearity, the authentic Romantics are more concerned with vertical sonority and orchestral opulence. While the abstractionists pursue canonic and fugal polyphony and the contrapuntal forms that have always delighted the craftsman, the authentics are rhapsodic in their expression, even when employing absolute forms, and not inclined to strict formal control.

The personal credo of Howard Hanson (1896–   ), as set forth in his oft-quoted statement about his own "Romantic" Symphony (No. 2: 1930), perhaps best sums up the feelings of all the Neoromantic composers of similar persuasion: "The symphony represents for me my escape from the rather bitter type of modern musical realism which occupies so large a place in contemporary thought. Much contemporary music seems to me to be showing a tendency to become entirely too cerebral. I do not believe that music is primarily a matter of intellect, but rather a manifestation of emotions." To this unfailing emotional Romanticism, Hanson has adhered without wavering from his First Symphony (the "Nordic") of 1922 to *Mosaics* of 1957.

STYLE AND ORCHESTRATION

Many critics claim that Hanson's musical style is closely akin to that of Sibelius, which the composer would certainly not deny; their instrumentation, however, is similar only in keeping orchestral "effects" at a bare minimum and bypassing all exaggerated coloristic devices. Thus string harmonics and col legno, for example, or wind flutter-tonguing and glissandi, are techniques rarely found in Hanson's scores. Nor is he drawn to unusual instruments or uncommon combinations of the traditional instruments.

Hanson's sonorities are achieved by way of the conventionally constituted orchestra, using fairly standard spacings and doublings. For example, he favors the brasses used in their family groups within the larger section: the four horns, the three trumpets, or the three trombones and tuba are usually kept in juxtaposition when utilized harmonically, rather than interlocked with the others. Hanson is partial to single-color solos in the woodwind choir, usually supported by a relatively uncomplicated background in the strings. The horn, too, is given great prominence as soloist, again with an essentially homophonic accompaniment (Example 82).

For the harp, treated in the nineteenth-century manner (as in Example 82), Hanson has a special fondness. And he makes full and highly effective use of standard percussion resources. His opera, *Merry Mount* (1933), includes an elaborate part for marimba, in addition to xylophone, tubular bells, temple blocks, and all the traditional members of the section. But the celesta, oddly enough, is missing from Hanson's instrumental palette except in *Mosaics* and the *Bold Island Suite* (1963), and he has never made the piano an orchestral resource—only a solo instrument in his jazz-oriented concerto of 1948.

Hanson's unique contribution remains the unmistakably personal aura with which he invests his Neoromantic orchestration of dramatically conceived music in absolute forms. His music, according to Joseph Machlis, "spoke persuasively to a generation of music lovers brought up on Franck, Brahms, and Sibelius, assuring them that twentieth-century music had something to say that they could understand. This needed doing in the Twenties and Thirties, and Hanson filled the need" (*The Enjoyment of Music*). Although his musical expression is not to everyone's taste, no one can deny the integrity of that expression.

The distinction ascribed to Hanson's orchestral style also applies to the scores of Samuel Barber (1910–   ). He is a composer whose music has always been notable for its lyricism and for an absence of strained sonorities and fractured rhythms. Like Hanson, he is a Romantic conservative—or conservative Romantic, if you will; just as his compositional

EXAMPLE 82
Howard Hanson: from Symphony No. 2, "Romantic," p. 55

N1301

style has been shaped by adherence to tradition, so his way with the orchestra partakes of the techniques of the late nineteenth century.

Barber's early *Music for a Scene from Shelley* (1933) shows a definite Impressionist influence in its orchestrational mannerisms, but the First Symphony (1936) and *First Essay for Orchestra* (1937) firmly established his inherent Romantic substance and expression. Not, however, until the Second Symphony (1943) and the *Medea* ballet score of 1947 do we discern in his scores the imprint of mid–twentieth-century musical thinking. *Medea's Meditation and Dance of Vengeance* (1955), the intense symphonic poem developed from this ballet, is possibly the most advanced work to come from Barber's pen. The boldness of the music, furthermore, is admirably complemented by its brilliant instrumentational investiture, in which the percussive qualities of the piano play an enormous part (Example 83).

The piano is also a prominent feature of Barber's Second Symphony. In both these works, however, it is employed largely to strengthen and highlight accented chords or ostinato lines. Seldom does the instrument have an independent part in the orchestral texture, or contribute its own unique coloristic qualities to the orchestral sonority. One might, in fact, question whether the piano is actually needed to the extent that the composer uses it in both scores. Nevertheless, the habit of using the piano as a doubling agent, welding heterogeneous woodwind, brass, and string tonal qualities, is common in much twentieth-century orchestration, from Prokofiev to Barber. With some contemporary composers its orchestrational use has become merely an annoying mannerism; with others, an unfortunate and uncontrollable vice.

In orchestrating his first opera, *Vanessa* (1956), Barber harks back to the earlier dramatic style of the First Symphony. Some sections of the opera are almost Puccinian, and rely heavily on the standard trappings of late Romanticism. The same is true of *Anthony and Cleopatra,* commissioned for the 1966 opening of the new Metropolitan Opera House in New York's Lincoln Center. Despite its many deft touches and its sense of spectacle, Barber's music and its orchestral garb were coolly received at the premiere.

Die Natali (1960), for all its contrapuntal intricacies and patrician craftsmanship, is orchestrally imbued with the same Romantic feeling as the operas, a feeling completely in keeping, however, with the essential simplicity of its religious materials. The 1962 Piano Concerto is perhaps more rhythmically complex than other Barber scores, but its orchestration is once again unmistakably Romantic in sound. A close parallel exists, texturally speaking, between the second movement of the concerto and

EXAMPLE 83

Samuel Barber: from *Medea's Meditation and Dance of Vengeance*, p. 40

43918

the slow movement of his First Symphony. The finale of the concerto, a driving toccata, is orchestrationally akin to *Medea's Dance of Vengeance*.

Barber's personal method of instrumentation, like Hanson's related concept of orchestral sonority, employs much interchoir mixing, with a minimum of pure timbre discernible. Consequently, the sound is thickly warm and opulent. Chords are usually closely spaced (see, for example, the slow movement of the Second Symphony [204]), and the entire chord-delineation is generally assigned to homogeneous instruments. This composer is not especially partial to unusual instrumental combinations or to exotic doublings; neither does he consciously exploit extreme ranges or the timbral devices endemic to Impressionist and Expressionist orchestration. Barber's instrumentation, like his basic musical concept, is unfailingly polished and rather aristocratic; his orchestral manner always sounds uncluttered and supremely confident. What it may lack in novelty or experimentation is amply counterbalanced by its incontestable logic and natural skill; this in turn may possibly account in part for the fact that Barber is one of our most frequently performed composers.

To describe the various orchestral works of other admirable Neoromantic composers in the United States would only overextend the analysis of trends and methodologies on previous pages. In our survey of the Neoromantic viewpoint we have encountered extensively for the first time the apparent contradiction between the compositional inclinations of the contemporary composer and the instrumental manner he employs for their realization. No one, for example, could convincingly maintain that the basic aesthetic of Ralph Vaughan Williams is analogous to that of Arthur Honegger, or that Ernst Toch's credo parallels that of Walter Piston or even of Samuel Barber. But these musically divergent composers share as Neoromantic orchestrators a common approach: without exception they consider the symphonic and operatic orchestra a rich aggregation of diverse instruments capable of a vast emotional range. Scoring from this commonly shared viewpoint, they release their frequently quite unrelated compositional styles into a common stream of instrumental atmosphere.

The Neoromantic composers view the orchestra, moreover, as a massive instrumental combination, and not as the artificially enlarged chamber ensemble that appeals to the Neoclassicist and the Expressionist alike. Stravinsky in his way, and Schoenberg, Berg, and Webern in theirs, often treated the symphonic (and operatic) orchestra more in terms of intimate, soloistic interplay than of massed orchestral sonority. The orchestral ethos of post-Romanticism, however, demands as its fundamental premise an instrumentation of power and opulence.

THE NEOROMANTIC ORCHESTRA

Just as late nineteenth-century Romanticism engendered a revolt against its excesses expressed in the countercurrents of Impressionism, Expressionism, and Neoclassicism, so the Neoromanticism of the twentieth century finds conflicting pressures in the exoticism and avant-gardism of today. The extent to which these two powerful centrifugal movements have altered the conceptual techniques of orchestration will be demonstrated in the chapters to follow. But regardless of the far-reaching changes brought about by current instrumentational experimentation, the vitality and validity alike of Neoromantic orchestration can never be relegated to museum status.

Notes

1. Compare this passage with one similarly orchestrated in Stravinsky's *Symphony in Three Movements* (Example 67, p. 184).

2. Arnold Schoenberg is credited with having introduced this effect to serious music in his symphonic poem *Pelleas und Melisande.*

3. Dmitri Shostakovich's youthful opera, *Lady Macbeth of Mtsensk* (1931) came into official disfavor, in part, for the erotic implications of its seemingly incessant trombone glissandi. In the composer's 1956 revision of his score, now titled *Katerina Ismailova,* most of the offending slides were excised—to the obvious improvement of the music.

4. Examples of this practice may be found in the first movement of the *Concert Music for Strings and Brass* (1930) ; the third movement of the *Concerto for Orchestra;* the two inner movements of *Symphonia Serena* (1946) ; and the fugue of the *"Turandot" scherzo* movement of the *Symphonic Metamorphosis on Themes by Weber* (1943) .

5. *Die Harmonie der Welt* was composed in 1951; six years later the composer wrote an opera on the same subject, preserving the title and using the same musical materials. On the other hand, his better-known symphony, *Mathis der Maler* (1934) , was derived from a previously composed opera of the same name (1930) ; the symphonic version, however, was premiered four years *before* the first performance of the opera.

6. See the first movement, between numbers 15–16, 18–19, for example.

7. First movement at number 19.

8. Final movement between numbers 115–116.

9. Compare this passage with Example 38, p. 89; though the instrumentation in each differs, the coloristic premises are nearly identical.

10. Refer to footnote 3, above.

11. The perceptive reader will surely have noticed the engraver's error in metrically lining up the percussion, harp, piano, and organ parts with the rest of the orchestra in the final measure of Example 75.

12. The flugelhorn also appears in Stravinsky's *Threni,* completed barely a year after Vaughan Williams's symphony was premiered.

13. Other notable instances of this technique occur in: *American Festival Overture* (1939) —strings alone, measures 84–167, followed by woodwinds, measures 168–185; *Judith* (1949) —woodwind choir, measures 88–94, followed by strings only, measures

95–122; *New England Triptych* (1956) —woodwinds alone, measures 34–62 of the third movement, followed by the string choir, measures 63–80; Third Symphony—rapid alternations of woodwind and string sections in the first movement, measures 320–337; woodwinds and percussion, measures 142–244 of the Toccata (last movement), followed by an elaborate cadenza for the strings, measures 244–320; Fourth Symphony (1941) — strings alone, measures 70–117 of the first movement, followed by the woodwind choir, measures 117–142; rapid alternations between strings and winds, measures 1–13 of the last movement; Sixth Symphony—winds alone, measures 94–104, answered by brasses and strings, measures 105–120; strings only, measures 169–189, followed by woodwinds and brasses, measures 190–206; *Undertow* (1945) —woodwind section, measures 244–269, followed by string choir, measures 270–286.

14. See *Circus Overture* (1944), measures 32–54; *Credendum* (1955), measures 435–438, 480–490; *Judith*, measures 231–241; *New England Triptych*, measures 159–163 of last movement; Third Symphony, measures 273–285 of the first movement and measure 394 of the final movement; Sixth Symphony, measures 132–142, 150–169, 683–687; Seventh Symphony (1960), measures 31–33, 64–73 of first movement, and measures 228–235 of the last movement.

15. Henry Cowell, who was the first composer to exploit tone clusters, in his early piano music, was also the first to apply the device consistently to his orchestral writing, notably in *Synchrony* (1930) and his Symphony No. 11 (1953).

9 ——————————

The Exotic Orchestra

Perhaps the art of orchestration has become too popular, and
interesting-sounding pieces are often produced for no better
reason than that which dictates the making of typewriters
and fountain pens in different colors.

Arnold Schoenberg,
Style and Idea

A high valuation of color and instrumental sonority is, as we have
already seen, a cardinal aspect of much twentieth-century music. Whatever the aesthetic—Impressionist or Neoclassic, Expressionist or Neoromantic—modern music usually immerses the listener in sounds remote
from previous tonal experience. But when the emphasis on instrumental timbre reaches exaggerated proportions, the resulting music may
be rightfully considered exotic.

As an aesthetic and as a specific technique, exoticism warrants separate consideration because its composers approach the orchestra (or
other instrumental aggregation) with a peculiar intent: unusual sound
for its own sake. This they may occasionally achieve by employing primitivist, archaic, or non-Western compositional techniques with a normal
orchestral complement—as, for instance, in Igor Stravinsky's *Chant du*

Rossignol (1919). But even more often, the wish to achieve irony, parody, or humor, to create a foreign atmosphere, or merely to indulge a healthy curiosity about unorthodox musical effects is fleshed out by nonconformist instrumentation.

The composer's exceptional intent manifests itself in and justifies the type of instrumental ensemble he calls for: an unconventionally constituted orchestra and the use of rare or non-orchestral instruments. It also accounts for the presence of any extramusical elements that the composer considers essential to his total effect. And it explains the degree of novelty, originality, experimentation—or, on occasion, outright freakishness—that may be counted upon to ensure audience titillation.

Though the exotic orchestra or ensemble may have produced more than its proportionate share of freak works, there is no valid reason to suspect all such motivated music of hollow showmanship. True, most exotic works are somewhat outside the main body of art music; hence it becomes all too easy to accuse the composer of being a musical mountebank, who depends upon queerness to cover his lack of significant ideas. But this attitude will not survive the light of reason, for one composer may be drawn to exoticism with the same creative integrity as another who is strongly influenced by Impressionism, Expressionism, or any other "ism."

Certainly no one is about to accuse Stravinsky of having concealed a lack of creativity behind any outré instrumentation in his catalogue of works. When he used the Hungarian cimbalom in his 1918 *Renard*, for instance, it was essential to the folk milieu of this witty score, just as it is in the Hungarian folk-opera, *Háry János* (1925–27) of Zoltán Kodály. *Renard* also has other attributes of exoticism: though it is scored for a chamber ensemble as background to the solo voices, the instrumental disposition is orchestral, comprising flute and clarinet; horn, cornet and trombone; one percussionist; and two violins, one viola, and a double bass.[1]

Even more patently exotic is Stravinsky's opera buffa, *Mavra* (1921), with its strident instrumental background in exaggerated and hilarious contrast to the *bel canto* voice-writing. These harsh instrumental timbres are assigned to a chamber orchestra consisting of four clarinets, four trumpets, three trombones, tuba, percussion, and a string nonet. Furthermore, the string group is weighted heavily on the bass side, there being three cellos and three double basses against only two violins and one viola—resources typical of Stravinsky's post-*Sacre du Printemps* experimentation.

In 1923 serious music's exotic catalogue was further enlarged by

THE EXOTIC ORCHESTRA

Stravinsky's *Les Noces* (begun in 1917) and Darius Milhaud's *La Création du Monde*. Each makes use of an uncommon instrumental ensemble, and each achieves a highly individual sonoric language such that
the two works are united by little more than chronology. The *Les Noces*
ensemble of four pianos and seventeen percussion instruments (played
by seven percussionists) supporting the vocal soloists and chorus creates a
primitive, at times barbaric, atmosphere that is unique in concert music.[2]

Milhaud's ingenuous little score calls for a number and variety of
percussion instruments almost equal to the battery for *Les Noces*. Instead of four pianos, however, Milhaud is content with one; his other
resources embrace a reduced, chamber-like wind and brass section (including alto saxophone, which occupies the score line normally taken by
the viola), two solo violins, one cello, and one double bass. With these
simple resources the composer produces an urbane sound-picture of
American jazz, as if photographed by a French camera (Example 84).
Interestingly enough, Milhaud's "blues" melody, with its characteristic
flatted seventh (205), predates by a scant three months the identical scale-
pattern in George Gershwin's *Rhapsody in Blue* (1924) (206). No
doubt the close similarity is completely fortuitous, just as when two sci-
entists arrive independently, yet simultaneously, at nearly identical dis-
coveries.[3]

Unusual instrumental resources combine with translated Oriental
compositional elements in a sizable number of American twentieth-
century works, among them Henry Eichheim's *Oriental Impressions*
(1928) and Henry Cowell's *Persian Set* (1957). Eichheim's score calls
for three woodwinds, piano, harp, a four-part violin section, and violas
(no cellos or double basses). An extensive percussion section requires
not only conventional instruments but Chinese drum and cymbals, fluctuating tam-tam, and "fish head" (a small wooden bell) as well. Cowell's
suite includes two woodwinds, a three-part violin section (no violas),
and cello and double bass on duplicating parts throughout. He also
uses piano and two native Persian instruments: the *tar* (somewhat like
a mandolin) and a Persian drum.

A number of Latin American compositions, naturally enough, also
combine exotic expression and instrumental means. One such work is
the primitive and tonally gritty *Sinfonia India* of Carlos Chávez
(1899–   ). Though written for fairly normal symphonic proportions,
the symphony is exotic in its Mexican-Indian materials, particularly its
group of native percussion instruments. These include *güiro,* rasping
stick, metal and clay rattles, Indian drum, water gourd, rattling string,
and maraca.

Many of Heitor Villa-Lobos's compositions show the same basic

247

EXAMPLE 84
Darius Milhaud: from *La Création du Monde*, p. 44

approach, adding Brazilian instruments and indigenous rhythms to his total expression. So, too, do the several orchestral and chamber works of the Mexican, Silvestre Revueltas (1899–1940), rely on the exoticism of native materials and instruments.

Of the numerous European scores in the category of exoticism, it will suffice to comment on only one: Olivier Messiaen's *Trois Petites Liturgies de la Présence Divine* (1944). For this work the composer called upon the following complement of instruments: celesta, vibraphone, piano, *ondes* Martenot, maracas, gong, tam-tam, and string orchestra. "Not a chamber orchestra, still less a full orchestra grouped in a classical fashion, it is rather a Europeanized Hindu or Balinese instrumentation" is the way Messiaen described his unusual resources.

It is obvious that an emphasis on percussive sound is paramount in this work, as indeed it is in nearly all of the exotically-motivated works cited thus far. It is in the field of percussion, of course, that the exotic orchestra often achieves its most telling and unorthodox effects. The very creation of the percussion orchestra is one of the notable innovations in twentieth-century composition, though the Western composer cannot claim that the basic idea is new to music, or unique to his mode of expression. Percussion ensembles of varying sizes are the base of Balinese and Javanese musical cultures, and figure prominently in the music of Chinese, Korean, Japanese, Burmese, Indian, and other Far Eastern societies. In this hemisphere, however, the concept of the percussion as a self-sufficient entity is relatively new.

The first occidental work to exploit the percussion-orchestra concept was the *Ballet Mécanique* (1926) by George Antheil (1900–1959). It was written, so the composer has told us, to exorcise the profound effect of *Les Noces* on his composition. Scored for no less than eight pianos and an immense aggregation of percussion instruments, it received at its Paris premiere a typical *succès du scandale*. A brainstorm of Antheil's manager—using an actual airplane propeller at the New York performance one year later (the composer's score calls only for the sound of a plane motor, mechanically simulated)—no doubt created a visual spectacle to rival the extraordinary auditory experience. As Antheil candidly admitted, the concert was worth a million dollars to him in publicity.

By common agreement, nonetheless, the first work of artistic significance in the new field of the percussion orchestra was the 1931 *Ionisation* of Edgard Varèse (1883–1965). Scored for some forty different instruments, to be manipulated by thirteen players, its extraordinary sonic effects must have stunned its listeners at its memorable premiere in New York in 1933 (Example 85). Since that date the large number of even more radical percussion works written, performed, and recorded has perhaps dulled for the experienced listener the sharp edge of Varèse's pioneering score, and its once strange sonorities—even including the sirens—now seem quite familiar.

In the intervening years we have heard, for instance, from John Cage (1912–   ), Lou Harrison (1917–   ), and Harry Partch (1901–1974), among the many composers of all nationalities whose percussive exoticism

EXAMPLE 85
Edgard Varèse: from *Ionisation*, p. 21

has frequently exceeded that of Varèse's genetic score. As a specimen of the resources required by these more recent composers, here is the list of "instruments" demanded by Cage for his *First Construction (in Metal)* (1939): thunder-sheet, orchestra bells (chimes), string piano, twelve graduated sleigh-bells, four brake drums, eight cowbells, three Japanese temple gongs, four Turkish cymbals, eight anvils or pipe lengths, four Chinese cymbals, four muted gongs, water gong, tam-tam, and suspended gong (normal, one supposes).

Cage's *Imaginary Landscape No. 3* (1942) makes use of these preternatural resources: oscillator, constant-frequency record, record of continuously variable frequency, tin cans (number and sizes unspecified), buzzer, generator whine, plucked coil, Balinese gongs, and marimbula. This last instrument, played with mallets, is an adaptation of the conventional marimba, strayed—like the refined Balinese gongs—into a foreign tone-scape. These two works illustrate vividly the lengths to which certain composers have gone in their search for new and startling means of expression. Even though the musical results do not invariably measure up to the overwrought efforts of the composers, such searchings are still essential to the life of musical art.

More conventionally musical than the Cage works mentioned are Henry Cowell's *Ostinato Pianissimo* (1934), Lou Harrison's *Canticle No. 3* (1941), Alan Hovhaness's *October Mountain* (1956), and Ernst Křenek's *Marginal Sounds* (1957). More unconventional than even the Varèse and Cage works are the experiments of the avant-garde in the fifties and sixties, of which the aleatoric *Zyklus* (1961) of Karlheinz Stockhausen is prototypical.

Harrison's *Canticle No. 3* calls for as eccentric a complement of instruments as one is likely to encounter: ocarina, guitar, six iron pipes (muted), five woodblocks, five brake drums (muted), three suspended brake drums, small xylophone, maracas, five dragon's mouths (temple blocks), five tongued *teponaztli* (slit-drums), five cowbells, large tam-tam, snare and bass drums, five tom-toms, large, medium, and small elephant bells, six water buffalo bells, wooden box, and two sistrums (rattles). For all their strangeness, however, these instruments are made to serve musical ends while they fulfill the special demands of instrumental exoticism.

The percussive ambience of an outstanding Latin American work, the 1960 *Cantata para América Mágica* of Alberto Ginastera (1916–), may be gauged by its extensive and primitivist resources. For dramatic soprano and percussion orchestra, the score requires the following instruments: six timpani, three Indian drums, snare and tenor drums, two bass drums, six temple blocks, four suspended cymbals, four pairs of cymbals, two cowbells, three tam-tams, two pairs of antique cymbals (tuned), two bongos, chimes, three triangles, two pairs of claves, three pairs of maracas, *güiro*, two sistrums, a pair of stones, sleigh bells, *reco-reco* (a bamboo *güiro*), *chocalho* (a dried gourd), large xylophone, marimba, glockenspiel, celesta, and two pianos.

These resources are well matched in both numbers and varieties in Carl Orff's one-act drama, *Antigonae* (1948). In addition to a sizable number of standard percussion instruments, the score calls for three xylophones, three glockenspiels, six tambourines, six pairs of castanets, three Turkish cymbals, ten large Javanese gongs, several stone slabs, a small wooden drum, and six pianos played normally and with plectrums and mallets.

Typical of the recent avant-garde approach to the percussion ensemble is the 1960 *Anaklasis* for string orchestra and percussion by Poland's leading composer, Krzysztof Penderecki (1933–). The passage shown here from this work (Example 86) is part of a long cadenza-like section for the six percussionists joined by celesta, harp, and piano (instruments that are treated by the composer as extensions of his percussive resources).

Of the American exotic composers, the most singular phenomenon is Harry Partch, whose utterly fascinating music is like no other known to Western listeners. The unique aesthetic of this experimenter led him to contrive new tonal resources, construct new instruments, and give music a completely new theatrical presence.

To take his radical inventions in chronological order: Partch first evolved a musical scale containing forty-three intervals to the octave, in just (as opposed to mean) intonation. In order to perform his music which used this microtonal succession of pitches, Partch then had to invent and construct instruments capable of negotiating his new scale. Probably no other composer past or present has originated and used so many new instruments as those built by Partch and his disciples. The extensive list includes, in part, "adapted" guitars and bowed string instruments, a chromelodeon, a surrogate kithara (a lyre-like instrument), harmonic canon (a form of zither), diamond marimba, boo (a marimba made of bamboo), and various sizes of glass cloud-chamber bowls.

Though these fascinating instruments can now only be heard in recordings, the variety and potential of the ensemble is strikingly demonstrated in Partch's *Oedipus* (1951), *Plectra and Percussion Dances*, (1952), the satire *The Bewitched* (1955), and the 1966 *And on the Seventh Day Petals Fell in Petaluma* (Example 87). None of these

EXAMPLE 86
Krzysztof Penderecki: from *Anaklasis*, p. 17

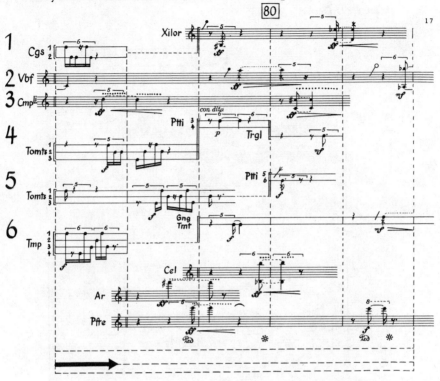

works, of course, qualify as orchestral music by conventional definition; hence Partch cannot be considered a direct contributor to exotic orchestral style. But his experiments nonetheless symbolize an important aspect of twentieth-century musical thinking—the intense preoccupation with new sound-materials and their meaningful application to original art music.

Possibly the most versatile of all the current avant-gardists drawn to exotic instrumental resources is Pierre Boulez. A superb conductor as well as a highly original composer, Boulez gradually moved away from his early preoccupation with total serialization to a compositional style based on the parameters of choice. His tendencies toward exotic orchestration are evident in all his works, even though he has relatively few compositions for full orchestra.

Described by the critic Heinrich Strobel as "Webern sounding like

253

EXAMPLE 87

Harry Partch: from *And on the Seventh Day Petals Fell in Petaluma* (MS.)

Debussy," Boulez's *Le Marteau sans Maître* (1955) is a unique chamber piece for solo soprano voice and six instrumentalists. Hardly an orchestral work, it nonetheless exemplifies the composer's predilection for exotic colorations, calling as it does for alto flute, viola, guitar, xylorimba (a cross between xylophone and marimba), vibraphone, and assorted percussion. These comparatively limited resources place the work in the same special category as Stravinsky's *L'Histoire du Soldat* and Schoenberg's *Pierrot Lunaire*. Stylistically, however, Boulez's score is related not at all to Stravinsky and only distantly to Schoenberg. Its instrumental exoticism is similar to that of many another gamelan-like composition (Messiaen's *Trois Petites Liturgies,* for example): a superrefined concept of instrumental timbre plus a striking unpredictability as to tonal juxtaposition and opposition.

This approach is applied even more cunningly in *Improvisation sur Mallarmé* (1957), a series again for soprano voice and a small chamber ensemble (Example 88). Though this score of Boulez uses only traditional instruments (the vibraphone used here had long since achieved this status), they are seldom treated in a conventional manner. The harp, for instance, is used percussively by Boulez, almost like a piano. Spiky-sounding chords, played close to the soundboard and nearly always non-arpeggiated, abound in the two *Improvisations*. The celesta provides delicate filigreed arpeggios; the pianist frequently is required to press down silent tone-clusters with the forearm.

Exoticism in contemporary music does not always rely on the utilization of unusual instrumental resources; a very pronounced and unambiguous exotic flavoring can be imparted to music written for a perfectly normal orchestra—as, for instance, with Igor Stravinsky's *Chant du Rossignol*. This is, without doubt, the most stunningly conceived of all the composer's exotically motivated works. Its orchestration, paradoxically, is a subtle and immensely skillful blend of Rimsky-Korsakov's methods with those of French Impressionism. Yet with these conventional materials Stravinsky establishes, by means of pentatonic melodic elements, quartal harmonies, and simulated Orientalisms, an atmosphere of Chinoiserie prophetic of a long line of quasi-Eastern essays from many other Western composers.

Such an extensive list of exotic works with an Oriental aura yet scored for the traditional symphonic ensemble would include Bartók's *The Miraculous Mandarin* (1919) —a marvel of incandescent orchestration—and Messiaen's *Turangalila-Symphonie* (1948) —a monument of orchestral obesity. Among American compositions there are also Colin McPhee's *Bali* and *Tabuh-Tabuhan* (both written in 1936), as well as

EXAMPLE 88
Pierre Boulez: from *Improvisation sur Mallarmé (II)*, p. 13

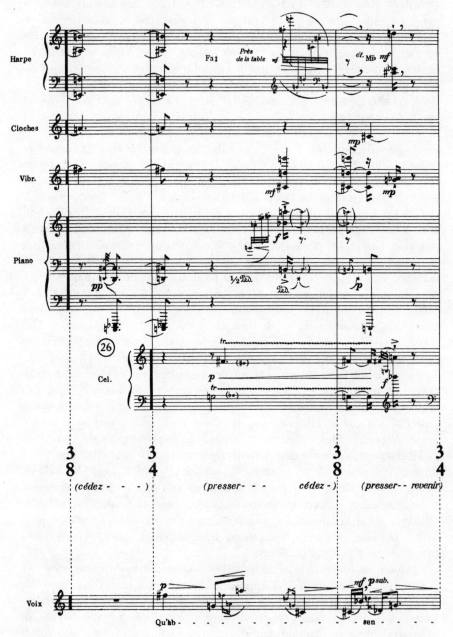

several accomplished scores of Bernard Rogers: *Three Japanese Dances* (1932), *The Song of the Nightingale* (1939; a title by no means exclusive with Stravinsky), and *The Dance of Salomé* (1940; not endemic to Strauss's domain, either). Peggy Glanville-Hicks's opera, *The Transposed Heads* (1952) and Cowell's *Ongaku* (1957) also qualify in this category. All of these compositions, however, owe their exoticism to simulated Oriental materials—harmonic, melodic, and rhythmic—rather than to novel instrumentation.

The prolific output of the American composer Alan Hovhaness (1911–   ) is the epitome of Eastern musical elements transmuted into Western modes of expression. Of Armenian heritage, Hovhaness has more consistently and more successfully than anyone synthesized the factors of Oriental and Occidental music into a composite personal language. He has largely dispensed with Western forms, with their correlative reliance on tonality, modulation, and sectional development. Instead, he employs the ancient ecclesiastical modes (but in a neomodal manner), a melismatic and improvisatory melodic style, endless chains of rhythmic figuration, and an orchestra or chamber ensemble that evokes the delicate exoticism of the Near East. Although the composer's orchestral resources are apt to be fairly standard, his chamber works frequently utilize unusual instruments or instrumental combinations.

One technical device that appears in one Hovhaness work after another was first used in his early piano concerto, *Lousadzak* (1944), a work which skillfully imitates a number of old Armenian instruments. One of these, the *kanoon* (somewhat like the Hungarian zither), is simulated by string pizzicati in rapid, nonrhythmical repetitions of single-pitch phrases. Since its early appearance in the concerto this particular, and peculiar, device has constantly been threaded through the Hovhaness instrumental works—as much a stylistic fingerprint as the *col legno battuto* passages in Mahler (see Example 89).[4] Hovhaness's wide-ranging use of this form of pizzicato tremolando has made this orchestral effect a staple genuinely enriching modern instrumentation.

Finally, exoticism of a very different sort is exemplified by John Cage's *Atlas Eclipticalis* (1961–62). Though ostensibly conceived for a normally constituted, yet numerically flexible, orchestra, Cage added an extramusical factor to his components—the scientific element of electronic circuitry. The work, however, is *not* electronic in the generally accepted definition of that term; the sounds are produced by conventional instruments and are not subjected to any modification other than changes of amplitude.

EXAMPLE 89
Alan Hovhaness: from *Meditation on Orpheus*, p. 23

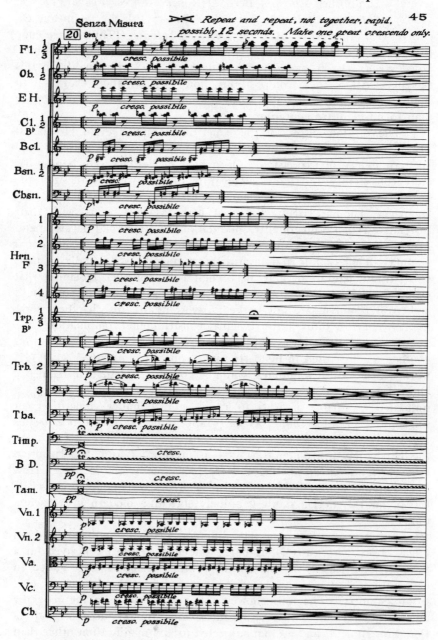

THE EXOTIC ORCHESTRA

The eighty-six instrumental parts of this piece, according to the composer, are "to be played in whole or part, for any duration, in any ensemble, chamber or orchestral, of the above performers; with or without *Winter Music* [a Cage composition for piano of 1957]; an electronic version is made possible by use of contact microphones with associated amplifiers and loudspeakers operated by an assistant to the conductor.

"Each part is written in space equal to a time at least twice as slow as clock time. . . . Space vertically equals frequency [pitch]. Since equal space is given each chromatic tone, notes not having conventional accidentals are microtones. Specific directives and freedoms are given regarding duration of times. Loudness is relative to the size of the notes. Tone production is never extraordinary. . . . The conductor's part is not a master score but gives information as to the details of the composition." That the Cage work has received few performances is perhaps understandable in the light of its unusual requirements.

From Stravinsky to Cage we have assembled and commented on a gallimaufry of exotic compositions. Yet an abstract of exotic style, particularly orchestrational style, is an obvious impossibility, for all exotic orchestration is by definition exceptional, if not unique. Even the instrumental resources of exotically oriented works cannot be neatly summarized, for there is no more standardization of instruments and quasi-instruments in exotic scores than there is a single type of sound in their performance. Every composer in this heterogeneous group has attempted something unprecedented for the sake of an unprecedented sound-totality. Yet exoticism, like Impressionism before it, is a potent influence in the music of the twentieth century. Unlike Impressionism, however, it is not merely a peripheral activity today, for it constitutes a major aesthetic in the very life of the musical avant-garde.

Categorization is even more difficult with music where an exotic orchestral style is employed for musical content that would seem not exotic at all. This factor would appear to be a direct contradiction of the premise stated in the Preamble of this book: that musical content and orchestrational expression are indissolubly interwoven, that genetic ideas and their instrumental realization are inseparable as an artistic whole. But when that creative totality is a twentieth-century work for orchestra, its wholeness must be a resolution of multifarious influences quite unknown to the eighteenth- and nineteenth-century composer.

When the first symphonic and operatic orchestras began to take definitive shape, composers were relatively circumscribed in their styles and forms of expression, as in their physical movements and communications in the world around them. In the Classical period no basically conflicting ideologies or revolutionary technical procedures competed to dominate the creative ambience. What is more, Classicism had a comparatively long tenure, for the tenets of Romanticism were conceived gradually, and novel techniques were only very slowly absorbed into the composer's total musical resources.

In contrast to this slow evolution and transition, the changes from Romanticism to Impressionism and then from Impressionism to Expressionism and Neoclassicism have occurred with progressive acceleration. In our own time so many contradictory philosophies and specialized techniques have appeared—full-blown, and insistent upon the composer's attention—that the present-day creator is literally overwhelmed by new styles and methodologies. The late–twentieth-century composer must master the techniques of a dozen or so widely varying musical aesthetics and then amalgamate them into an expression distinctly his own.

Let us reemphasize, then, that when Hindemith dresses basically Neoclassical or Baroque forms in the style of an incontrovertibly Romantic orchestra, he is making a personal resolution of the gravitational pulls of opposing styles. When Messiaen writes exotic music for an Impressionist orchestra, or Carl Orff orchestrates primitive music for an exotic ensemble, these are individual reconciliations of strong and influential twentieth-century movements. No work by these three men, or by any other significant composer of our time, negates the fundamental premise that musical content and orchestrational style cannot be convincingly divorced. But the musical creativity of our century, with its incredibly complex resources, can take shape only in a complex and eclectic style.

It is still true that, for example, the orchestral manner of the eighteenth century does not fit the musical aesthetic of the late nineteenth century. And certainly no contemporary composer with integrity can yield to the layman's frequent pleas (when he is not showing indifference) to write music of immediate accessibility. But the new Classicism of *our* time, for instance, *can* be welded to a coexistent post-Romantic orchestral style, just as non-exotic compositional ideas can take shape in terms of unusual instrumentation. Thus the apparent contradiction of musical content and instrumental expression is not an anomaly; it may even be the truest expression of our times.

Notes

1. To give another example of the composer's typical cunning in instrumentation, the sarrusophone and flugelhorn in *Threni* are made to seem equally inevitable in the general tonal ambience.

THE EXOTIC ORCHESTRA

2. Similar instrumentational externals appear in Carl Orff's archaic trilogy: *Carmina Burana* (1936), *Catulli Carmina* (1945), and *Trionfo di Afrodite* (1951). The musical substance of these works, however, is slight and wholly conventional.

3. Attention might also be directed to the similarity of a theme in Hindemith's *Concert Music for Strings and Brass* (pp. 45–46) to the Gershwin and Milhaud themes.

4. A closely similar, yet durationally restricted, effect was used by Rimsky-Korsakov in *Scheherazade* (second movement, measures 162–164), and by Sir Edward Elgar in his Violin Concerto (pp. 88–89).

10

The Avant-Garde Orchestra

Style is not a quality that one can, and even less that one should,
pursue for itself. . . . The composer's task is to establish
homogeneity, to forge unity out of the elements he manipulates—
elements whose centrifugal force is often prodigious.

Pierre Boulez,
Boulez on Music

Whereas a few measures are usually sufficient to identify a work by
Bartók, Hindemith, Webern, or Stravinsky (in his various periods), this
quick certainty is unlikely with the scores of Penderecki, Stockhausen,
Ligeti, or Berio. What is more, it is almost impossible to identify the
musical fingerprint as, let us say, Argentinian, Swedish, Canadian, or
Polish. For orchestrators of the late twentieth-century avant-garde—
divergent though they are in their personal aesthetics and in their reliance on current aleatoric principles—achieve a quality of expression more
universal than particular. National, if not personal, style is thereby
effectively obliterated.

Because the so-called "liberation of sound" is the focus of most experimental musical expression today, avant-garde symphonists every-

where have made use of five primary instrumentational techniques aimed at extending the range of orchestral timbre: (1) They exploit *extreme ranges* on all instruments capable of extending their outer register limits; (2) they consider the *tone cluster* of paramount importance, elevating its orchestrational usefulness above all other tonal structures; (3) using *soloistic divisi,* they divide and subdivide the orchestra into a multitude of independent voices; (4) they introduce *percussive effects* even on non-percussion instruments; and (5) they requisition *extramusical devices* that frequently stress the visual as well as the aural.

Because avant-garde orchestration relies so heavily on these specific techniques, our discussion will be related to each concept in turn rather than to a chronological survey of individual composers and their works. Of the five basic techniques characteristic of vanguard instrumentation, the exploitation of extreme instrumental range is not, of course, exclusive with today's avant-garde; it was very much a factor in the orchestral styles of the exotic composers (who were and are, after all, a subspecies of the avant-garde of their day), and appeared as well in the scores of the late Romantics (Strauss and Mahler, in particular) and the Expressionists (principally Schoenberg and Berg). Before the present era of highly experimental orchestration, however, extreme pitches were always specific (and possible) and were so notated. Today, such instances of extreme instrumental pitches are often only approximate, notated with non-specific symbols and, usually, the added directive "as high as possible" or "as low as possible." The presence of these extreme pitches in the typical vanguard score imparts a tense, strained tonal quality—often like a piercing shriek or an ominous rumble, in which indeterminate sound rather than definite pitch is the most crucial factor for the composer.

A second primary technique in vogue with vanguard orchestrators is the extensive use of the tone cluster, or sound-mass. Foreshadowed by Charles Ives and quintessential with Henry Cowell, the cluster is now a firmly rooted orchestrational cliché. Most experimental composers score this device throughout the entire orchestral range, including even the pitched percussion instruments. New works by Krzysztof Penderecki and György Ligeti, in particular, show massive clusters on almost every score page.

Cluster-formations may be comprised of diatonic, chromatic, or microtonal intervals—the latter applied equally to woodwind, brass, and string dispositions. Generally, the contiguous tones of such cluster-blocks are assigned to family groups or to homogeneously voiced instruments. And often (as illustrated in Example 90) the clusters are apt to

EXAMPLE 90
Krzysztof Penderecki: from *De Natura Sonoris (I)*, p. 16

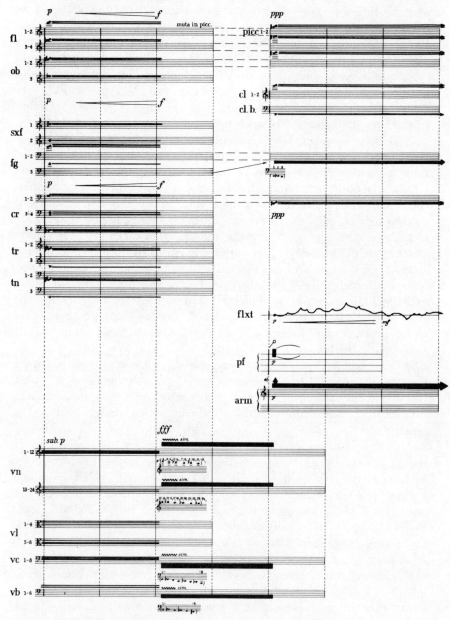

264

be positioned at the very top and the very bottom of the orchestral range for startling tonal contrast.

It will be noted in the Penderecki example that the wind-brass clusters of the first two measures are diatonic, outlining the two possible whole-tone scales. The succeeding string cluster is chromatic, as is the wind and harmonium tone-block that follows. An added coloristic touch is provided by the flexatone—an exotic addition to the composer's percussive resources—and by the pianist playing (inside the piano) on the highest strings with a soft mallet.

In Penderecki's *Threnody for the Victims of Hiroshima* (1960) (207) for fifty-two stringed instruments, the prevailing clusters are con-structed microtonally. Swelling by means of slow glissandi from narrow tonal bands to wide strata, or the reverse, the composer's dense sound-masses resemble electronic "white noise" far more than they do conven-tional string tone. Their distinctive flavor is a signature, not only of Penderecki's style, but of all vanguard orchestration.

Almost the entire orchestrational premise of *Atmospheres* (1961) by the Hungarian György Ligeti (1923–   ) is that of the tone cluster. The huge blocks of sound appear to erase all timbral differences between the various instruments, so that an all-encompassing color prevails. In Ligeti's *Requiem* (1963–65) and *Lux Aeterna* (1966) the sound-masses are applied to choral as well as to instrumental voices. The greatly divided choral parts blend so unobtrusively with the orchestral instru-ments that no timbral distinctions can be easily perceived. Considered collectively, the works just discussed create a vivid profile of the manner in which tone clusters have been applied to contemporary orchestral technique and indicate their immense importance in the sound world of the twentieth-century experimental composer.

Soloistic divisi, the third factor of avant-garde instrumentation to be considered, is a technique by which all the orchestral instruments are assigned independent parts, either as components of vertical sonic struc-tures or as melodic voices. This means that instrumental doubling is minimal; when notes are duplicated it is nearly always in an octave rela-tionship rather than at the unison. If unison doubling does occur, al-most invariably it is between like instruments of closely similar timbre.

The purpose of soloistic divisi is to provide an all-encompassing heterophony to the orchestral mass—to figurate in an almost infinite number of ways the component pitches of vertical sonorities or of separate thematic lines (as in Example 91). The principle of *Klangfar-benmelodie* is thus applied to the orchestral totality; no hierarchy of instruments exists, for all are considered equal in the tonal web. This is

EXAMPLE 91
György Ligeti: from *Lontano*, p. 23

the fundamental concept of chamber music applied to full orchestra, used not for power or weight but as an artificially enlarged color spectrum where the orchestrator obliterates all timbral differences, homogenizing the acoustic ensemble as far as possible. This soloistic concept, then, does not regard an oboe, let us say, as a nasal, sweetly pungent quality in the composer's arsenal of instrumental resources as much as an element of a cluster or a component in a multiplicity of horizontal strands.

The citation from Ligeti's work (Example 91) typically demonstrates the amount of vertical space on the score page required for extensive soloistic divisi. Because every instrument is frequently occupied with its own rhythmic patterns as well as its individual pitch-sequences, it is quite common to find avant-garde scores containing as many staves as there are individual instruments requisitioned. The rather unwieldy physical proportions of such scores, it might be added, create certain problems for conductors and librarians alike.

Fourth in the list of specialized technical procedures is the application of every percussive effect possible, even to instruments inherently non-percussive in nature.[1] Among the woodwinds and brasses this takes the form of audible finger-tapping on the keys or valves, or else striking the instrument itself with the flat hand, fingers, or fingernails. Furthermore, brass players are often directed to strike the outside of the instrumental bell or the tubing with a metal object, such as a mechanical mute. Sometimes the player is instructed to rattle the mute inside the bell itself, a sound that can have wide dynamic variance.

For the strings, the nontraditional percussive effects (exclusive, that is, of pizzicato and col legno) range from striking the instrument frame or tailpiece with the bowstick, to slapping the body with the palm or flat fingers, to tapping with fingernails or fingertips on various parts of the wooden frame. Also, the four strings themselves may be forcibly struck with the fingers or hand. A delicate, faintly rustling murmur highly attractive to many avant-garde orchestrators is achieved by audibly fingering a sequence of specific pitches without drawing the bow across the strings.

Not percussive, but pertinent here in that they exploit new timbre potentials, are other string devices common to vanguard instrumentational style: the glassy, indeterminate sounds produced by bowing behind the instrument bridge; the use of extended and multiple-voiced glissandi, both arco and pizzicato (see, for instance, the *Achorripsis* of 1958 [**208**], or almost any other score, by Iannis Xenakis); all possible harmonics; col legno effects, both *battuto* and *tratto;* and the effect caused by letting a plucked string vibrate against the left-hand fingernail, which produces a faint metallic buzz—a sound much admired by Ligeti and the Argentinian composer Mauricio Kagel in particular.

As logical extensions of the percussion section, the piano and harp have been fruitful sources of nontraditional effects. Today the piano is played, more often than not, in its interior, directly on the strings, using mallets of varying degrees of hardness or softness, picks, metal objects, or fingertips and nails. Furthermore, the metal crossbars inside are utilized for percussive sounds, as are the outside areas of the instrument—the top, sides, underside, pedals, and so on. When the orchestral vanguardist uses the keyboard itself, it is usually to create massive tone-clusters played with the flat palm or the entire forearm—the keys are either struck forcibly or are silently depressed to create overtones.

Harpists are required by many experimental orchestrators to use their instrument percussively rather than as a vehicle for conventional, idiomatic arpeggios and glissandi. They are directed to strike the soundboard with the flat hand, the knuckles, or fingernails, or to hit the front column or the metal plate at the top of the instrument with such objects as a stick or the ubiquitous tuning key. They must also frequently stroke the strings with the flattened fingers or with a wirebrush, glide vertically on a low string with the tuning key, or play on the very lowest strings with timpani mallets. In addition, they must on occasion pluck the strings very close to the tuning pins or else near the soundboard, execute glissandos with the pedals alone (first plucking the string and then moving the pedal from notch to notch), or audibly change pedal positions without plucking the strings at all—in short, engage in any number of quite unconventional, esoteric, and even unidiomatic playing techniques.

As might reasonably be anticipated, the bona fide percussion instruments in the avant-garde orchestra are made to produce effects that in no way can be considered standard. The list of devices to be found in the vanguard scores of the last twenty-five years or so is far too extensive to catalogue here, but it would contain such procedures as scraping the gongs, tam-tams, and suspended cymbals in a circular motion with a metal stick; playing with drum sticks on a tambourine laid flat; creating quarter-tone inflections on the vibraphone and glockenspiel by exerting gentle finger-pressure on the bars; muting cowbells by stuffing a piece of cloth inside the bell; damping the tone of triangle or chime by grasping the metal with one hand while striking with the other; placing a small cymbal or a tambourine or even a coin on the timpani-membrane to produce a metallic rattle—the list of such unusual devices could be extended ad infinitum. By no means mere exotic tricks, these procedures are legitimate explorations of natural and contrived sound, and are basic to the avant-gardist's schema.

THE AVANT–GARDE ORCHESTRA

In addition to manipulating familiar instruments in unfamiliar ways, vanguard orchestrators experiment widely with extramusical effects. Instrumentalists must also produce inhaled and exhaled breath sounds while playing; must hum, sing, speak, shout, or whistle. In multimedia works that stress both visual and aural events, the musicians are often called on for hand clapping, finger snapping, foot stamping or shuffling, and striking of chairs, stools, or music stands with some object (a bow-stick, mallet, or their hands, for instance).

For heightened theatrical effect, players of avant-garde music may even move about the stage, enter or exit while playing, and perambulate around the auditorium during performance.[2] These visual elements are as much a part of vanguard orchestrational style as any of the more specialized instrumental techniques we have discussed, although their contribution to the totality is only viable in live performance.

The instrumentational techniques treated above—extreme ranges, tone clusters, soloistic divisi, percussive experiments, and extramusical devices—are only one side of the coin of avant-gardism. The obverse side is a new profile of the composer's approach to his orchestra, a new conceptual manner of regarding the orchestral entity. Most notably it features unorthodox seating arrangements, multiple instrumental groups, incorporation of jazz elements (group improvisation), various aleatoric procedures, and the inclusion of electronically produced sound.

To consider these approaches in order: Many of the avant-garde, in their pursuit of fresh ways of dealing with orchestral sound, have in essence gone back to the antiphonal and spatial theories of Giovanni Gabrieli.[3] These composers have transferred to our contemporary concert halls Gabrieli's practice of stationing various instrumental groups in different parts of St. Mark's Cathedral in Venice. This they accomplish either by rearranging the traditional platform-seating of the orchestra or by dividing the players into smaller units dispersed around the auditorium. Either procedure is undertaken to ensure a pronounced stereophonic effect upon the listener, so that sound literally comes from several different directions, perhaps from all sides.

In general, orchestral players are seated on the concert platform in unorthodox fashion because the composer wants autonomous groups heard in timbral antiphony. One of the earliest contemporary scores to be based on a non-traditional seating plan is *Spectra* (1958) by Gunther Schuller (1925–). In this work the wind, brass, and percussion instruments (including harp and celesta), are divided into five unequally constituted and essentially non-homogeneous groups, while the string section is split into a solo group of twenty-one and a tutti group of forty-six

269

players. The composer's musical materials are specifically designed to pass from one ensemble to another, to be juxtaposed, blended, or sharply differentiated—all to create a stereophonic movement through the entire orchestra of pure timbre, pointillistic melody, or massed sonority.

A parallel concept informs the first movement of Schuller's *American Triptych* (1965), which he calls "a study in texture." Inspired by Alexander Calder's mobile *Four Directions,* Schuller's analogous musical ideas are made to rotate spatially in different directions and at different speeds among the orchestral players. Although the ensemble is seated conventionally for this work, the composer's musical lines travel around the orchestra in preassigned circular orbits, each line having its own specific complement of instruments. As Schuller says in his notes, "The spatial placement of sounds is no longer left to chance, but incorporated into the very conception of the work, thereby creating—as an added dimension—a counterpoint of space" (Example 92).

Another work premised on an unorthodox seating plan is *Doubles* (1957) of Pierre Boulez. The basic motives of this score have complementary "doubles" grafted onto them—that is to say, variant aspects of each musical figure modify each other, "refracting" their substance as a prism refracts light rays. The novel seating arrangement of the orchestra here is designed to enhance that process and is not done, in the composer's words, "for the sake of a more or less superficial stereophony."

Diario Polacco (1958) of the Italian-born Luigi Nono (1924–   ) combines unconventional seating of the players with the concept of the *multiple orchestra.* The work is scored for four orchestras of identical size and instrumental composition, the players within each ensemble being seated according to a non-traditional plan. A somewhat later *Sinfonia para tres grupos instrumentales* (1963) by the Spaniard Cristobal Halffter (1930–   ) divides the traditional orchestra into three groups: Orchestra A consists of four woodwind, two brass, and five string instruments; Orchestra B comprises all the percussion—a sizable array—and piano; Orchestra C is made up of four woodwind and two brass instruments plus the balance of the string section. The three large groups are positioned on the stage to the left, in front of, and to the right of the conductor.

When the vanguardist composer moves his players offstage and into the auditorium it is to explore further the effect of music in space. He may position multiple orchestras around his listeners, or may divide the single orchestra into autonomous groups separated spatially in the hall. One of the first experiments in this direction was made by Henry Brant (1913–   ) in his *Antiphony One* (1953). The composer divides his

EXAMPLE 92

Gunther Schuller: from *American Triptych*, p. 27

orchestra into five differently constituted groups distributed around the auditorium, each with its own conductor taking his cues from the chief conductor on stage. Thus the audience hears the music coming from all directions, a truly stereophonic listening experience.

Brant continued his experiments in *December* (1955), *Atlantis* (1960), and *Voyage Four* (1963). Each score fulfilled his primary intent that spatial music should be conceived "in accordance with the premise that there is no optimum position in the hall for each listener, and no one optimum distribution of the players in only one ideal hall." Should a precisely controlled sonic result be deemed essential, he thinks, then the spatial distribution of the players must be made according to a specific plan, allowing always for adjustments of detail. Spatial music, Brant affirms, "must be written in such a way that the composer is able to accept what he hears as a listener regardless of his position in the hall."

The composer acknowledges that the physical resource of space is even today considered by most composers a peripheral—or at best, optional—aspect of contemporary composition. He believes, however, that for a composer to attempt the writing of spatial music without a fixed scheme of performer distribution in mind is akin to composing without specific controls of time-values or of pitches. That nearly all aleatorically oriented composers do not rigorously control time-values or specific pitches lends a certain unintended irony to Brant's observation.

Other notable essays in stereophonic positioning include Stockhausen's 1957 *Gruppen* for three orchestras, his *Carré* (1960) for four orchestras, and four works by Xenakis: *Duel* (1959), *Strategie* (1959–62), *Terretektorh* (1965–66), and *Polytope* (1967).

Gruppen of Karlheinz Stockhausen (1928–   ) arranges its three different orchestras in the form of an open-ended square, each ensemble having its own conductor and operating largely under its own conditions of tempo and meter (Example 93). At the time of its first performance, the composer took pains to point out that the spatial aspects in this work were completely functional rather than decorative. "One finds oneself listening," he says, "in the midst of several temporal-spatial manifestations which together create a new musical time-space."

Duel and *Strategie* of Iannis Xenakis (1922–   ) are both elaborately contrived "games" for two orchestras and their two conductors. The losing conductor, according to the composer, should not be considered less efficient than the winner, who wins simply because he adheres more closely to the rules of the game. The "riddle" canons of the early Netherlands contrapuntal school may surely be considered the logical ancestors of this recent and popular avant-garde gamesmanship.

EXAMPLE 93
Karlheinz Stockhausen: from *Gruppen*, p. 33

STYLE AND ORCHESTRATION

Xenakis's *Terretektorh,* on the other hand, is written for a normally constituted single orchestra of eighty-eight players which is scattered among the audience rather than grouped conventionally on the concert platform. The conductor is stationed at the center of the axis of the hall, so that players and audience surround him on all sides. According to Xenakis the scattering of the orchestral musicians "brings in a radically new kinetic conception of music which no modern electro-acoustical means could match. For if it is not possible to imagine eighty-eight magnetic tape tracks relaying to eighty-eight loud speakers disseminated all over the auditorium, on the contrary it is quite possible to achieve this with a classical orchestra of eighty-eight musicians. The musical composition will thereby be entirely enriched throughout the hall both in spatial dimension and in movement."

In many ways *Terretektorh* sustains the conviction the composer offered in his notes for *Metastaseis* (1953–54) : that the human orchestra can still surpass in novel sonorities and in subtle expression any new electronic techniques being developed. The same conviction informs the orchestrational styles of many other contemporary composers today, writers whose outlook on the current musical scene can by no stretch of the imagination be considered reactionary.

The instrumental components of *Polytope* differ from the other Xenakis scores in that the work is designed for four identical orchestras to be positioned each at one of the four cardinal points of the concert hall. Furthermore, the makeup of the orchestras is somewhat unconventional (although each includes woodwind, brass, percussion, and string instruments) : piccolo, E-flat clarinet, contrabass clarinet, and contrabassoon; trumpet and trombone; a large gong, a Japanese woodblock, and four tom-toms (played by one percussionist) ; four violins and four cellos (no violas or double basses) .

The rearrangement of the orchestra, on stage or off, is the most immediately evident avant-garde manipulation of the familiar. However, symphonic music today has been far more drastically reshaped by the prevalence of the aleatoric [4] elements that currently dominate the musical scene. The principle of including the unexpected is, of course, fundamentally an approach to composition, and only secondarily an influence on orchestrational style. As such, it ranges from the briefest of improvisatory passages to the near anarchy set in motion by musical graphics. This wide soundscape, and the universe of notational innovation it comprises, can only be suggested here by citing various aspects of the improvisational approach.

One area of music-making in which improvisational elements would seem to reside most gracefully and naturally is that of jazz expression. A number of composers convinced of the viability of jazz as the original source of modern improvisational techniques have combined the jazz band or the core jazz-combo with the full symphonic orchestra. They have hoped in this way to create a "third-stream" [5] music, partaking of the best of both musical worlds.

From Rolf Liebermann's 1954 *Concerto for Jazz Band and Symphony Orchestra* to Gunther Schuller's *Concertino for Jazz Quartet and Orchestra* (1959) to Larry Austin's *Improvisations for Orchestra and Jazz Soloists* (1961), composers of inquiring minds have sought to weld the freedoms of jazz to the disciplines of serious music. Stylistically, however, one must say that this marriage has appeared so far an unfruitful union of incompatible personalities.

Outside the "third-stream" group there are numerous composers who inject the freshness of improvisation through passages framed by music traditionally notated and performed. Significantly, this approach does not preclude prior composition, nor does it relegate determinacy to a subsidiary position. Characteristic of this approach are the two versions of *Time Cycle* (1960) by Lukas Foss (1922–), a work for soprano and orchestra concerned with "clocks, bells, and time."

At stated points in one version a selected group of instrumentalists improvises on thematic elements of the various songs. In the other version of *Time Cycle* the interludes are independent of the composed sections' thematic or harmonic elements. Instead, an improvising group (clarinet, cello, piano, and percussionist) contributes extensions of the mood of the preceding vocal text, the players being free to add their own individual displays of technical virtuosity. It is precisely this latter element, however, that constitutes the most hazardous aspect of group improvisation. A performer who is not also a composer may present a dazzling technical display, but he is less likely to create spontaneous material of enduring, or even of minimally interesting, substance.

In works where improvisation is extended to the full ensemble, the term may refer to spontaneous composition within the composer's framework of style and basic idea; or, in a narrower sense, to the application of personal choice to a number of structural or parametral options.

Poesis (1963) by the Swedish composer Ingvar Lidholm (1921–), for example, often carefully specifies the desired rhythmic values, but allows the players to apply them to a sequence of indeterminate sounds (Example 94). Exactly the opposite approach appears at times in *Tempi concertati* (1960) by Luciano Berio (1925–), performed by an orchestra divided into four groups separated onstage as much as possible. Pre-

EXAMPLE 94
Ingvar Lidholm: from *Poesis*, p. 29

276

cisely indicated pitches enclosed in boxes ("frame notation") in the individual parts are to be played in any order and in any rhythmic pattern, the duration of each sequence being determined by its visual relationship to horizontal space (Example 95).

For the ultimate degree of orchestral improvisation on both pitches and rhythms—not to mention tempos, articulations, and dynamics—we must turn to the *musical graphic*. These graphics are abstract designs, in contradistinction to conventional notational symbols, intended to stimulate the performer to react in terms of sound to what he experiences visually. No better example can be cited than *Maandros* (1963) of the Greek Anestis Logothetis (1921–). This unusual work is constructed on the principle of an open maze; it has a clearly defined beginning, middle, and end, but is designed to be improvised from beginning to end according to the visual stimuli in the score. As is customary with all graphic compositions, the performers read not from individual parts but from their own copy of the complete "score."

To many listeners, if not to numerous performers, too, productions of *Maandros* might be summed up in terms of critic Robert Henderson's comment on aleatoric music in general: "Total liberty ceases to be liberty at all and becomes merely chaos." In contrast to this graphic aesthetic, Witold Lutoslawski (1913–), the dean of Polish vanguard composers, holds to a more controlled application of aleatoric factors. "I am not interested in music entirely determined by chance," he says. "I want my piece to be something which I myself have created, and I would like it to be the expression of what I have to communicate to others."

From the composer's standpoint, this would seem to be an unassailable tenet. Nonetheless, improvisation—whether controlled or free—is an obvious antidote to the intellectual rigors of total serialization and a strong and viable attempt to restore flexibility to the art of music. The aesthetic of aleatory has, moreover, shaped too significant a body of music to be dismissed out of hand. But wide use of chance elements in music also carries implicit dangers.

From the audience standpoint, chance composition may be bad (and boring) as well as good (and emotionally stimulating). Audiences are taxed, too, by split reactions in listening—with one type of reaction to composed material, another to improvised and structurally random passages.

But the greater hazard is to music as an art. Improvisation by its very nature is transitory and impermanent; it never happens the same way twice, and it is never fixed, either in performance or on score paper. In what way, then, can this kind of musical expression achieve sufficient

EXAMPLE 95
Luciano Berio: from *Tempi concertati*, p. 52

permanence to be considered an orchestral style? If, as Maurice Ravel so succinctly remarked, true art leaves nothing whatsoever to chance, then one hopes that some composers, at least, will opt for art.

Whatever the ultimate potential of all types of improvisation, including aleatoric devices, the avant-garde has developed other strong resources for a fresh view of the symphonic-operatic orchestra. In 1954, when the Louisville Orchestra commissioned the Otto Luening-Vladimir

THE AVANT–GARDE ORCHESTRA

Ussachevsky *Rhapsodic Variations for Tape Recorder and Orchestra,* they initiated a fecund sequence of performances of pieces simultaneously presenting orchestral materials (traditional and experimental) and sounds created by an electronic generator or synthesizer. Though the piece is hardly to be regarded as a significant work of art—what pioneering composition is an unqualified masterpiece?—the score deserved its *succès d'estime.* Later essays by these two composers more successfully overcame the inherent limitations of the *Rhapsodic Variations,* in which fairly conventional orchestral material was at stylistic variance with the experimental sounds on tape.

Also in 1954 Edgard Varèse composed his unique *Déserts* for a large ensemble of woodwinds, brasses, percussion, and piano, with interpolated sections of what the composer called "organized sound" on tape. Soon numerous other composers in Europe and the United States began to create works combining conventional—sometimes not-so-conventional—instrumental sounds with the radically new tonal materials of electronicism. In 1956 the Dutch composer Henk Badings created his electronic ballet, *Cain and Abel,* for symphonic orchestra and prerecorded magnetic tape. A little later Pierre Boulez composed his *Poésie pour Pouvoir* (1958), which called for two orchestras, both unconventionally seated on stage, to be joined by taped, electronically generated sounds. In 1960 Luigi Nono wrote his highly controversial opera, *Intolleranza,* which followed by one year the immensely successful appearance of the Swedish composer Karl-Birger Blomdahl's "space opera," *Aniara* (1959). Both stage works made extensive use of electronic effects; in the case of *Aniara,* the other-worldly generator music seemed to grow logically from the nature of the work itself, creating a true expression of art rather than a technique artificially imposed.

Most of the recent contemporary works that combine orchestral and electronic sound do so from the antiphonal standpoint—a kind of give and take between the instrumental and the generator or synthesizer sounds. The range of effects extends, therefore, from traditional instrumental timbre through an electronic duplication and synthesis of these timbres to nonassociative electromagnetic "pure" sound. When orchestral and electronic sound is presented simultaneously, usually the one or the other is given a momentarily subsidiary role. Seldom do the two sound-sources operate together on completely equal terms, a factor determined more by acoustical considerations than by compositional preference.

If a style can be ascertained from these procedures, it is one that contrasts, mixes, or synthesizes the two basic sound elements, the orchestra (traditionally constituted or otherwise) and the tape recorder. Some

279

composers purposely juxtapose rather conventional orchestral effects with highly experimental electronic sound for the sake of exaggerated contrast. Others combine unusual instrumental sounds with near-standardized procedures on tape, almost as a mechanized parody of the live orchestral sound. It is evident, then, that the electronic group of composers, with these contrasts and various mixes, has not as yet synthesized a real vernacular that can be termed an electronic style.

One of the most convincing essays in melding instrumental and electronic sound is not orchestral, but a chamber work—Leon Kirchner's *Quartet No. 3 for Strings and Electronic Tape* (1966). The composer's remarks about this score are entirely applicable to any recent composition attempting to reconcile the two sonic worlds represented by human performers and by electronically produced sound-materials: "More interesting to me [than electronic music alone] are combinations of [conventional] instruments with electronic sound and filters. The instrumental qualities are then somehow reflected, extended, and enlarged. . . . I set out to produce a meaningful confrontation between 'new' electronic sounds and those of the traditional string quartet—a kind of dialogue-idea in which the electronics are quite integral."

Kirchner has admirably achieved his stated aim, and in so doing has proved that a valid future for electronic music depends wholly on the artistic stature of those who work in the medium. Unlike the earlier attempts to join the sonic worlds of jazz and "serious" music, efforts to create a new art-form by fusing manmade and synthesizer-produced music hold immense promise for the future.

"Though the standard orchestra is not yet an anachronism," Stravinsky once observed, "perhaps it can no longer be used standardly except by an anachronistic composer." It is precisely this creative dilemma that the contemporary composer must solve to his own personal satisfaction. The period of experimentation, of the exploration of sound sources, of the development of new techniques and of new instruments, is far from over; on the contrary, it gives every indication of being intensified in the years ahead. The current orchestrational style of the avant-garde, therefore, may be only a transitory manifestation. By the year 2000 orchestral style may be as multitudinous as the composers themselves—or as impersonal as the computers that could come to stand as surrogates of human performers.

Although a modern composer may be essentially unsympathetic to the world of *musique concrète,* digital computers, and technological instruments in general, his reaction ought to be positive rather than nega-

THE AVANT–GARDE ORCHESTRA

tive. Backed by strong personal conviction and perfection of instrumentational technique, the composer should attempt to restore to the symphonic orchestra a fresh viewpoint and an individual approach. In this direction may lie his own salvation as a potent creative artist in a difficult period in musical history. Moreover, it may prove the only possible manner in which to preserve the symphonic-operatic orchestra as a viable medium for composers of the future.

Notes

1. These, and the following instrumental effects described, are more fully discussed and illustrated in the author's *Contemporary Instrumental Techniques* (see Bibliography).

2. George Crumb's Pulitzer Prize-winning *Echoes of Time and the River* (1967) is a prime example of orchestral perambulation.

3. Refer to Chap. 1, page 11 for a discussion of Gabrieli's instrumental practice.

4. Structural and parametral ambiguity, choice, chance. The term "aleatory" is derived from the Greek *alea,* meaning "chance." An *aleator* is a thrower of dice; hence an aleatoric composer depends upon chance or random elements in his expression.

5. The term "third-stream" was coined by Gunther Schuller.

Postscript

> It [instrumentation] has . . . also served only too often to mask the poverty of a composer's ideas, to ape real energy, to counterfeit the power of inspiration, and even in the hands of really able and meritorious writers it has become a pretext for incalcuable abuses, monstrous exaggerations, and ridiculous nonsense.
>
> Hector Berlioz,
> *Treatise on Instrumentation*

In spite of the prophets of doom—of whom contemporary music has more than a normal share—the orchestra, symphonic and operatic, is still alive in this final stage of the twentieth century. It is not, however, entirely well. In many ways the great symphonic-operatic orchestras of the Western world now serve as tonal museums for the past rather than as viable showcases for our own time. Given reluctant conductors and instrumentalists and intellectually demanding music, the gulf between serious composition and its potential audience unhappily increases day by day.

As a consequence, symphony and opera orchestras may already have passed their greatest era and entered a period of inevitable decline. With the composer's incentive of potential performance at a low ebb, and the tangible rewards for an occasional hearing minimal indeed, the contemporary musical climate stultifies significant orchestrational development and consolidation.

Sonic probings are, of course, very much in evidence. But if they are not directed solely to electronic sound, they are applied more often to chamber groups and solo performers than to the full orchestral ensemble. Thus the symphonic orchestra no longer presents the ultimate challenge to the instrumental composer.

As for the twenty-first century—the orchestral styles of the future may well be geared to a technological machine, some complex and sophisticated piece of laboratory equipment that would supersede the 80 to 100 human performers who now comprise the major orchestras of the Western hemisphere. The ubiquitous tape recorder may become the sole performer of orchestral music, and the reel of magnetic tape the composer's only score. Printed music as we know it would then survive simply as the relic of an extinct style, to take its place in museums alongside the crumbling parchments and cuneiform tablets of dead civilizations.

This prognostication may sound implausible, but it is no less likely than were many current commonplaces that once seemed only bizarre possibilities. How many mid–nineteenth-century composers would have believed that the bedrock of tonality would be cracked within fifty years and reduced to rubble within seventy-five? How many would have dreamed of a world of musical creativity in which melody and rhythm are ionized, form and structure liberated, and the theory of probability a predominant factor?

Perhaps, however, the future of symphonic music is threatened less by its electronic rival than by the current preoccupation of the avant-garde with technique over content, with the *how* rather than the *why* of current musical expression. The composers of our time can literally orchestrate anything set before them; no style, no technical problem seems to blunt an easy virtuosity that would have been the envy and despair of many a pioneer of orchestrational art. But unhappily this technical refinement is not always at the service of a powerful and unique expression.

"Sound," said Arnold Schoenberg, echoing the sentiments of that pioneer avant-gardist, Hector Berlioz, "once a dignified quality of higher music, has deteriorated in significance since skillful workmen—orchestrators—have taken it in hand with the definite and undisguised intention of using it as a screen behind which the absence of ideas will not be no-

STYLE AND ORCHESTRATION

ticeable" (*Style and Idea*). If the modern orchestral mountain continues to labor and bring forth only a musical mouse, the historic glory of the orchestra can have no relation to the present. The future of the orchestra is assured only when composers have something deeply felt to communicate in terms of the orchestral entity.

List of Score References

285

STYLE AND ORCHESTRATION

LIST OF SCORE REFERENCES

STYLE AND ORCHESTRATION

No.	Composer: Work	Edition: Score Page
105	F. Liszt: *Mephisto Waltz No. 1*	Schuberth: 67
106	_____: *Eine Faust-Symphonie*	Eulenburg: 147ff.
107	J. Sibelius: *Tapiola*	Breitkopf: 51–55
108	_____: *En Saga*	_____: 83–85
109	R. Strauss: *Don Quixote*	Philharmonia: 52ff.
110	_____: *Don Juan*	Kalmus: 44–47
111	_____: *Till Eulenspiegels lustige Streiche*	_____: 56
112	_____: *Ein Heldenleben*	Eulenburg: 29ff.
113	_____: *Die Frau ohne Schatten*	Boosey: 20
114	_____: *Ein Heldenleben*	Eulenburg: 81ff.
115	_____: *Salome*	Furstner: 202ff.
116	_____: *Don Juan*	Kalmus: 79–82
117	_____: *Symphonia Domestica*	Associated: 74–89
118	_____: *Also Sprach Zarathustra*	Eulenburg: 97
119	_____: *Till Eulenspiegels lustige Streiche*	Kalmus: 1
120	_____: *Don Quixote*	Philharmonia: 39
121	_____: *Ein Heldenleben*	Eulenburg: 45ff.
122	_____: *Also Sprach Zarathustra*	_____:127ff.

CHAPTER 5

No.	Composer: Work	Edition: Score Page
123	C. Debussy: *Jeux*	Durand: 27
124	_____: *Ibéria*	_____: 75
125	_____: *Printemps*	_____: 35
126	_____: *Sirènes*	_____: 103
127	_____: *La Mer*	_____: 105
128	_____: *Le Martyre de Saint Sébastien*	_____: 44
129	_____: *La Mer*	_____: 39
130	_____: *Gigues*	_____: 2
131	_____: *Rondes de Printemps*	_____: 13
132	_____: *La Mer*	_____: 29ff.;60;81ff.
133	_____: *Ibéria*	_____: 54
134	M. Ravel: *Daphnis et Chloé*	_____: 84
135	_____: _____	_____: 180–181
136	_____: _____	_____: 269
137	_____: *L'Enfant et les Sortilèges*	_____: 132
138	_____: _____	_____: 126–131
139	J. Ibert: *Suite Symphonique*	Peters: 16–20
140	_____: *Escales*	Leduc: 37–46
141	J-L. Martinet: *La Trilogie des Prométhées*	Heugel: 28–35
142	I. Stravinsky: *Le Sacre du Printemps*	Kalmus: 133–139
143	F. Delius: *Eventyr*	Augener: 27
144	O. Respighi: *The Pines of Rome*	Ricordi: 67

CHAPTER 6

No.	Composer: Work	Edition: Score Page
145	A. Berg: *Wozzeck*	Universal: 236;266;435
146	_____: *Lulu*	_____: 34;276;514

LIST OF SCORE REFERENCES

No.	Composer: Work	Edition: Score Page
147	A. Schoenberg: *Five Pieces for Orchestra*	Peters: 28
148	A. Berg: *Wozzeck*	Universal: 248
149	_____: _____	_____: 350

CHAPTER 7

No.	Composer: Work	Edition: Score Page
150	I. Stravinsky: *Symphony of Psalms*	Boosey: 16ff.
151	_____: _____	_____: 4–6
152	_____: *Orpheus*	_____: 30
153	_____: *Le Sacre du Printemps*	Kalmus: 20
154	_____: *Chant du Rossignol*	Boosey: 55
155	_____: *Agon*	_____ 26;70
156	_____: _____	_____: 59;74
157	_____: *Oedipus Rex*	_____: 15
158	_____: *Threni*	_____: 48–50
159	_____: *Orpheus*	_____: 30
160	_____: *Perséphone*	_____: 135
161	_____: *Threni*	_____: 66

CHAPTER 8

No.	Composer: Work	Edition: Score Page
162	B. Bartók: *Music for Strings, Percussion and Celesta*	Philharmonia: 94
163	_____: *Dance Suite*	_____: 59
164	_____: *Deux Images*	Boosey: 44–46
165	_____: *Suite No. 2*	_____: 91–94
166	_____: *Violin Concerto No. 2*	_____: 1
167	_____: *Concerto for Orchestra*	_____: 22
168	_____: *Dance Suite*	Philharmonia: 43ff.
169	_____: *Music for Strings, Percussion and Celesta*	_____: 81ff.
170	_____: _____	_____: 22
171	_____: *The Miraculous Mandarin*	Philharmonia: 58ff.
172	_____: *Concerto for Orchestra*	Boosey: 29–46
173	_____: _____	_____: 17–20
174	_____: _____	_____: 73
175	P. Hindemith: *Kammermusik* No. 1	Schott: 67;111
176	_____: *Concerto for Woodwinds, Harp and Orchestra*	_____: 51–53
177	_____: *Symphonic Metamorphosis on Themes by Weber*	Associated: 31–32
178	_____: *Symphonia Serena*	Schott: 62ff.
179	S. Prokofiev: *Piano Concerto No. 3*	Boosey: 142
180	_____: *Symphony No. 5*	_____: 65
181	_____: *Scythian Suite*	_____: 48
182	_____: *Chout*	_____: 21;125;135
183	_____: *Symphony No. 5*	Leeds: 82
184	_____: *Symphony No. 6*	_____: 39

STYLE AND ORCHESTRATION

Select Bibliography

Bartolozzi, Bruno. *New Sounds for Woodwind*. London: Oxford University Press, 1967.

Bekker, Paul. *The Story of the Orchestra*. New York: Norton, 1936.

Berlioz, Hector. (Ed. Richard Strauss.) *Treatise on Instrumentation*. New York: Kalmus, 1948.

Brindle, Reginald Smith. *Contemporary Percussion*. London: Oxford University Press, 1970.

Carse, Adam. *The History of Orchestration*. 1925. Reprint. New York: Dover Publications, 1964.

_____. *The Orchestra*. New York: Chanticleer Press, 1949.

_____. *The Orchestra from Beethoven to Berlioz*. London: Heffer, 1948.

_____. *The Orchestra in the XVIIIth Century*. London: Heffer, 1940.

Casella, Alfredo, and Mortari, Virgilio. *La technica dell'orchestra contemporanea*. Milan: Ricordi, 1950.

Coerne, Louis. *The Evolution of Modern Orchestration*. New York: Macmillan, 1908.

Donington, Robert. *The Instruments of Music*. London: Pitman Publishing, 1951.

Elson, Arthur. *Orchestral Instruments and Their Use*. Philadelphia: Theodore Presser, 1923.

Erpf, Hermann. *Lehrbuch der Instrumentation*. Mainz: Schott's Söhne, 1959.

Forsyth, Cecil. *Orchestration*, 2nd ed. New York: Macmillan, 1935.

Gevaert, François A. *New Treatise on Instrumentation*. Paris: Lemoine, 1885.

Geiringer, Karl. *Musical Instruments*. London: Allen and Unwin, 1943.

Guiraud, Ernest. *Traité practique d'instrumentation*. Paris: Durand, 1933.

STYLE AND ORCHESTRATION

Henderson, William J. *The Orchestra and Orchestral Music.* New York: Scribner's, 1920.

Howes, Frank. *Full Orchestra.* London: Secker and Warburg, 1942.

Jacob, Gordon. *The Elements of Orchestration.* London: Jenkins, 1962. Reprint. New York: October House, 1966.

___. *Orchestral Technique,* 2nd ed. London: Oxford University Press, 1965.

Kennan, Kent. *The Technique of Orchestration,* 2nd ed., rev. Englewood Cliffs, N.J.: Prentice-Hall, 1970.

Kling, Henri. *Modern Orchestration and Instrumentation.* New York: Carl Fischer, 1905.

Koechlin, Charles. *Traité de l'orchestration.* Paris: Eschig Editions, 1954.

Lavoix, Henri. *Histoire de l'instrumentation.* Paris: Firmin-Didot, 1878.

Leibowitz, René, and Maguire, Jan. *Thinking for Orchestra.* New York: Schirmer, 1960.

Marescotti, A. F. *Les instruments d'orchestre.* Paris: Jobert, 1950.

McKay, George Frederick. *Creative Orchestration.* Boston: Allyn and Bacon, 1963.

Malipiero, Gian Francesco. *The Orchestra.* London: Chester, 1921.

Piston, Walter. *Orchestration.* New York: Norton, 1955.

Prout, Ebenezer. *The Orchestra,* 2 vols. London: Augener, 1897.

Rauscher, Donald J. *Orchestration: Scores and Scoring.* New York: Free Press, 1963.

Read, Gardner. *Contemporary Instrumental Techniques.* New York: Schirmer Books, 1976.

_____. *Music Notation: A Manual of Modern Practice,* 2nd ed., rev. Boston: Crescendo Publishing, 1972.

_____. *Thesaurus of Orchestral Devices.* 1953. Reprint. New York: Greenwood Press, 1969.

Reed, H. Owen, and Leach, Joel T. *Scoring for Percussion.* Englewood Cliffs, N.J.: Prentice-Hall, 1969.

Rimsky-Korsakov, Nikolay. *Principles of Orchestration.* 1922. Reprint (2 vols. in 1). New York: Dover Publications, 1964.

Rogers, Bernard. *The Art of Orchestration.* New York: Appleton-Century-Crofts, 1951.

Sachs, Curt. *The History of Musical Instruments.* New York: Norton, 1940.

Terry, Charles Sanford. *Bach's Orchestra.* London: Oxford University Press, 1932.

Wagner, Joseph. *Orchestration: A Practical Handbook.* New York: McGraw-Hill, 1959.

Wellesz, Egon. *Die Neue Instrumentation.* Berlin: Hesses Verlag, 1928.

Widor, Charles Marie. *The Technique of the Modern Orchestra.* New York: Schuberth, 1906.

Index

INDEX

INDEX

INDEX

INDEX

INDEX

INDEX

INDEX

INDEX

INDEX

INDEX